RURAL HEALTH AND AGING RESEARCH: THEORY, METHODS AND PRACTICAL APPLICATIONS

Edited by:

Wilbert M. Gesler

Department of Geography,
University of North Carolina at Chapel Hill

Donna J. Rabiner

National Center for Health Promotion,
Veterans Administration Medical Center, Durham, North Carolina

Gordon H. DeFriese

Director, Cecil G. Sheps Center for Health Services Research,
University of North Carolina at Chapel Hill

Jon Hendricks, Editor
SOCIETY AND AGING SERIES

Baywood Publishing Company, Inc.
Amityville, New York

Library of Congress Catalog Card Number: 97-28444
ISBN: 0-89503-183-3 (Cloth)

Library of Congress Cataloging-in-Publication Data

Rural health and aging research : theory, methods, and practical
   applications / edited by Wilbert M. Gesler . . . [et al.].
      p.   cm. - - (Society and aging series)
     Includes bibliographical references and index.
     ISBN 0-89503-183-3 (cloth)
     1. Rural aged- -Medical care- -United States. 2. Rural health
services- -United States. I. Gesler, Wilbert M., 1941-
II. Series.
RA771.5.R858 1998
362.1′ 04257′ 08460973- -dc21
                                                         97-28444
                                                           CIP

Table of Contents

CHAPTER
1

Introduction to Research on Rural Health and Aging Issues

*Wilbert M. Gesler, Donna J. Rabiner,
and Gordon H. DeFriese*

It has been recognized for some time that older adults living in rural areas face problems that make health care delivery to them particularly difficult: relatively high levels of illness, geographic isolation, and low levels of health resources available, among many others. As we show below, these problems are well documented. What is lacking is a comprehensive set of research methodologies which can be used to investigate, and hopefully alleviate, the health care problems of rural older adults.

The purpose of this book is to make available to researchers a set of approaches that an interdisciplinary group of academic and health care practitioners, working together under the umbrella of a grant from the National Institutes of Aging, within the National Institutes of Health to the Cecil G. Sheps Center for Health Services Research, have actually used in their studies. The theoretical background, strengths and weaknesses, and the use of both quantitative and qualitative techniques to define problems, measure levels of illness and health, and evaluate practices, are described for a variety of approaches.

More specifically, what we set out to do in this book includes the following:

1. We will describe a wide-ranging set of research approaches which have been used to study the health care problems of adults living in rural areas.

1

2. We will show how the research approaches can be used to define health care problems, measure levels of illness and health, and evaluate health care practices.
3. We will provide a theoretical background for the use of these approaches from the health care delivery literature.
4. We will provide details of how these approaches can be carried out in the field, as well as their strengths and weaknesses.
5. We will describe studies using these approaches, both from the literature, and, most importantly, studies carried out by the authors.

This volume provides an overview of several very different approaches to the study of the most salient issues in the field of rural health and aging. By presenting to the reader various approaches to the study of specific interventions designed for older adults in rural settings, we believe that our methods will become more accessible and understandable to a wide range of individuals who are interested in learning more about these techniques for building a scientific basis for public policy and clinical or social interventions in the future.

This chapter sets the stage for what we are attempting to do in this book. First, we review literature on the health status and health care needs of older adults who live in rural areas, as well as critical policy issues which form the background to the need for research on rural health and aging. We then proceed to a description of the North Carolina Rural Aging Program (NC•RAP) because we wish to show that we have practiced what we preach in this book. That is, we advocate the establishment of an interdisciplinary group of academicians and health practitioners who engage in a variety of studies of older persons in rural areas using diverse methodologies, and NC•RAP is an exemplar of that kind of group. Many of the specific strategies described throughout the book have already been tried in the field by various members of NC•RAP. The next section of this chapter shows how this volume arose out of discussions among NC•RAP members about the wide variety of methods they were using in their research, the need to bring some order into these methods, deficiencies in the literature on research approaches, and the need to both share strategies among themselves and disseminate them to a wider public. The chapter closes with brief notes on the book's intended target audience and its overall organization.

AN OVERVIEW OF THE STUDY OF
RURAL HEALTH AND AGING ISSUES

In recent decades, social gerontologists and health services researchers have become increasingly interested in studying the distinctive experiences of older persons living in less densely populated areas. Early investigations of the unique circumstances and health conditions of rural elderly populations indicated that rural older adults had relatively more functional limitations, more chronic conditions, and more accidental falls than their more urban counterparts [1, 2]. More recent assessments, however, have found that fewer urban-rural differences in health status have remained once important sociodemographic factors (such as age, gender, and income) were included in subsequent multivariate model estimations [3-6].

Coward, Miller, and Dwyer used data from the 1984-1986 Longitudinal Study of Aging of the National Health Interview Survey to assess residential differences in a variety of health indicators among older adults ages seventy and above at the time of the initial interview [1]. Of the twenty-six health indicators they examined, 61.5 percent ($n = 16$) exhibited statistically significant differences by residence. In particular, 75 percent ($n = 12$ of 16) of the significant differences reported indicated a rural disadvantage. Other early residential comparisons suggested that rural elders, relative to their more urban counterparts, had a higher probability of suffering from both chronic disease conditions, and the limitations in activities that accompanied these conditions [7, 8]. Similarly, Krout [9], and Lassey and Lassey [10] reported a persistent rural disadvantage in the physical health of rural elderly individuals once several control variables were introduced into the analyses.

Despite the importance of the findings from the early 1980s, since the term "rural" has not been defined consistently in the literature, it has remained difficult for researchers to systematically assess the relationship between residential location and subsequent patient health and utilization outcomes, and to synthesize prior study findings [11]. "Urban" and "rural" are multidimensional concepts that include structural, ecological, social, and cultural dimensions. Due to this complexity, most definitions of the urban-rural continuum have been based largely on structural characteristics.[1]

More recent assessments of the impact of residential location have begun to use more refined residential groups to assess variation in health status across a wider range of urban-rural community types. These studies generally have revealed that differences in health status do not vary along a clear urban-rural continuum. Instead, there seem to be a number of significant differences within the rural population along a number of specific health dimensions. Coward and

---

[1] Federal policies generally rely on a dichotomous grouping, with areas classified either as urban/rural or metropolitan/nonmetropolitan. For example, the Office of Management and Budget (OMB) designates a metropolitan statistical area (MSA) as including a large population center and adjacent counties that have a high degree of economic and social integration with that center. Similarly, the Bureau of Census' definition of an urban area includes densely settled "urbanized areas" plus places with populations of 2,500 or more outside urbanized areas [11]. According to these classification schemes, "rural" areas are designated by exclusion; they are those locations not classified either as MSA or urban [11]. Since most extant data sets on older adults have relied on the OMB or Bureau of Census definition of residential setting, it has remained difficult for rural aging health services researchers to include an examination of the variability in health status and service usage across a "continuum" of community settings.

Dwyer, for example, reported that non-farm, nonmetropolitan-dwelling elders had the poorest health status of any residential group in the aging population [2]. However, the differences reported by Coward and Dwyer have not been found to be universal across all indicators of health, nor have they always placed the rural elderly at a disadvantage [3, 6, 12-15].

Beaulieu recently relied on data from the 1988 National Health Interview Survey (NHIS), a national probability sample of noninstitutionalized persons, to assess urban-rural differences in the prevalence of chronic disease and mortality [12]. Although age-adjusted activity limitations were more prevalent among nonmetropolitan-based older persons, the percentage differences were small (ranging, for example, from 45.3% for nonmetropolitan-based adults aged 75+ with activity limitations, to 40.7% in more metropolitan areas). In addition, while NHIS data indicated that circulatory conditions and respiratory conditions were generally more prevalent in the nonmetropolitan areas, "mortality caused by selected chronic conditions, including cardiovascular disease, cancer, chronic obstructive pulmonary disease, and diabetes is not greater for rural residents when the data are controlled by age, sex, and race" [12, pp. 232-233].

Cutler and Coward's study based on National Health Interview Survey Data found that residence exerted a significant effect on five measures of health and impairment when mean values were compared by four residential categories (central city, Standard Metropolitan Statistical Area (SMSA)-non-central city, non-SMSA-non-farm, and non-SMSA-farm) [3]. In particular, older adults from rural non-farm areas reported having the poorest profile of health of any residential group in the aging population. However, when they reexamined the health differences by residence after adjusting for distributional differences in four sociodemographic characteristics known to be associated with both residence and health (i.e., age, gender, living arrangements, and education), some of the residential differences no longer existed. More specifically, while the number of medical conditions, the number of functional limitations, and perceived health status remained less favorable for rural non-farm elders, the number of activities of daily living (ADLs) and instrumental activities of daily living (IADLs) performed with difficulty no longer differed for any residential sub-category.

In addition, Van Nostrand [13] and Braden and Van Nostrand [14] used data from the 1986 National Health Interview Survey and the 1987 National Medical Expenditure Survey to examine urban-rural differences in the proportion of the population with physical and functional difficulties. While Van Nostrand found that a greater proportion of elderly individuals from nonmetropolitan areas rated their health as "fair" or "poor," Braden and Van Nostrand found that "there were no significant differences between nonmetropolitan and metropolitan elderly in the proportion with difficulties in activities of daily living (ADLs) or instrumental activities of daily living (IADLs), which are often used as indicators of the need for long-term care" [14, p. 63].

To complicate matters further, Ortega, Metroka, and Johnson studied a representative sample of 2,500 Nebraskans, aged eighteen to eighty-two-plus living in different community settings (farm/rural/town/city/metropolitan area) and found a linear, yet favorable, impact of rural residence on self-reported health [16]. Even after controlling for sociodemographic characteristics, those individuals living on farms were found to have the best self-reported health; respondents living in small towns or villages (with populations between 2,500-10,000) were reported to have the next highest overall level of health; and those from cities and larger metropolitan areas perceived their overall level of health status to be the worst.

Similarly, researchers from the University of North Carolina at Chapel Hill analyzed recent data from a national probability survey of the non-institutionalized older adult population, known as the National Survey of Self-Care and Aging (NSSCA), to compare the functional status and self-care practices of older adults residing in metropolitan and nonmetropolitan communities and to identify differences associated with residential location [15]. They performed weighted bivariate and multivariate logistic regression analyses in order to examine the relationship between metropolitan and nonmetropolitan residential location and self-reported ability to perform basic, mobility, and instrumental activities of daily living, and to assess the degree to which the levels and types of functional limitations affect metropolitan versus nonmetropolitan older adults' performance of self-care activities.

Bivariate logistic analyses pointed to modest, often insignificant metropolitan versus nonmetropolitan differences in the ability to perform functional tasks. However, larger positive effects of nonmetropolitan residence were generally observed once other factors likely to account for some of these differences were taken into account. Older adults from nonmetropolitan areas were more likely to report being able to perform functional activities, but were also more likely to report performing self-care activities both in the presence and absence of disability. The authors concluded that non-metropolitan older adults may discount the significance of declining functional status, thus "normalizing" the trajectory of aging in a different way than do their metropolitan counterparts.

In summary, given the range and variability in reported study findings, considerable uncertainty remains regarding the extent to which urban-rural differences in the physical and functional health of older adults may be attributed to effects of residence per se, rather than to differences in other factors that co-vary with residence [3, 17]. According to Coward and colleagues, the answer to the question—Is the health of the rural elderly (population) different from that of older persons who live in more urban settings?—"is neither easy nor straightforward, and a great deal of further research will be needed to clarify these issues fully" [5, p. 19]. Particularly lacking is theoretical and methodological research designed to expand the state-of-the-art in rural health and aging research in order to: 1) enhance our understanding of the very complex set of issues faced by researchers studying the impact of social, economic, and physical environment on the health and well-being of rural- and urban-dwelling older adults; 2) clarify, and better synthesize prior study findings; and 3) ultimately, eliminate any remaining disparities in the health and well-being of older Americans from rural community settings.

The characteristics and special problems associated with the health status and health care needs of the rural elderly population are topics of considerable health policy significance [5, 18]. Recent research (described above) has revealed that the issues faced when studying the health and well-being of rural older adults are very complex, and that our knowledge of older adults' comparative health status and access to health care remains incomplete. Given that there is a lack of consensus regarding the health status, accessibility, utilization, and quality of health care services to older adults, additional research is needed to further elucidate the critical ways in which the aging process and its associated life-style adjustments are influenced by the social, economic, and physical environment in which older adults live. What is particularly lacking is an easily accessible, and comprehensive overview of available and practical research methodologies that can be used to investigate, and hopefully, alleviate, the unique health care problems of rural older adults.

HISTORY AND DEVELOPMENT OF THE NORTH CAROLINA RURAL AGING PROGRAM (NC•RAP)

Acknowledging that older rural Americans continue to have special needs, experience unique economic, social, and physical conditions, and have more limited access to health services than their more urban counterparts, the U.S. Congress called for the funding of several Rural Health and Aging Exploratory Research Centers. In 1990, the National Institute on Aging (NIA) within the National Institutes of Health (NIH) responded to this call by establishing four rural health and aging exploratory research centers. The objective of each center was to "promote research through the funding of small-scale pilot projects" [19]. Projects chosen for funding were designed to address specific gaps in the existing knowledge about the health of older Americans living in rural settings. Particular emphasis was placed on helping scholars to develop full research proposals to be subsequently submitted to outside funding agencies. The ultimate goal of these research efforts was to improve the health and well-being of older adults in rural community settings.

Although each of the centers emphasized the importance of interdisciplinary approaches to the study of the health and aging of rural Americans, each center defined a unique research focus. The North Carolina Rural Aging Program (NC•RAP) was established in the fall of 1990 within the Cecil G. Sheps Center for Health Services Research at the University of North Carolina at Chapel Hill (UNC-CH). The grant was funded as an extramural, interdisciplinary (P-20) center/program for the study of ". . . the social, economic, psychological, environmental, and biomedical factors affecting the aging processes and the health and effective functioning of older people in rural areas." The explicit goal of the P-20 center/program was to create within the structure of UNC-CH an active and viable research program which could bring into effective relationship with one another a multidisciplinary faculty with interests in the special problems of older adults living in rural areas. The center/program was derived from an interest in four topical issues:

1. the promotion and maintenance of the capacity for independent living;
2. the use and intersection of formal and informal care;
3. the positive, proactive aspects of aging; and
4. the methodological aspects of rural health research involving older adults.

Over the initial two years of activity of NC•RAP, eight exploratory studies were launched which spanned these four topical areas. These ambitious small-scale studies were fashioned around a core set of activities already underway which involved scholars from the UNC–Chapel Hill campus who had been studying particular aspects of health and aging involving rural elderly populations. In some cases, these studies were undertaken by clinicians who happened to be concerned with the distinctive patterns of response to symptoms and subsequent use of formal health care services for particular health conditions, such as dizziness, lower back pain, or the early warning signs of impending stroke. For others, there were concerns with the way in which certain types of conditions common to older adults were treated by health care practitioners in rural areas, such as stroke, diabetes, trauma, arthritis and other musculoskeletal disorders, or dental disease. There were other researchers who were focused on the potential for significant health improvement through physical exercise interventions offering training to build muscle strength, motor function, and general enthusiasm for life activities and self-confidence in their performance among frail older adults. Still other researchers were interested in the patterns of self-care and the social support offered by close family members and friends which could help make independent living possible despite the experience of serious functional limitations among older adults. Finally, there were research colleagues at UNC-CH who were interested in studying the ecology of aging in rural areas, with a particular focus on the range, complexity, and infrastructure supports for health and social programs to serve this population.

In its three-year extension, the North Carolina Rural Aging Program consolidated its efforts in the two laboratory settings, launched new research activities in these and other sites, and linked the research taking place under the North Carolina Rural Aging Program with other ongoing projects addressing intersecting research issues. Projects funded during this phase covered two themes: 1) the influence of rural social and cultural context on health perceptions and behaviors (described in Chapters 6 and 8); and 2) the clinical, social, and economic impact of limited access to health care services on rural community settings (described in Chapter 2). During both the initial and extended periods, NC•RAP gave visibility to the set of studies which were taking place. Research results were disseminated to a wide audience of persons and organizations with an interest in the special health problems of older persons in rural areas. This book, in fact, is one product of that dissemination process.

The emphasis of NC•RAP was to design and conduct studies which relied on primary data collection, as well as studies which combined both clinical and social science orientations. Studies were also launched which used large data sets collected for other studies (e.g., the national longitudinal study of self-care practices among older adults being conducted with support from NIA) as secondary data sources. Other collateral studies, such as work on the secondary and tertiary prevention of stroke, used national Medicare data.

Of utmost importance to the themes of this book was the creation by NC•RAP of two community-based research laboratories for the study of rural aging issues; one in Johnston County and the other in Northampton and Halifax Counties (described in greater detail in Chapter 5 of this volume). In conjunction with the UNC-CH Center for Health Promotion and Disease Prevention and the Thurston Multipurpose Arthritis Center, also at UNC-CH, NC•RAP developed a social science and epidemiological research laboratory in cooperation with a non-profit, community-based organization created in rural Johnston County in eastern North Carolina. The effort led to the incorporation of Rural Health Research, Inc. of Johnston County, with a distinguished board of directors from the community appointed to oversee the effort to bring the benefits of organized health care research to the people of the county, in partnership with several centers and institutes at UNC-CH. Some of the small-scale studies mentioned above were carried out in Johnston County. One of the projects of greatest interest here is a multi-year natural history study of osteoarthritis (OA), where CDC has funded a project to locate and then to follow several hundred older adults who are, at baseline, without the symptoms of OA. NC•RAPs interest is in following those in rural areas with these symptoms over time in order to better understand the spectrum of health and social services used by these populations, with particular emphasis on levels of disability and work disability associated with OA of the hip and knee.

NC•RAP has responded to an equally promising opportunity in the northeastern corner of North Carolina, in Northampton and Halifax Counties. In this location, we have been invited by the Roanoke-Amaranth Health Center and its affiliated nursing home to undertake several projects designed to enrich the range of services and programs available to older adults in those two counties. A monthly geriatric assessment team clinic has been organized in Jackson, the site of the Roanoke-Amaranth Health Center. Using a regular clinical case conference format, several researchers in the Program on Aging of the UNC-CH School of

Medicine have begun a series of exploratory studies of African-American and Native-American social and cultural attitudes, beliefs and behaviors related to health, as well as a study to demonstrate the potential adjunctive benefits of a multidisciplinary approach to geriatric case management in this rural setting.

It should be clear from this description of NC•RAPs work that researchers have been engaged in a very wide range of studies. However, as members of the P-20 center talked among themselves, they discovered that their interests intersected in many ways. For example, the work done on resource availability in rural communities had much to do with the impact that formal health care providers and systems may have in assisting rural residents with functional limitations in managing these in such a way that independent living arrangements can be maintained.

THE EVOLUTION OF THIS BOOK FROM NC•RAP

This volume arose out of conversations among colleagues working under the aegis of NC•RAP. In hindsight, one could say that there were three (not necessarily chronological) phases to the book's inception: a recognition of the deficiencies in the existing literature on methodologies to study the rural elderly, an expressed need to share knowledge about diverse strategies within the group, and the desire to disseminate the group's collective knowledge to other researchers as well as to health care planners and managers.

When we began our program of research on the special problems of rural elderly populations, the formal literature in this field appeared to be limited, both in its extent and in the rigor of the research it summarized. John Krout and his colleagues [9, 20] and Raymond T. Coward and G. R. Lee [21] clearly helped to dispel the notion that the literature was without depth. Yet, the amount of overall attention paid by the health and social sciences to the set of issues addressed in this literature was not impressive. Probably no more than twenty researchers had devoted significant career attention to this area since the mid-1960s, these mainly from the fields of rural sociology, social work, and agricultural economics. The sheer range of issues of great importance to the social and physical health and safety of persons who grow old in rural communities suggested a complex field of study, but the volume and variety of research taking place in relation to these issues was anything but overwhelming.

As we began to bring some degree of cohesiveness to the many strains of research taking place on our own campus, we discovered something common to all who have chosen to work in this field, Our interests, we found were extremely diverse, and the requirements for our respective research endeavors were highly varied as well. For some of us, there were requirements for access to major secondary data sets, such as the Medicare beneficiary files or the trauma registries maintained at the state level across the nation, in order to carry out our research. For others, there were heavy demands for intensive primary data collection involving in-person and in-depth interviews with older rural persons. For still others, there were needs for extensive clinical databases, or special arrangements for the collection of data from the clinical case encounters with older patients as they were seen in a variety of health care settings in rural communities.

Despite the enormous interest in the research we had undertaken, and the widespread support we had received from NIA, the American Association of Retired Persons (AARP), and area agencies on aging in our own state and elsewhere, we were immediately aware of the fact that an increased focus on questions in the field of rural health and aging would involve a much broader spectrum of research strategies than we had previously operationalized for any other multidisciplinary programs of health research then occurring under the umbrella of the Sheps Center for Health Services Research. In order to study, in any comprehensive way, the health and social situation of rural elders, we would have to include interests in health status, health care utilization, quality of life and well-being, the demography of aging, the use of both formal and informal systems of care, health-related life styles, and the economics of rural social and family life.

Research strategies and instruments for measuring these aspects of health and life in the general society would have to be made applicable (i.e., relevant and valid) for application in the study of rural elder populations. Both quantitative and qualitative methods would be required. In addition, opportunities for the study of these interrelated aspects of rural social life, aging, and health would have to be created and maintained. Our own interest in and commitment to population-based health research necessitates that we more fully explore the possibility of a close working relationship with defined local communities wherein these studies could take place, and where the results of this research might possibly be employed in the interest of improving the health and social circumstances of those we would study.

As we met on numerous occasions over the first three years of support from NIA, we discussed at great length the variety of research approaches we seemed to be using in an equally varied number of research settings in an effort to understand these phenomena of relevance to the health and social circumstances of the rural elderly in our society. In our discussions, representatives of area agencies on aging, local senior centers, and clinics offering special services for older adult populations spoke often about the unique demands which certain kinds of research seemed to place on these agencies as they sought to find ways to facilitate our collection of data and the understanding of special problems of older rural community residents. We were made aware of the fact that the methods themselves, and the special demands that certain types of study designs and instrumentation place on both rural elderly subjects and the agencies and professionals who facilitate our access to these persons, are simply not easily understood or appreciated. Moreover, the eventual utility of such information in achieving a greater understanding of fundamental questions in the field of rural aging are not self-evident. It was out of these discussions, occurring over several months, that we decided to launch the project represented by the chapters appearing in this volume.

TARGET AUDIENCES

The chapters in this volume either present a method or approach felt to offer promise with respect to the understanding of a particular issue or problem in the field of rural health and aging; or they describe a method or approach often seen as disruptive or otherwise a problem itself, as a method, by persons who are asked to facilitate, support, or arrange for its use in a particular community or organizational setting. The chapters were written with several audiences in mind. They were motivated by the desire to make these methods individually accessible and understandable to a non-researcher audience of interested professionals and educated laypersons from a wide range of disciplines—including public health, geriatric medicine, public policy, planning, social work, education, and rural health—who may have a need to know more about these techniques for building a scientific basis for public policy and social interventions in relation to older adults. At the same time, we have tried to make the chapters interesting and useful to some of our research colleagues who may gain further insight into the use of these methods for their own research in other settings, and with regard to different questions and issues than they have studied previously. In this way, we hope to stimulate the growth and development of this aspect of the science of gerontological research, and to ultimately attract colleagues from an even wider array of disciplines to the field.

ORGANIZATION

The book is divided into three sections, covering: 1) the definition and presentation of health problems of older adults living in rural areas; 2) the measurement of levels of illness and health; and 3) the evaluation of health care practices. Each substantive chapter will: 1) state how a particular research approach can be used to solve some problem or problems experienced by rural older adults; 2) provide a theoretical background for the use of this approach; 3) describe the strengths and weaknesses of the approach; 4) show how the approach has been operationalized in previous studies and in studies currently being carried out by the authors; and 5) make a final assessment of the utility of the approach. We hope that publication of this volume will help to illustrate the special problems and opportunities which lie ahead in the field of rural health and aging research. It is our thesis that through well done and highly salient research, the lives of rural older adults can be made better.

REFERENCES

1. R. T. Coward, M. K. Miller, and J. W. Dwyer, The Role of Residence in Explaining Variation in Reported Health and Dysfunction of the Elderly in the United States, in *Study of Models to Meet Rural Health Care Needs Through Mobilization of Health Professions Education and Services Resources,* National Rural Health Association (eds.), Contract No. HRSA-240-89-0037, National Rural Health Association, Kansas City, Missouri, 1992.
2. R. T. Coward and J. W. Dwyer, *Health Programs and Services for Older Adults in Rural America: A Review of the Life Circumstances and Formal Services that Affect the Health and Well-Being of Older Adults,* National Resource Center for Rural Elderly, Kansas City, Missouri, 1991.
3. S. J. Cutler and R. T. Coward, Residence Differences in the Health Status of Older Adults, *Journal of Rural Health, 4*:3, pp. 11-26, October 1988.
4. J. A. Krout, Epilogue, in *Providing Community-Based Services to the Rural Elderly,* J. A. Krout (ed.), Sage Publications, Thousand Oaks, California, 1994.
5. R. T. Coward, C. N. Bull, G. Kukulka, and J. M. Galliher (eds.), *Health Services for Rural Older Adults,* Springer, New York, 1994.
6. E. P. Stoller and L. E. Forster, Patterns of Illness Behavior Among Rural Elderly: Preliminary Results of a Health Diary Study, *Journal of Rural Health, 8*:1, pp. 13-26, 1992.
7. National Center for Health Statistics, *Vital Statistics of the United States, 1984, Volume II, Section 6, Life Tables,* CCHS Publication No. [PHS] 87-11,04, Government Printing Office, Washington, D.C., 1987.
8. R. A. Rosenblatt and I. S. Moscovice, *Rural Health Care,* John Wiley and Sons, New York, 1982.
9. J. A. Krout, *The Aged in Rural America,* Greenwood, Westport, Connecticut, 1986.
10. W. R. Lassey and M. L. Lassey, The Physical Health Status of the Rural Elderly, in *The Elderly in Rural Society,* R. T. Coward and G. R. Lee (eds.), Springer, New York, 1985.
11. M. Hewitt, Defining 'Rural' Areas: Impact on Health Care Policy and Research, in *Health in Rural North America,* W. M. Gesler and T. C. Ricketts (eds.), Rutgers University Press, New Brunswick, New Jersey, 1992.
12. J. E. Beaulieu, Services for the Rural Elderly and Disabled, in *Rural Health Services: A Management Perspective,* J. E. Beaulieu and D. E. Berry (eds.), AUPHA/Health Administration Press, Ann Arbor, Michigan, 1994.
13. F. Van Nostrand (ed.), Common Beliefs About the Rural Elderly: What do National Data Tell Us? National Center for Health Statistics, *Vital Health Statistics, 3*:28, 1993.
14. J. Braden and J. F. Van Nostrand, Long-Term Care in Common Beliefs About the Elderly: What do the National Data Tell Us? J. F. Van Nostrand (ed.), National Center for Health Statistics, *Vital Health Statistics, 3*:28, 1993.
15. D. J. Rabiner, T. R. Konrad, G. H. DeFriese, J. E. Kincade, S. L. Bernard, A. Woomert, T. A. Arcury, and M. G. Ory, Metropolitan Versus Nonmetropolitan Differences in Functional Status and Self-Care Practice: Findings from a National Sample of Community-Dwelling Older Adults, *Journal of Rural Health,* 1997.

16. S. T. Ortega, M. J. Metroka, and D. R. Johnson, In Sickness and in Health, in *Aging in Rural America,* C. N. Bull (ed.), Sage Publications, Newbury Park, California, 1993.
17. C. L. Longino and M. H. Smith, Epilogue: Reflections on Health Services for Rural Older Adults, in *Health Services for Rural Older Adults,* R. T. Coward, C. N. Bull, G. Kukulka, and J. M. Galliher (eds.), Springer, New York, 1994.
18. R. T. Coward and S. J. Cutler, Informal and Formal Health Care Systems for the Rural Elderly, *Health Services Research 23*:6, pp. 785-806, 1989.
19. National Institute on Aging (NIA), *The Rural Health and Aging Exploratory Research Centers: 1990-1993, Activities Report,* National Institute on Aging, Washington, D.C., 1994.
20. J. A. Krout, Correlates of Service Utilization Among the Rural Elderly, *The Gerontologist, 23,* pp. 500-504, 1983.
21. R. T. Coward and G. R. Lee (eds.), *The Elderly in Rural Society: Every Fourth Elder,* Springer, New York, 1985.

PART ONE

Defining the Health Issues and Problems of Rural Elderly: Context, Experience, Statistical Profiles, and Indicators

Secondary Data and Statistical Profiles of Older Rural Americans

Mary Anne P. Salmon and Thomas C. Ricketts, III

Confronted with a question about aging or older adults in a rural setting, the researcher or human services professional will probably assume a need for *primary data,* that is data collected by the team through surveys, interviews, focus groups, or other methods for the sole purpose of answering this research question. However, *secondary data analysis* (the use of data collected by someone else for some other purpose) provides a relatively quick and inexpensive overview of the status of older adults living in rural areas and can hint at the emergence of issues in rural aging. Depending on the level of aggregation and the time period over which data are examined, a planner, practitioner, or researcher can capture major trends in the functional, economic, and health status of this group, as well as their use of formal services.

This chapter will briefly discuss the more common uses of secondary data in rural gerontological research. Then it will detail the steps involved in secondary analysis—locating and selecting an appropriate data set, approximating research questions with the data at hand, presenting the data, interpreting secondary data, and refining the question.

USES OF SECONDARY ANALYSIS

Formal presentations of secondary data analysis in the field of rural aging have typically fallen into three general categories—compiling atlases, data books, and online statistical profiles; comparing rural and urban areas; and studying specific rural areas. Each of these three requires a somewhat different approach to assembling, interpreting, and presenting data, and each has its own challenges. Let us examine them separately before going on to explore the steps common to all three.

Compiling Atlases, Data Books, and Online Statistical Profiles

Assembly of secondary data into a profile or atlas is not, in the strictest sense, research, but it can be a valuable tool in facilitating program development for rural elders, a predecessor to comparative research, and a powerful force in shaping rural aging policy. Widely known examples of print compilations include *The National Rural Health Policy Atlas* [1], *Old and Alone in Rural America* [2], *Common Beliefs about the Rural Elderly: What Do the National Data Tell Us?* [3], *Statistical Handbook on Aging Americans* [4], and *Statistical Record of Older Americans* [5]. The World Wide Web is an exciting new medium for both retrieving and displaying secondary data. By the very nature of the Internet, exemplary sites appear almost weekly. An excellent source of information on sites relevant to all areas of aging is Joyce Post's regular column in *The Gerontologist,* which began appearing in January 1996 [6].

Although the three purposes of such materials (planning, research, and policy) often overlap in practice, there are some basic differences in the choice of data items for these purposes. The statistical profile for program development is often commissioned by a public or private agency such as an area agency on aging (AAA), a state or local department on aging, or the marketing branch of a large home health or nursing home corporation specifically for service planning or provision. The agency commissioning the profile needs information for a specific purpose and will be involved in identifying its particular data needs or the questions that the assembled data should be able to answer. The contracting agency's ability to articulate these needs may be naive or extremely sophisticated, but the essential first obligation of the research team accepting such a commission is to identify them as accurately and completely as possible and to check periodically that there is continuing agreement on this point.

The statistical profile as a predecessor to research is more theoretically-based, and the choice of variables is usually at the discretion of the research team. For example the team may assemble data to answer the question, "Do the resources provided to a rural county by the in-migration of retirees offset or fall short of the increased demand for amenities and services?" The broad research question may be theoretically-derived or grounded in past empirical findings. The data gathering is shaped by what potential factors can be derived from theory and/or identified in the literature review (e.g., the relative affluence and health of in-migrants, their likelihood of continuing to receive some medical care from providers in their place of origin) and which relevant variables can be identified in secondary data sources (e.g., median income and education, real estate and personal property tax assessments, public service utilization). Publishing atlases or data books and/or making these focused data elements part of a web site or other online resource provides a tool for the research community that shares an interest in the broader research question. At the same time, looking at the data that is already available will help the research team to refine and focus the questions that remain unanswered.

The statistical profile used to influence policy may grow out of an academic research interest, but more often it grows out of the desire of an advocacy group to provide credible support for their cause. For example, a group interested in expanding in-home services in a rural area where commissioners are looking at expanding nursing home facilities may wish to produce a "fact book" that includes such data as the numbers of elders with activities of daily living (ADL) impairments living at home relative to those in facilities, the comparative daily public costs of in-home and institutional care, the initial capital outlay for expanding the two types of services, and the estimated increase in jobs under the alternative plans. At the national level, advocates for older adults, for rural health and social services, or both, may choose to publish and post data that emphasize the problems of rural elders and point out gaps in services and resources.

As in the case of the data collection commissioned for program planning, the research team will need to work closely with those whose policy agenda their work is intended to support. However, there is a much trickier ethical issue for researchers in this case. They must, within the bounds of ethical practice, honor the legitimate wish of the sponsoring agency to shape the content of its product, while guarding against subtle or less-than-subtle pressure to suppress data or otherwise mislead the reader, for example, by omitting data that show rural elders faring as well as, or better than, urban elders in some respects.

Comparisons of Rural and Urban Areas

Secondary data are widely used in state- and national-level studies about health and social services for older adults in rural settings. This is primarily because of the logistical problems of primary data collection over a large, representative sample of rural places. Historically, much of this research has focused on comparisons of rural states or counties to urban ones using data from public records or comparing urban subjects to rural ones using subsets of larger surveys. A variety of questions have been addressed in this manner. Do rural elders have poorer health [7]? Do they have greater service needs [8]? Do they use more formal and informal support [9]? Do they have less access to health and social services through specific funding streams such as those funded by Title III [10],

Title XX [11], and Medicare-funded home health [12-15]? Is rurality a legitimate factor in intrastate funding formulae for Older Americans Act funds [16]?

Increasingly, however, advocates for rural studies, including Coward and Cutler [17], have suggested that rural elders are of interest in an of themselves and need not be defined by how they differ from, or are disadvantaged relative to, urban elders. This sentiment almost exactly echoes that of advocates for the study of ethnic minority elders (see, for example, [18, 19].) These authors point out that this constant comparative approach leads to the view of ethnicity (or in our case, rurality) as a social problem.

A separate, but related, perspective is the call for better recognition and measurement of the diversity *among* rural areas, and by extension, among urban ones. For example, Cutler and Coward revisited the question of whether rural or urban elders have poorer health and conclude that rural, non-farm-dwelling elders have more medical conditions and more functional impairment than their metropolitan counterparts (both central city and non-central city), but that farm-dwelling elders had better health than any of the other groups [7]. The complexity of this and other relationships is lost if data are gathered according to either the urban/rural or the metropolitan/nonmetropolitan dichotomies.

Ricketts et al. have provided an overview of the various ways in which rural versus urban places are described and how intra-rural differences are classified for policy and research purposes [20]. In the two most common policy definitions, rurality is a subtractive term. In the Census Bureau's definition, urban places and populations are classified first and the remainder are considered "rural." Similarly, the Office of Management and Budget determines what counties are considered metropolitan, while those not attaining that status are non-metropolitan. There are, however, positive definitions of rurality and descriptions of ruralness. The field of rural sociology has developed and tested several constructs and theoretical approaches to the description of rural, rural people, and rural places [21]. These descriptions are often attached more to personal perceptions of place and social interaction rather than to specific boundaries and places. The key lesson that can be drawn from a structured analysis of "what is rural?" is that it is many things and that there are many different types of "rural" [22]. In comparing secondary data, however, the same problems face the reviewer as face the policymaker—divisions and boundaries must be drawn to contract the data or to apply policies. This necessary requirement and its flaws must be accepted if we are to move ahead.

The classification of populations as urban or rural in the chapters that follows and in the specific examples we cite below, will follow one of the two major classification schemes: the Census Bureau's urban-rural delineation which is person-specific, or the Office of Management and Budget metropolitan designation which follows county lines. These are the most common and most accepted systems. Alternatives that identify sub-county jurisdictions or postal geography are occasionally proposed, but rarely applied.

Studies of Specific Rural Areas

Most studies of rural elders that do not employ comparisons to urban areas are focused on counties or county groups (such as hospital or mental health catchment areas), often ones targeted for some rural health or services intervention. These studies are somewhat less likely to use secondary data than the broader comparisons of rural to urban states or counties, simply because the collection of primary data is not as difficult for a relatively small, clearly defined area. However, even when primary data are collected, contextual variables gleaned from secondary sources may contribute prior to data collection, during the analysis, or subsequent to analysis of the primary data.

Prior to the collection of primary data, secondary data may indicate some characteristics of the population that should be taken into consideration in design and analysis of primary data. For example, a bi-modal income distribution in county census data on older adults might suggest the presence of two distinct groups that need to be adequately represented in the survey (e.g., in-migrant retirees and indigenous elders and/or a large ethnic minority). Hospital discharge data may show an unusually high or low rate of a mental condition, which may have an impact on service utilization, suggesting the need to collect data to be able to control for this diagnosis.

During primary analysis, secondary data may be incorporated into the primary data set for analysis. For example, in researching why neighboring rural counties differ from each other in the services they offer older adults, subjective and interpretive data from interviews with service providers, political figures, and consumers might be supplemented with objective secondary data on the two counties' poverty rates, voting records, ethnic composition, age structure, and leading cause of hospital admittance.

Secondary data can also be used to help interpret unexpected findings in primary analysis. For example, if a relationship is found that is substantially different from findings reported in the literature, secondary data may be used to examine ways the population in the rural area of interest is different from that of the rural areas presented in the literature. Secondary data can also be used to compare participants in a program (or other intervention) with the underlying geographic population or the population at risk of needing the service. For example, if an adult day care program has an exclusively female enrollment, it is tempting to assume that either the outreach to male clients has been inadequate or that the service is unacceptable to men in some way. However, assuming that clients are usually unmarried and must be both functionally impaired and dwelling in the community, using secondary analysis to examine gender differences in marital status, level of impairment, and living arrangement might show that the number of unmarried, community-dwelling, functionally-impaired men in the study community is so small that their absence in day care is accounted for.

STEPS IN SECONDARY ANALYSIS

Locating and Selecting Appropriate Data Sets

There are a variety of standard data sets that may be used for secondary analysis. These can be classified into six broad categories—population-based health data sets; sample-based health data sets; synthetic estimates of health data; health resource data sets; social, demographic, and general data sets; and indirect data sets. These vary in the availability and in the advantages and disadvantages associated with their use.

Population-Based Health Data Sets

Some sources of data attempt to include events for an entire population. These include vital statistics data, national registries of specific diseases or conditions, Medicare data, and Medicaid data. Institutional admissions/discharge data provide figures for the entire population receiving tréatment, but the appropriate choice of denominators to calculate rates from these data may be challenging.

Each state maintains and publishes regular reports from the licensure of births, marriages, divorces, and deaths, as well as selected reports on special topics. For those involved in issues of rural health, data on the cause of death and underlying conditions from death certificates may provide some information on the variation in morbidity and mortality among rural counties or between rural and urban ones. The annual vital statistics publications provide counts of events (births, deaths, marriages), which must be combined with census data or projections that provide a denominator for calculating rates. However, many states publish reports on special topics, including cause of death, which already include denominators from other sources. These data, which are typically available at the county level, are available directly from state data centers as well as in combined national form available from the National Center for Health Statistics (NCHS). Some products are available online from the NCHS web site (http://www.cdc.gov/nchswww/nchshome.htm).

Many states maintain registries of reported and substantiated cases of elder abuse or neglect, which may also be of interest to those connected with the health of rural elders. Typically, these data are available at the county level. However, comparisons among states or among counties in different states may not be possible because they vary widely in their definition and inclusion criteria. For example, in North Carolina, this registry includes people reported for self-neglect—that is, mentally or physically disabled people, judged not to have the capacity to make their own decisions, whose behavior constitutes a threat to their own health and safety. In other states, only abuse or neglect by a caregiver is reported. States also differ in their definitions of caregiver and in their inclusion or exclusion of younger disabled adults.

Medicare data are made available semi-annually on public use tapes from the Bureau of Data Management and Strategy of the Health Care Finance Administration (HCFA) in Baltimore. About 85 percent of these data pertain to beneficiaries aged sixty-five or older (the remainder are younger disabled people whose care is funded through specific Medicare programs), and most older adults are covered. The primary source of omissions is older participants in HMOs whose Medicare participation does not follow the traditional fee-for-service reimbursement pattern and thus is not easily incorporated into the data. Beneficiary data include both county and zip code identifiers for identifying rural places. Additional data on health resources are also available (see Health Resource Data Sets on p. 24).

Medicaid data are available from the agency that administers it in each individual state, which determines the geographic units for which the data can be made available. (In North Carolina it is administered by the Division of Medical Assistance.) Although data are collected nationally by the Health Care Finance Administration (with selected states sending data files on tape directly), it is difficult to obtain national data and even more difficult to work with it. Eligibility requirements differ from state to state, and among populations within states. For example, in some states pregnant women and children are eligible if their family income is at the poverty level, while older adults in the same states might need incomes less than 50 percent of the poverty level to qualify.

Some Medicaid data, for instance, physician visits of older adults, are duplicated on the Medicare files. Data on Medicaid nursing home and other long-term care expenditures, on the other hand, are available only through Medicaid, and Medicaid is a major funder of these services. Medicaid is also responsible for the "Minimum Data Set" (MDS), containing standardized assessment measures for all residents of Medicare- and/or Medicaid-certified nursing facilities. (See references [23, 24] for information about this data set.)

Sample-Based Health Data Sets

Probably the most widely used national sample survey of health issues is the National Health Interview Survey (NHIS). This annual survey of the noninstitutionalized civilian population is conducted by the National Center for Health Statistics, and results are published in their Vital and Health Statistics, Series 10. The National Institute on Aging's "Established Populations for Epidemiologic Studies of the Elderly" and the "National Institute of Mental Health's Epidemiologic Catchment Area Program" are other examples. The National Archive of Computerized Data, sponsored by the NIA is a major source of such sets, some of which are available online.

Synthetic Estimates of Health Data

When population data on the prevalence of a disease or condition are not available but good estimates are essential to policy and planning, some form of synthetic estimation technique is used to produce these data. Although the exact procedures and the assumptions that underlie them differ in their particulars, all synthetic estimation techniques involve two basic steps: 1) use sample data or data for a small population such as the residents of an epidemiologic catchment area to produce prevalent estimates for demographic subsets of the population (typically age by race by gender, and sometimes metropolitan/nonmetropolitan); and 2) apply these prevalent rates to the population composition of the geographic area in question (see, for example, [25, 26]).

Synthetic estimates vary in quality with the external validity of the study producing the prevalent measures and the accuracy of the population projections used. However, even the best are limited by the weakness of correlation between health conditions and these basic demographic characteristics. Take, for example, differences in the rates of hypertension for older white and African-American men. Differences come from a complex mix of economic, educational, and cultural factors, overlaid with the effects of overt discrimination in access to services (during much of the lives of today's older adults, even if not in the present) and possible genetic differences in predisposition. If we apply national race- and sex-specific rates to some of the poorest rural counties in the Deep South, the differences in the two groups will be exaggerated by synthetic estimation because both African-American and white men will have little education, a lifetime of poverty, limited access to preventive health care and screening, and a diet high in animal fats and salts.

Health Resource Data Sets

While much of the research on the health of rural elders is focused on consumer-level variables, policy questions often include a need to measure available resources such as provider personnel. Prior to 1990, the National Center for Health Statistics published a series 14 on health manpower and facilities. Some of these data have been included in the National Health Care Survey after 1990.

In addition, states maintain data on physicians, registered and practical nurses, physical therapists, and a variety of other health professionals who are licensed by the state in which they practice. A smaller number of states require the licensure of social workers and of paraprofessionals such as in-home aides and nursing assistants. Typically, registration data will include the county in which the professional practices, specialty (where applicable), and year of first certification, making them a good source for assessing county labor force in the helping professions serving older adults. Access to these data is controlled by the licensing authority, usually the professional association of the group in question, which may vary in the conditions for and limitations on potential users of the data.

Medicare maintains data about hospitals, nursing homes, physicians (Part B), and HMOs, although this would not cover those institutions that are not Medicare-certified or physicians who do not accept Medicare assignment. The

January issue of each years' *Health Care Financing Review* provides expenditure data on this and a variety of other public health expenditures.

Resource data may be gleaned from budgets and other records of public provider agencies. Some kinds of resource data may also be available from the trade associations of private not-for-profit, and even proprietary agencies. However many proprietary agencies are reluctant to provide such data about their operations.

Social, Demographic, and General Data Sets

There are a variety of secondary data sources for social and demographic variables relevant to both policy and specification of research models. One of the most widely known and used sources is the U.S. decennial census. The great advantage of census data is the breadth of coverage and the geographic detail for which data are available. An essential set of demographic questions are targeted to the entire population, and a supplemental set are asked of a large representative sample. The disadvantage of the census is its relatively small number of variables and the length of time between data collection and publication in print or on tape, although the time lag grows shorter with each decade. The 1990 census has two features that improve its usefulness to the gerontologist: its inclusion of a question about functional impairment, and the availability of the special tabulation on aging.

For many years gerontologists have bemoaned the lack of data on impairment that cover a wide range of specific geographic areas. In the absence of such data, we have been forced to rely on synthetic estimation techniques. Finally, in 1990, the census added the following item to the sample supplement to their questionnaire.

> 19. Because of a health condition that has lasted for 6 or more months, does this person have any difficulty—
>   a. Going outside the home alone, for example, to shop or visit a doctor's office? (yes, no);
>   b. Taking care of his or her own personal needs, such as bathing, dressing, or getting around inside the home? (yes, no)

These questions have their limitations. For example, there is no way to distinguish between a person with a single moderate functional impairment, such as the inability to bathe without assistance (which rarely leads to the use of formal services) and a person with several severe impairments. Similarly, the mobility question makes no distinction between the person who is unable to use public transportation without assistance, from the person who cannot take even a few steps. Nevertheless, the availability of good sample data that measures impairment, covers the entire nation, and is available for small geographic units, is a real advance for those interested in any aspect of formal or informal services to older adults.

The special tabulation on aging was designed by state units on aging and area agencies on aging to provide the census data most useful to them in their work. (Data are available on 16 compact discs—one for the U.S. summary, and each of the 50 states on the remainder—which may be purchased separately.) These files contain most census variables for the population age sixty and older, with enough detail that subgroups (e.g., those 65 and older) can be identified. Of interest to gerontologists in rural studies is the rich geographic detail. These data not only give the standard rural/urban and metropolitan/nonmetropolitan breakdown, but they also give data from "rural portion of county," "rural portion of Planning and Service Areas (PSAs)," as well as small areas, down to the census block level. As always in census data, frequencies for any specific variable are not available at a level where that information would compromise confidentiality. (For example, income is not reported by Hispanic status in tracts with small numbers of Hispanic residents.)

The Census Bureau Home Page (http://www.census.gov) makes finding popular data elements extremely quick and convenient and provides links to other federal agencies that provide statistics, including the Bureau of Economic Analysis, the Bureau of Labor Statistics, the Bureau of Transportation Statistics, the National Science Foundation, and the National Center for Health Statistics.

In addition to the decennial census, the Bureau of the Census also conducts the current population survey and publishes findings in the *Current Population Reports*. These data are collected monthly on a rotating set of demographic and economic topics from hundreds of sample areas representing every state and the District of Columbia. The survey is designed to be representative of its universe—the civilian, noninstitutionalized population of the United States. Like the sample component of the census, it is representative but not random. Its advantage is that it has the same quality of data collection and handling as the U.S. census, it is available much more quickly, and thus it covers more recent time periods. The disadvantage is that the sampling methods involved do not make it appropriate for use in studying small areas such as counties or county groups, especially when looking at a specialized group such as older adults. However, for those wishing to get up-to-date information on rural states, this is an important source. Like the census, it is available on tape and CD-ROM, in print, and through the Census web site.

The Statistical Abstract of the United States provides public data from a wide variety of other sources, including information about weather, the labor force, the economy, demography, and politics. Its advantage is that it usually has the latest "official" statistics on a wide variety of topics. Its disadvantages are that it provides little geographic detail, primarily national and state statistics, and little depth in any topic.

University data centers like the University of North Carolina's Institute for Research in the Social Sciences or the University of Michigan's Institute for

Social Research may have their own large state, regional, or national data sets from which a subset of subjects age sixty-five and older may be selected for additional analysis. They may also own copies of Gallup, Roper, and other public opinion polls, which can be used in the same way.

Indirect Data Sets

Indirect data sets are reports, directories, medical or service provider records, and other resources from which data sets can be built. Time-consuming to use, but readily accessible sources of data about health and social resources in rural areas, are directories of services or facilities. These directories may include a fair amount of data, including ownership, area served, acceptance of Medicaid, and capacity. Researchers who choose directories should be sure they know exactly who is included and excluded from the listing. For example, does this directory list all licensed domiciliary care facilities in the state or only those which accept Medicaid clients? Does this list of home-delivered meals programs include those funded entirely by churches and civic organizations or only those that receive some federal funding? Another question to ask is whether the provider agency only offers services in the county where it is located or to surrounding areas as well.

Using the telephone "yellow pages" listings requires a greater leap of faith because there is no clear definition of their contents. For example, large or marketing-wise medical groups, facilities, and other service providers may be listed in the directories of all surrounding counties, while other smaller, less marketing-wise groups or providers offering the same services may be listed only in the county in which they are located. Further, services provided by religious, civic, or other largely volunteer efforts may not be listed at all, or they may be listed separately in a "Community" section of the directory. On the other hand, the telephone book is probably where the average older adult or family member first tries to locate services. Thus, in the absence of more precise measures, the variable "number of home-health agencies listed in a county telephone directory" has an intrinsic meaning about choice for the consumer.

The work setting of the agency or organization that funds applied or policy research may provide access to a wealth of additional secondary data. Provider agencies, for example, may have data sets established to track funding or compliance. These may be used to provide data on units of service provided, cost per unit, and even some characteristics of service recipients. State-mandated data sets such as files of elder abuse reports and substantiations are a similar source of valuable research data. When working with a small rural agency, it is especially important to remember that secondary data often does not reside on diskette or compact disc. Sometimes they are in a file cabinet crammed with twenty years worth of annual reports.

Approximating Research Questions with the Data at Hand

There can be no rules of thumb or easy guidelines about whether the variables measured by other researchers come close enough to the question the current research demands. The first task is to read the documentation and, if possible, talk to people involved in the initial data collection/preparations. This should clarify how the question was actually asked and reveal any hidden limitations of the data. The unfortunate reality is that data sets will vary enormously in the completeness and accuracy of their documentation. In addition, when faced with data such as annual reports from a variety of subsidiary agencies, one has little but others' opinions as a basis for judging the accuracy and consistency of the data. For example, local home health agencies may be required to file an annual report including the unduplicated count of people receiving services from their agencies. Do all of these agencies keep records by social security number or other unique identifier, or are some of the respondents guessing based on average daily counts and an estimate of their rate of turnover? Are clients truly unduplicated within the agency, but duplicated across agencies?

Armed with as much information as possible about data quality, the research team must weigh the value of using the data already collected, in a known format, with a known response rate, and a known variation in responses (for better or worse), against the potential value of asking a better-focused, more precise question (assuming your team is relatively sure it can write a question that will provide a better measure of the concept), in a hypothetical format, with an unknown response rate, an unknown variation in the response, and a much longer turn-around time. It is a rare user of secondary data who has not had at least one disaster from using a data set with undocumented inconsistencies or some other hidden land mine. On the other hand, it is a rare researcher who never has a failed question in the primary data-gathering effort, and these mistakes show up many months and dollars later.

Most often, in studying rural aging, the research team will be combining secondary and primary data. Thus, primary data from a survey of service needs and preferences or of county spending priorities may be supplemented with secondary data about the subunits of the area surveyed, including such variables as poverty rate, presence or absence of a rural hospital, liberal or conservative voting history, death rates from occupation-related illnesses, and many others.

Methods of Presentation

When secondary data are used for analysis, they are simply merged with the primary data set or used separately in performing the analysis. (See, for example, Chapter 11 about the use of macro- and micro-data in statistical models.) However, when the data are being used to assemble a statistical profile or data book, presentation becomes a key issue.

Statistical profiles may range from a simple summary of variable values covering a single geographical area, to a more elaborate affair providing descriptions of multiple areas and explicit comparisons among them. The more elaborate versions may include some of the methods of data presentation discussed in Chapter 3, including choroplethic mapping as well as tables and charts. Figures 1 through 5 show some examples of presentation styles that can be used.

Figure 1 shows a simple and widely used presentation style when data are compiled for a number of units (counties, states, service areas) [27]. In this case, an identical two-page spread is presented for each county in North Carolina with variables related to need for services (age, race, poverty, rurality, impairment) appearing on the left hand page, and variables representing resources (supply of health professionals, hospital and nursing home beds, per capita expenditure for services) on the right. Comparisons to the other counties in the Area Agency on Aging region and the state are provided for each variable.

Figure 2 is a simple bar graph showing the gender- and race-specific prevalence estimates of severe cognitive impairment with metropolitan/nonmetropolitan comparisons for a single state [28]. The advantage of this type of graphic (bar charts, pie charts, and line graphs) is its accessibility to less-sophisticated readers. This makes it a good choice for presentations to both providers and legislators who are seldom able to devote time to studying more esoteric formats.

Figure 3 is a set of population pyramids representing the age and gender composition of two rural counties and illustrating the heterogeneity of rural places [1]. Smith County in Texas shows the near-rectangular shape of an older and stable population (one with the same low rate of natural increase year after year), while Sweetwater County in Wyoming shows the pyramidal shape of a young and growing population. The population pyramid conveys detailed information about population composition while using a visual and accessible format. A time series of such pyramids is one way to convey the aging of a population. Figure 4 uses a pair of choroplethic maps to convey a smaller amount of information, but still make a somewhat more dramatic statement about the projected increase of the oldest old in North Carolina. Figure 5 illustrates the real value of choroplethic mapping in giving county-specific detail and allowing for a variety of quick comparisons among counties and across regions [1]. In this example, the county and regional differences in number of people per physician offering patient care is illustrated.

In addition to these sorts of figures, traditionally used in both publications and slide presentations, the Internet publisher has a variety of sound, animation, and video options for presentation. In deciding on presentation styles for web sites, site managers must balance sometimes conflicting goals. The goal of making the site visually appealing is facilitated by the use of graphs, tables, video and audio clips, and animation. However, the goal of usefulness is even more important. If the graphics files are so large that they take an uncomfortably long

County Aging Profiles

Northampton

	No. in County	County	AAA Region	State
Demographics of Aging				
Population age 65+, 1990	3,436	15.1%	13.3%	12.5%
Population age 65+, 2010	4,137	18.3	15.5	15.1
Age 65+ nonwhite, 1990	1,746	50.8	35.6	18.4
Age 65+ living alone (1980)	N/A	26.0	27.4	26.4
Age 65+ in rural areas (1980)	N/A	100.0	53.7	51.7
Population age 85+, 1990	311	1.4	1.1	1.1
Population age 85+, 2010	620	2.7	2.2	2.2
Economics of Aging				
Median income (1979, in 1988 dollars):				
Households with heads age 65 or older	N/A	$14,160	$14,658	$15,928
Unrelated men age 65 or older	N/A	6,498	6,235	6,103
Unrelated women age 65 or older	N/A	5,478	5,692	5,883
Age 65+ in poverty (1980)	N/A	30.4%	28.4%	23.9%
Receiving SSI (1987)	490	15.4	12.4	6.7
Receiving Social Security (1987)	3,047	95.5	91.7	92.2
Receiving Medicaid (FY 88–89)	763	23.2	17.9	11.4
Receiving Medicare (1985)	3,152	100.0	98.8	96.5
Receiving food stamps (FY 88–89)	551	16.8	14.1	7.2
Receiving special assistance (FY 88–89)	80	2.4	2.4	1.6
Problem housing conditions (1980):				
Substandard/nonexistent kitchen	N/A	14.7	8.7	4.6
Substandard/nonexistent plumbing	N/A	19.5	11.7	6.3
No telephone	N/A	13.2	11.6	8.4
No central heating	N/A	68.2	53.6	41.2
No air conditioning	N/A	60.1	44.8	50.8
Functionally Impaired, Age 65+				
Three or more ADL impairments,1990	273	8.1	7.5	6.9
IADL impairments, 1990	314	9.3	8.6	7.7
Mental Health and Aging, Age 65+				
Severe cognitive impairment, 1990	192	5.6	4.2	3.4
Other mental illness, 1990	354	10.3	9.2	7.6

	Deaths per 1,000 People Age 65+		
Mortality Statistics	County	Region	State
Deaths from all causes (1988)	58.3	54.4	50.6
Deaths from cardiovascular disease (1988)	28.5	28.9	25.6
Deaths from cancers (1988)	10.5	10.8	10.4

150 CARES for the North Carolina Division of Aging

Figure 1. Sample data book pages.

Northampton

	Total $	$ per Person Age 65+		
	County	County	Region	State
Community Services				
Mental health centers	$35,127	$10.68	$8.18	$7.27
Adult day care	0	0.00	2.08	1.36
Adult protective services	60	0.02	0.55	0.98
Meals (congregate & home)	72,115	21.93	18.54	19.66
Transportation	10,063	3.06	3.47	6.84

	Per 1,000 Residents Age 65+		
	County	Region	State
Active Health Professionals			
Primary care physicians	1.5	2.7	3.8
Total physicians	1.8	8.1	12.9
Registered nurses	6.1	40.2	53.9
Licensed practical nurses	6.1	15.6	18.4
Physical therapists	0.3	1.2	1.6

	Total $	$ per Person Age 65+		
	County	County	Region	State
In-Home Services, Adults 65+				
Medicare hospice/home health	$172,220	$52.38	$49.96	$64.84
Medicaid hospice/ home health	59,509	18.10	9.20	12.64
OAA home health	0	0.00	1.63	0.54
State home health services program	5,417	1.64	3.72	3.18
Medicaid CAP	0	0.00	6.86	16.63
Medicaid personal care	193,137	58.74	26.23	12.61
OAA in-home services	44,462	13.52	8.68	7.17
SSBG in-home services	94,996	28.89	9.72	6.13
State in-home services	32,846	9.99	7.22	6.02

	Beds per 1,000 People Age 65+		
	County	Region	State
Institutional Care			
Total nursing home (SNF & ICF)	20.8	34.6	34.0
Domiciliary care (family & HA)	39.6	31.5	27.8
Acute care hospital	0.0	29.2	33.9
Residents 65+ in state mental hospitals	1.5	3.1	1.2

	County	Region	State
Housing			
HUD-subsidized public housing units	306	4,866	75,789
HUD & FHA housing for the elderly	62	1,607	30,951
Continuing care facility independent living units	0	150	4,294

CARES for the North Carolina Division of Aging   151

Figure 1. (Cont'd.)

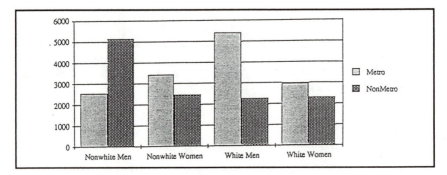

Figure 2. Bar chart of estimated number of residents aged sixty-five and older with severe cognitive impairment: North Carolina, 1988.

time to view on older equipment, or if the presentation uses a new application or "plug-in" not readily accessible to the majority of browsers and equipment in use, this goal is sacrificed.

In *presenting* data, as in selecting items, the purpose for which the collected data is to be used is an important consideration. For example, when comparisons among counties are made as a basis for building future research, the focus may be on conceptual issues (e.g., "Do counties that contain at least one urban place have a higher ratio of primary care physicians to population?"), but when comparisons are made for planning purposes, there is more interest in identifying relative strengths and weaknesses (e.g., "Which of the council of government's region counties have the highest and lowest per capita spending for adult day care? Which areas of a county are not reached by medical transportation services?").

The level of detail reported may also vary with the purpose of the research. For example, while the research community and the policymakers may be interested in the absolute and relative *rates* of impairment in Activities of Daily Living (ADLs) in farming and non-farming rural areas, the planning group may be more interested in the actual *number of people* with ADL impairments in the area for which they must budget services.

Interpreting Secondary Data

Understanding the Data

Accurate interpretation of a variable drawn from secondary data, like the decision about whether this variable is usable, should be based on as thorough a grounding as possible in the original question, the method of collecting the data, and any oddities about the data set. Mistaken assumptions about these can lead to wildly inaccurate conclusions. Once the original research is understood, interpretation of secondary data is very similar to interpretation of primary data.

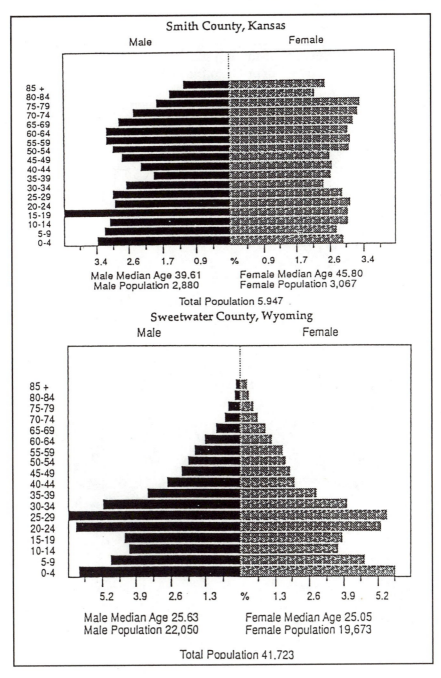

Figure 3. Comparison of population pyramids.

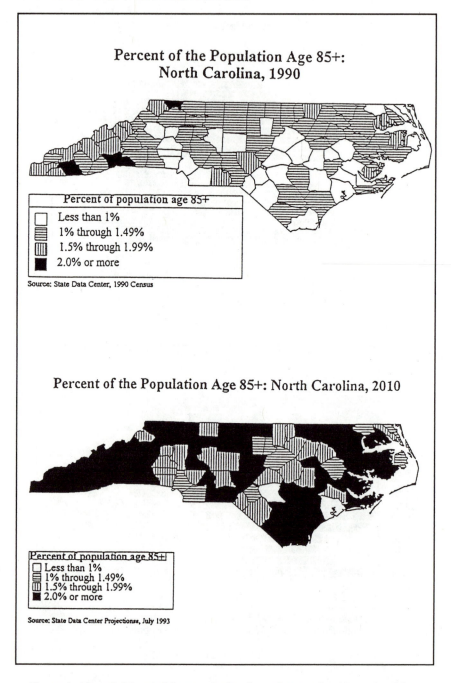

Figure 4. Use of choroplethic mapping to show changes in age composition.

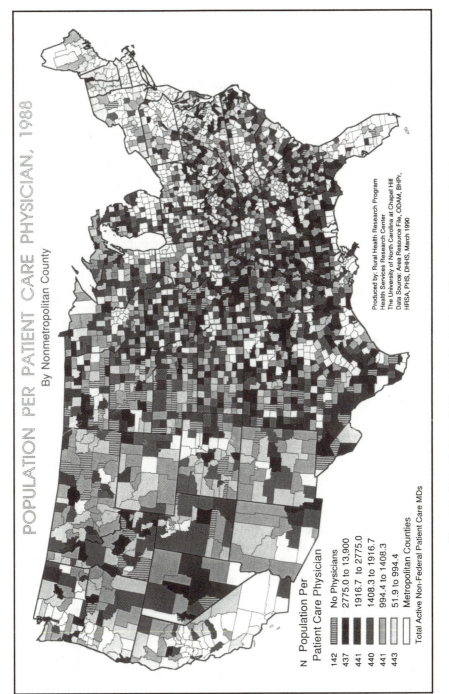

POPULATION PER PATIENT CARE PHYSICIAN, 1988
By Nonmetropolitan County

N Population Per
Patient Care Physician

142   No Physicians
437   2775.0 to 13,900
441   1916.7 to 2775.0
440   1408.3 to 1916.7
441   994.4 to 1408.3
443   51.9 to 994.4
      Metropolitan Counties

Total Active Non-Federal Patient Care MDs

Produced by: Rural Health Research Program
Health Services Research Center
The University of North Carolina at Chapel Hill
Data Source: Area Resource File, ODAM, BHPr,
HRSA, PHS, DHHS, March 1990

Figure 5. Use of choroplethic mapping to show inter-county comparisons.

However, there are three additional dangers that are not unique to the task, but which may be considered secondary analysis "risk factors": overinterpreting proxy variables, the ecological fallacy, and overinterpreting central tendencies.

Proxy Variables

As the name implies, a proxy variable is used to stand in for a variable that is not available. For example, a research team examining the demand for home health services is doing secondary analysis of a data set from a national survey. Most of the variables they would like to study are in this data set, but they find, inexplicably, that there is no question asking whether or not the respondent had any chronic diseases or conditions. Since those with chronic conditions are likely to make different demands on the type, level, and duration of services, the team feels this is an essential control variable for their analysis. A person with little knowledge or experience in the field might think that self-reported health status had good face validity as a proxy variable. Surely a person with a chronic condition would be more likely to report fair or poor health than a person with only acute health problems. As most readers know, experience does not support the validity of this proxy. Even people with very severe disabilities and chronic illnesses seemingly adjust their answer to a baseline which includes that disability as a given. Thus, for example, people with diabetes will rate their health as good, apparently with the unspoken qualifier, "for a person with diabetes."

For a younger population, the team might be able to use a variable reporting days of work missed due to personal illness in the past year as a proxy for chronic conditions. Even in a younger population this would be imperfect both because of gender differences in workforce participation and because of the possibility that, in a given year, a large number of work days were missed due to a severe acute illness rather than a chronic condition. In an older population, in which labor force participation is both low and highly variable, this would not be a useful proxy at all.

Let us say that the data set does include a variable about the need for assistance in bathing, dressing, and grooming. This is a far from perfect proxy for chronic illness, both because many people with fairly serious chronic conditions can usually or always bathe and dress themselves, and because some people may be unable to bathe or dress themselves as the aftermath of an acute episode such as a stroke. On the other hand, as a control variable for variation in underlying need for assistance, the original intent of including chronic conditions, this may be a satisfactory, or at least the *most* satisfactory, solution.

However, it is incumbent on the team to make clear that the variable is a proxy in all communication about its analysis. It is too easy to slip into writing and even *thinking* of the variable as "chronic health problem" when it is in fact "ability to bathe and dress." It is perfectly reasonable, in discussion, to posit the link between the two variables, but it is important to remember that this is an assumption.

Ecological Fallacy

The ecological fallacy is the logical error of interpreting data at an inappropriate level of analysis (e.g., making a micro-level interpretation of macro-level data or a macro-level interpretation of micro-level data). Research into the need, availability, and access to health and social services in rural areas is particularly susceptible to this problem, because the data are usually macro-level (e.g., per capita spending on respite for Alzheimer's caregivers, average case mix for home health agencies), yet many of the underlying research interests are about individual rural elders.

It is very easy to slip into this fallacy. Take, for a moment, a not-quite-hypothetical case in which the researchers want to know whether a new allocation formula for a given funding stream is reaching the target population better than the old formula. Two target groups for this funding, which are not mutually exclusive, are rural elders and African-American elders. Analysis using aggregate demographic data and the new funding formula shows that a larger proportion of the money is now going to nonmetropolitan counties in which the proportion of the citizens who are African Americans is larger than the average for the state. Does the new formula improve targeting?

When the question is spelled out directly, most readers will see the problem at once. Getting the money to counties that have large numbers of rural and/or African-American elders is necessary, but not sufficient, to show improved targeting. A predominantly white urban county might be spending every penny of its allocation on African-American elders in the central city area and on white elders in a rural corner of the county. At the same time, a disproportionately African American, predominantly rural county might be spending most of its allocation on white clients who live in the county's one moderate-sized town.

Does this mean that macro-level data or ecological/contextual analysis is useless, or is it a poor substitute for individual level data? No. In fact, in 1994 both the *American Journal of Public Health* and the *American Journal of Epidemiology* devoted substantial space to arguments about the strengths and weakness of group-level analysis. While some of these commentaries have perpetuated the idea that ecological analysis is useful primarily for generating hypotheses or when no individual-level data are available, most are detailed methodological arguments for not throwing out the ecological baby with the fallacious bathwater [29-35].

Schwartz argues that widespread, unthinking concern about the ecological fallacy has encouraged three new fallacies: "1) that individual-level models are more perfectly specified than ecological-level models, 2) that ecological correlations are always substitutes for individual-level, and 3) that group-level variables do not cause disease" [33, p. 819]. If we view "disease" more broadly as "outcome variable," the relevance of the latter two points to the study of rural elders is immediately obvious.

First, we are often interested in macro-level outcomes as well as macro-level predictors. For example, what characteristics of a rural county predict the level of public services it will offer or the number of health providers it will be able to recruit? The ecological fallacy is irrelevant to this analysis because it is performed and interpreted at the macro level. Second, we see clearly that macro-level variables may have a different meaning for the individual than the individual variables from which they are aggregated. For example, coming from a poor community (i.e., local poverty rate) may have a number of influences on health and social services available to an individual citizen, irrespective of that citizen's financial status. Thus, at the individual level, the macro-level variable poverty rate has a separate influence from the micro-level variable poverty status. (For a discussion of the methodological issues in mixing variables from multiple levels of analysis, see Chapter 11.)

These problems are relevant to the first point, whether individual-level models are more perfectly specified than ecological-level models. The dangers of misspecification and sources of bias at the two levels of analysis are complex, and beyond the scope of this chapter. It seems clear that ecological analysis may be distorted more severely, and in somewhat different ways from microanalysis by omission of interaction terms and other misspecifications. The bottom line is eloquently stated by Susser, "Equipped with an understanding of the dimensions involved at ecological and individual levels and of the relationships between them, one is in a position to exploit the public health potential of the ecological approach. Effective researchers do not despair in the face of confounding and error; they guard against them and search them out" [34, p. 829].

Overinterpreting Central Tendencies

A third danger lies in overinterpreting central tendencies. For example, the most rural counties in North Carolina have a lower mean per capita supply of nursing home and domiciliary beds than more urban counties. However, viewing only the mean supply hides the nearly bimodal distribution of beds. In fact, while many rural counties are undersupplied, there are several rural counties for which large facilities are a sort of local industry.

Refining the Question

Preliminary research using secondary data can help to refine the research question in a variety of ways. First, it can help researchers avoid wasted time and effort by pointing out unexpected relationships or showing that expected relationships do not exist for the area or population under study. For example, those of us who study rural aging tend to take for granted that rural counties have higher poverty rates for older adults than urban counties do. However, in those rural counties of great natural beauty which have attracted high levels of retirement migration, the poverty rates for retirees may be unusually low. (Of course, this does not mean that there might not be a subgroup within the county with very high poverty rates, such as indigenous loggers, farmers, or fishermen (see "Over-interpreting Central Tendencies," p. 38).)

Another way of using secondary data for refining the question is to "round up the usual suspects." For example, suppose people from remote parts of a rural county have very low participation rates in community-based services such as adult day care or health screenings held at senior centers. An applied researcher might want to conduct a survey of potential consumers, asking them to identify attractions and barriers to participation. However, an initial look at demographic and service data might reveal several potential explanations that could be further explored without a full-fledged survey effort. Perhaps there are no transportation services or funds for transportation available to people in that part of the county. Perhaps the people in that part of the county are substantially different from those in the remainder by level of education, income, race, or length of time in the county. Even if a survey is still contemplated, this knowledge will help to shape the areas of inquiry.

A third way is the serendipitous finding. For example, when beginning to look at predictors of public services expenditures among rural and urban counties, Salmon, Nelson, and Rous fully expected to see lower per capita expenditures in the rural counties, but a preliminary review of the secondary data revealed that this traditional view was supported for adult day care and protective services, but not for other home and community services [36]. What we learned accidentally was of more significance than our findings for the question we had originally planned since it challenged a popular view, raised a larger research question about the wide variation of services among demographically similar counties, and strengthened the case for greater analysis among rural counties rather than between rural and urban ones.

SUMMARY

This overview of secondary data use for rural gerontological research had made the following key points.

- There are three primary uses for secondary data gathering and analysis in rural gerontological research: 1) atlases, data books, and online statistical profiles; 2) comparisons of rural and urban areas; and 3) studies of specific rural areas.
- Atlases, data books, and statistical profiles are arrays of secondary data assembled for program planning, as a research tool, or to influence policy decisions. The types of elements and, to a lesser degree, the way they are presented, is a function of the primary purpose.

- Comparisons of rural and urban areas are a very common form of rural gerontological study using secondary data. Although this has been an important piece of the development of the rural aging literature, some researchers fear that this approach casts rurality as a problem to be overcome, rather than a form of diversity to be embraced.

- Studies of specific rural areas are less likely to use secondary data because primary collection is less prohibitive in terms of time and cost. However, there is value to combining primary and secondary data in studies of this type.

- The steps involved in secondary analysis are: 1) locating and selecting an appropriate data set, 2) approximating research questions with the data at hand, 3) interpreting secondary data presenting the data, and 4) refining the question.

- Some major sources of secondary data are the *U.S. Decennial Census; Current Population Reports;* the *Statistical Abstract of the United States;* state vital statistics data; state medical licensure data; directories of services or facilities; phone books; and data sets controlled by universities, agencies, or associations.

- A variety of methods are available for presenting data in profiles. The decision to use tables of numbers or such graphics as bar charts, flow graphs, or choroplethic mapping depend on whether the purpose is to reveal major trends, or provide precise information, and on the needs of the audience for whom the presentation is intended.

- Four potential pitfalls in interpreting secondary data are: 1) not understanding how the original data were collected, 2) reifying proxy variables, 3) the ecological fallacy, and 4) overinterpreting central tendencies.

- Analysis of secondary data is one of the tools for further refining a research question, leading to primary research, or further analysis of the secondary data.

REFERENCES

1. Rural Health Research Program, *National Rural Health Policy Atlas,* prepared by Health Services Research Center, University of North Carolina at Chapel Hill, Chapel Hill, North Carolina, HSRC, 1991.
2. R. T. Coward, G. R. Lee, J. W. Dwyer, and K. Seccombe, *Old and Alone in Rural America,* AARP Public Policy Institute, 1993.
3. J. F. Van Nostrand (ed.), Common Beliefs about the Rural Elderly: What Do National Data Tell Us? National Center for Health Statistics, *Vital Health Statistics, 3*:28, 1993.
4. F. L. Schick and R. Schick (eds.), *Statistical Handbook on Aging Americans* (number 5), Oryx Press, Phoenix, Arizona, 1994.
5. C. A. Dorgan (ed.), *Statistical Record of Older Americans* (2nd Edition), Gale Research, Detroit, Michigan, 1996.

6. J. A. Post, Internet Resources on Aging, *The Gerontologist, 36*:1, pp. 11-12, 1996.

7. S. Cutler and R. Coward, Residence Differences in the Health Status of Elders, *The Journal of Rural Health, 4,* pp. 11-26, 1988.

8. R. A. Leinbach, Differences in Need among the Rural and Urban Aged: Statistical Versus Practical Significance, *The Journal of Rural Health, 4*:3, pp. 27-34, 1988.

9. R. Blieszner, W. J. McAuley, J. K. Newhouse, and J. A. Mancini. Rural-Urban Differences in Service Use by Older Adults, in *Aging, Health, and Family: Long-Term Care,* T. H. Brubaker (ed.), Sage Publications, Newbury Park, California, pp. 162-174, 1987.

10. J. L. Meyer, R. A. Lusky, and A. Wright, Title III Services: Variation in Use Within a State, *Journal of Applied Gerontology, 10*:2, pp. 140-156, 1991.

11. G. M. Nelson, A Comparison of Title XX Services to the Urban and Rural Elderly, *Journal of Gerontological Social Work, 6*;1, pp. 3-23, 1983.

12. A. E. Benjamin, Determinants of State Variations in Home Health Utilization and Expenditures under Medicare, *Medical Care, 24*:6, pp. 535-547, 1986.

13. J. Hammond, Analysis of County-Level Data Concerning the Use of Medicare Home Health Benefits, *Public Health Reports, 100*:1, pp. 48-54, 1985.

14. G. M. Kenny and L. C. Dubay, Explaining Area Variation in the Use of Medicare Home Health Services, *Medical Care, 30*:1, pp. 43-57, 1992.

15. J. H. Swan and A. E. Benjamin, Medicare Home Health Utilization as a Function of Nursing Home Market Factors, *Health Services Research, 23,* pp. 479-500, 1990.

16. R. T. Coward, W. B. Vogel, R. P. Duncan, and R. Uttaro, Should Intrastate Funding Formulae for the Older Americans Act Include a Rural Factor? *The Gerontologist, 35*:1, pp. 24-34, 1995.

17. R. T. Coward and S. J. Cutler, Informal and Formal Health Care Systems for the Rural Elderly, *Health Services Research, 23*:6, pp. 785-806, 1989.

18. J. W. Green, Aging and Ethnicity: An Emergent Issue in Social Gerontology, *Journal of Cross-Cultural Gerontology, 4,* pp. 377-383, 1989.

19. E. P. Stanford and D. L. Yee, Gerontology and the Relevance of Diversity, *Generations, 15*:4, pp. 11-14, 1991.

20. T. C. Ricketts, L. A. Savitz, W. Gesler, and D. Osborne (eds.), *Geographic Methods in Health Services Research,* University Press of America, Lanham, Maryland, 1994.

21. M. K. Miller and A. E. Luloff, Who is Rural? A Typological Approach to the Examination of Rurality, *Rural Sociology, 46,* pp. 608-625, 1981.

22. M. Hewitt, Defining "Rural" Areas: Impact on Health Care Policy and Research, in *Health in Rural North America,* W. M. Gesler and T. C. Ricketts (eds.), Rutgers University Press, New Brunswick, New Jersey, pp. 25-34, 1992.

23. C. Hawes, J. N. Morris, C. D. Phillips, V. Mor, B. E. Fries, and S. Nonemaker, Reliability Estimates for the Minimum Data Set for Nursing Home Resident Assessment and Care Screenings (MDS), *The Gerontologist, 35*:2, pp. 172-178, 1995.

24. E. E. Lipowski and W. E. Bigelow, Data Linkages for Research on Outcomes of Long-Term Care, *The Gerontologist, 36*:4, pp. 441-447, 1996.

25. L. K. George and D. Blazer, Psychiatric Disorders and Mental Health Service Use in Later Life: Evidence from the Epidemiologic Catchment Area Program, in

Epidemiology and Aging, J. A. Brody and G. L. Maddox (eds.), Springer, New York, pp. 189-219, 1988.

26. A. Unger and W. Weissert, *Data for Long Term Care Planning: Application of a Synthetic Estimation Technique,* Report No. 1466-24 (revised), The Urban Institute, Washington, D.C., May 1983.

27. Center for Aging Research and Educational Services (CARES), *North Carolina Come of Age,* prepared by the Center for Aging Research and Educational Services, School of Social Work, University of North Carolina for the North Carolina Division of Aging, CARES, Chapel Hill, North Carolina, 1990.

28. Center for Aging Research and Educational Services (CARES), *Aging in North Carolina,* prepared by the Center for Aging Research and Educational Services, School of Social Work, University of North Carolina for the North Carolina Division of Social Services, CARES, Chapel Hill, North Carolina, 1989.

29. B. L. Cohen, Invited Commentary: In Defense of Ecologic Studies for Testing a Linear–No Threshold Theory, *American Journal of Epidemiology, 139*:8, pp. 765-768, 1994.

30. S. Greenland and J. Robins, Invited Commentary: Ecologic Studies—Biases, Misconceptions, and Counterexamples, *American Journal of Epidemiology, 139*:8, pp. 747-760, 1994.

31. J. S. Koopman and I. M. Longini, Jr., The Ecological Effects of Individual Exposures and Nonlinear Disease Dynamics in Populations, *American Journal of Public Health, 84*:5, pp. 836-842, 1994.

32. S. Paintadosi, Invited Commentary: Ecologic Biases, *American Journal of Epidemiology, 139*:8, pp. 761-764, 1994.

33. S. Schwartz, The Fallacy of the Ecological Fallacy: The Potential Misuse of a Concept and the Consequences, *American Journal of Public Health, 84*:5, pp. 819-824, 1994.

34. M. Susser, The Logic in Ecological: I. The Logic of Analysis, *American Journal of Public Health, 84*:5, pp. 825-829, 1994.

35. M. Susser, The Logic in Ecological: II. The Logic of Design, *American Journal of Public Health, 84*:5, pp. 830-835, 1994.

36. A. Salmon, G. M. Nelson, and S. G. Rous, The Continuum of Care Revisited: A Rural Perspective, *The Gerontologist, 33*:5, pp. 658-666, 1993.

CHAPTER
3

Methods for Assessing Geographic Aspects of Health Care for Older Adults in Rural Areas

Wilbert M. Gesler, Lucy A. Savitz, and Peggy S. Wittie

INTRODUCTION

A high proportion of older persons in our society have a complex set of health care problems; these problems are often more challenging in rural areas. Of particular concern to medical geographers is physical accessibility to care. Many older residents in rural areas are isolated, must travel relatively long distances to receive care, and have difficulty obtaining transportation. In addition, accessibility varies for different subgroups of the older population.

This chapter describes several specific geographic techniques that can aid in the assessment of geographic accessibility. An overview of the geographic perspective on health care delivery precedes a discussion of the main issues in health care provision for rural adult populations that can be addressed with such techniques as maps and graphs. These issues include descriptions of the distributions of both older persons and health care resources, availability of resources, and the accessibility to and utilization of resources. These descriptions and analyses complement other methodologic approaches to better ensure adequate and effective health care.

HEALTH CARE PROBLEMS OF OLDER PERSONS
IN RURAL AREAS

Why perform geographic analyses that address the health care problems of older persons who reside in rural areas? The U.S. population is increasing and life expectancy continues to lengthen. By the year 2020, it is estimated that 21 percent of the population will be over the age of sixty-five [1] with the most rapidly growing segment of the elderly population being women over the age of eighty. Since older persons have greater needs for health care services and place greater demands on the health care systems than other segments of the population, we need to make special efforts to ensure that health care is made available to them, and efficiently and effectively delivered to them. This matching of needs and services is difficult because of the complexities of geriatric care. Besides routine physician office visits and visits to hospitals for minor problems, older persons have a relatively high proportion of chronic conditions with economic, social, and mental health as well as medical implications. The complexity of these cases requires additional attention, often including an array of services and providers. Moreover, the provision of long-term care must be expanded [2].

Health and health care access are greater problems for older persons living in rural areas than they are for their urban counterparts [3]. For example, older persons in nonmetropolitan areas are twice as likely to have to travel more than thirty minutes to reach their usual source of care, and face limited or no public transportation services. Further, a higher proportion of nonmetropolitan older people have reported their health as fair or poor [4].

Rural older persons often have special needs: transportation may be an especially important concern and isolation can be a serious problem. Those who live alone have a poorer health profile than those who have other residential arrangements [5]. There may also be a problem of kin support. A study by Powers and Kivett showed that expectations of kin assistance among rural older adults were much higher than actual levels of support, and that level of support was mainly a question of geographic distance to kin and norms of obligation [6].

America's older population is heterogeneous. Important subgroups include the very old, women, poor people, and those from various ethnic groups [7]. The population of older people who are members of ethnic minority groups is growing more rapidly than the overall population. In 1990, 10 percent of the population over the age of sixty-five belonged to an ethnic minority (African American, Hispanic, Asian, and others). By 2025 it is estimated the figure will be 15 percent. In North Carolina, which provided many of the examples used in this chapter, the 1990 Census showed that the population over sixty-five was 81.9 percent white, 17.3 percent black, 0.6 percent Indian, and 0.2 of Asian origin. Many ethnic minorities have relatively high rates of poverty, malnutrition, and poor health care. Disparities continue to persist among ethnic groups in terms of access to health care [8].

THE GEOGRAPHIC PERSPECTIVE

Providing effective health care to older people requires an interdisciplinary approach. Geographers have their own perspective, emphasizing the spatial distributions of health care consumers and providers as well as the relationship between them. A major focus is on understanding the barriers to physical accessibility. A great amount of work by geographers and others has been done in this area over the last twenty to thirty years [9-11]. Since geographic analysis is usually accompanied with visual aids such as maps and graphs, it enables one to actively *see* the salient issues in the utilization of health services for older adults. It is this latter point that we wish to emphasize in this chapter, in the spirit of "a picture is worth a thousand words." With recent developments in map-making computer software, visual presentations can be constructed rapidly and manipulated quite easily to display many different facets of a health care situation.

The geographic techniques that we present in this chapter are both descriptive and analytical. They describe the spatial distributions of older adults and potential health care resources. They allow examination of relationships between consumers and providers, including comparisons between different subgroups of older populations based on age, ethnicity, gender, and other population characteristics. We also show how statistical information and cartographic displays complement each other. That is, tables and maps tell a story from complementary perspectives.

Geographic techniques can only provide partial answers to practical health care delivery problems; other important (and often interrelated) variables must also be considered. The results of geographic analysis must be interpreted within their wider cultural, social, political, and economic context. For example, the main reason that some elderly people do not go to a particular facility may have more to do with their individual and cultural attitudes than with their distance from the facility [12, 13]. Nonetheless, the geographic analysis can identify important considerations and suggest alternative explanations.

The ultimate goal of this chapter is to assess the health care needs, resource availability, geographic accessibility, and utilization patterns of older adults living in rural areas. Table 1 is a list of questions to direct the geographic inquiry toward achieving this goal. Questions 1 through 3 examine the geographic distribution of the elderly population. Relevant concerns include the overall distribution, how subgroups are distributed, and how some important diseases are distributed. The next set of questions, 4 and 5, address the availability of health care resources. The issue here is how these resources are distributed and whether there are inequalities in resource availability among subgroups. Finally, questions 6 and 7 inquire about the interaction between older people and health care resources. Interactions are of two types: accessibility is a measure of *potential* utilization and utilization, or *realized* accessibility is a measure of the *actual* use of resources [9]. Access and utilization depend on the volumes and distances of consumer to provider flows, how areas within which people move when seeking

Table 1. Issues for Elderly People Which Lend Themselves
to Geographic Analysis

Spatial Description of the Population of Older Adults in Rural Areas

What are the main features of the overall geographic distribution of older
people in the study area?

What are the distributional characteristics of various subgroups of older
persons?

What is the distribution of health problems among older adults?

Availability of Health Care Resources

Where are the facilities and health personnel located that can meet the
needs of older adults?

Are there geographic inequalities in health care supplies for older adults?

Accessibility and Utilization

What geographic accessibility do older adults have to health care?

What are the health care utilization patterns for elderly people?

---

health care compare to areas in which they move in carrying out their daily
activities, and how well the locations and movements of older adults tie in with
the infrastructure of the study area.

ISSUES AND GEOGRAPHIC TECHNIQUES

Spatial Description of the Population of
Older Adults in Rural Areas

*What are the Main Features of the Overall Geographic
Distribution of Older People in the Study Area?*

A first step in obtaining a picture of where the target population is would be
to construct a *dot map*. On a dot map, points, circles, squares, or other symbols
are placed at the address of each older person. Symbols of a larger size might be
necessary to indicate where several older people resided (e.g., in a nursing home).
Dot maps can tell us quickly whether or not older adults are concentrated or
dispersed, and whether they tend to live in certain sections of the study area more
than in others. The dot map shown in Figure 1 depicts the distribution of people

over the age of sixty-five in Johnston County, a rural county in North Carolina. Within each of the seventeen townships and places within the county, the appropriate number of dots (each dot represents 250 older persons) was placed to approximate the population base since exact addresses were not known. Knowing addresses would, of course, produce a more accurate map.

If the addresses of people are not known, but census data are available in such geographic subunits as zip code areas, census tracts, or counties, we can also develop a picture of their distribution by constructing a *choropleth map*. Suppose that we are interested in the distribution of older adults in relation to the total population. We begin by looking at the entire distribution of ratios of older people to the total population in each subunit and then order the distribution from high to low. Next we divide the distribution into several groups (between 4 and 6 is usual). Geographic subunits whose ratios fall into the various categories are shaded the same way on a map. Subunits of the study area with relatively high proportions of older adults can be easily seen. For Figure 2, we have taken the same data used in Figure 1, divided the number of older people by the total population in each of the seventeen townships of Johnston County, and constructed a choropleth map.

An alternative to choropleth shading is to construct a *three-dimensional* (3-D) choropleth map with bars of various heights to represent the same information. To illustrate a 3-D map, we used the same total population data used for Figure 1 to construct Figure 3. Information in this format may be useful for local government efforts aimed at targeting community-based service programs for this subset of the population.

It might be of interest to know what *proportion* of the total older population in each geographic subunit fall into different age categories. To show this cartographically, we can place *pie charts* in each subunit that shows the percent of older adults who fall within these age ranges: sixty-five to seventy-four, seventy-five to eighty-four, and eighty-five and older (see Figure 4).

It is often useful to know how the distribution of a target population compares to the distribution of some other phenomenon. For example, thinking of one aspect of their accessibility to care, where does the older population live in relation to road networks? To make a comparison between people and roads, a dot map of the residences of older adults can be superimposed on a road map. This is called a *map overlay* and is readily done using a Geographic Information System (GIS), described below. A simple map overlay was produced (Figure 5) by superimposing Figure 1, the dot map which showed the distribution of older persons, over Johnston County's road network. Maps of the distribution of older populations could also usefully be overlaid with maps depicting the location of health facilities, health personnel of various types, topography (an indicator of time distance to care), and so on. In this way, a sense can be obtained of how many older people are isolated with respect to the transportation and health service infrastructure of a study area.

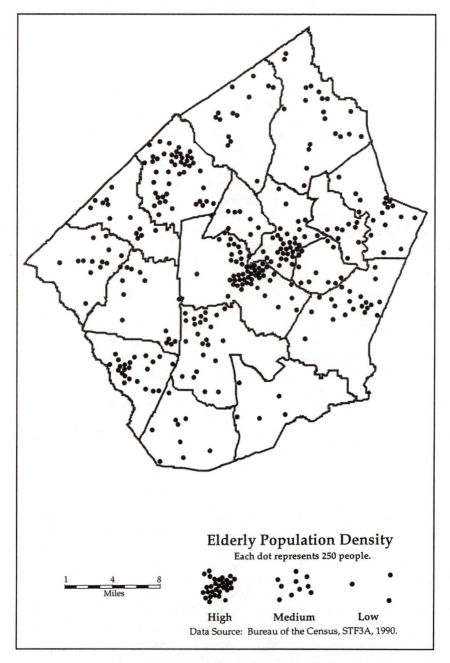

Figure 1. Elderly population, 1990, in townships
Johnston County, North Carolina.

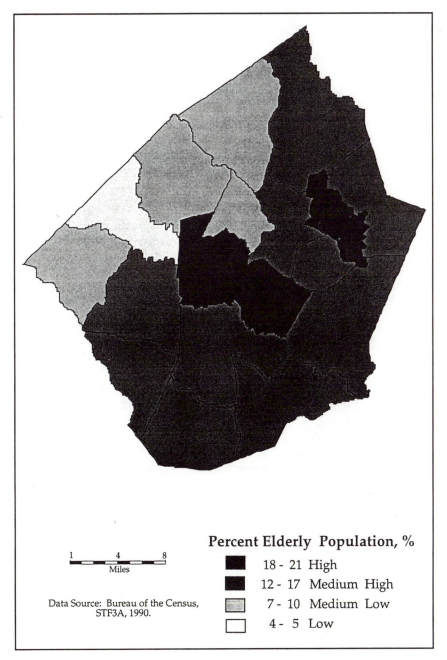

Percent Elderly Population, %

18 - 21 High
12 - 17 Medium High
7 - 10 Medium Low
4 - 5 Low

1   4   8
Miles

Data Source: Bureau of the Census,
STF3A, 1990.

Figure 2. 1990 elderly as percent of total population within
each township in Johnston County, North Carolina.

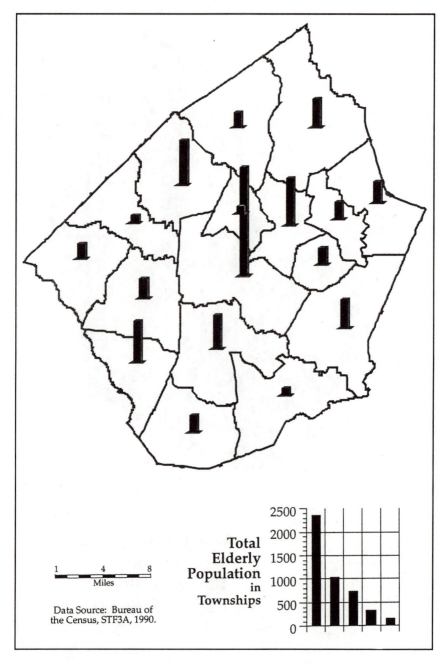

Total Elderly Population in Townships

Data Source: Bureau of the Census, STF3A, 1990.

Figure 3. 1990 total elderly population in townships, Johnston County, North Carolina.

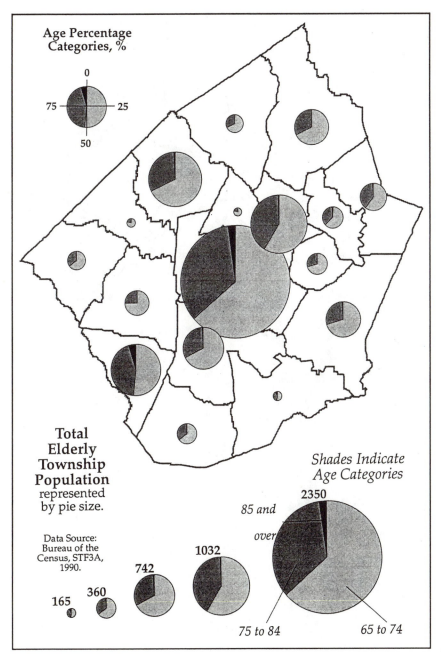

Figure 4. 1990 elderly population,
Johnston County Townships, North Carolina.

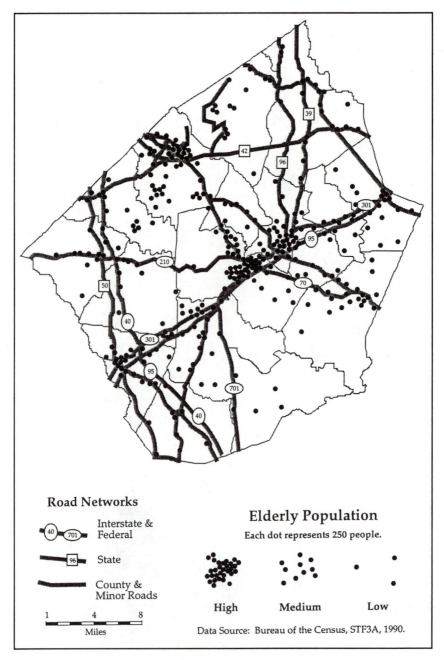

Figure 5. 1990 elderly population in
Johnston County Townships, North Carolina.

What are the Distributional Characteristics of Various Subgroups of Older Persons?

In order to target at-risk subgroups or to compare subgroups, it is often necessary to make maps that look at the entire older population broken down by such characteristics as age, gender, ethnicity, or income. If something is known about these variables, all of the maps discussed above can be constructed: dot, choropleth, overlay, or 3-D. For example, separate dot maps could be made for whites and nonwhites or they could be joined in one map, using different symbols for the two ethnic categories. The distributions of those age groups sixty-five to seventy-four, seventy-five to eighty-four, and eighty-five plus could also be compared in choroplethic maps.

What is the Distribution of Health Problems among Older Adults?

The task here is to discover where specific health needs of older people are located. Are there, for example, certain areas within the study area where heart diseases seem to be more prevalent? Again, dot, 3-D, choropleth, and overlay maps can be of assistance in targeting specific diseases. Disease maps can be compared to the entire distribution of older adults. They can, of course, also be developed for population subgroups.

If a population characteristic such as disease is being considered, it is often useful to map rates of the characteristics per population. This is best done on choropleth maps. Rates for each geographic subunit can be calculated (and perhaps adjusted for such factors as age, sex, and race), ranked, categorized, and shaded to show in which parts of the study area rates are relatively high or low. Figure 6 is a choropleth map showing tuberculosis rates per 100,000 for the counties of North Carolina in 1990. Especially in sparsely populated rural areas, however, the analyst may be forced to calculate rates over multiple time periods to accommodate instability in rates associated with small numbers.

Choropleth disease rate maps may be deceiving. This is because the areal extent of spatial units does not necessarily correspond with the size of the target population. Take, for example, a map which shows a disease whose prevalence rate is high in the Western and Mountain states of the United States. These states would stand out visually in the map patterns, although most of the states have relatively small populations. Thus, undue importance might be attached to these states in comparison to, say, Rhode Island or Washington, D.C. A *demographic base map* corrects this visual distortion. The basic idea is to alter the "real" map so that the size of each geographic subunit is proportional to the size of the target population in that subunit. Contiguity of subunits is maintained as much as possible. Actually designing a demographic base map takes some graph paper and a bit of patience, but it can produce a more "realistic" picture that reflects the underlying population base. Figure 7 uses a demographic base map to show pneumonia and influenza per 100,000 for 1985-1989 in the eleven-county Health

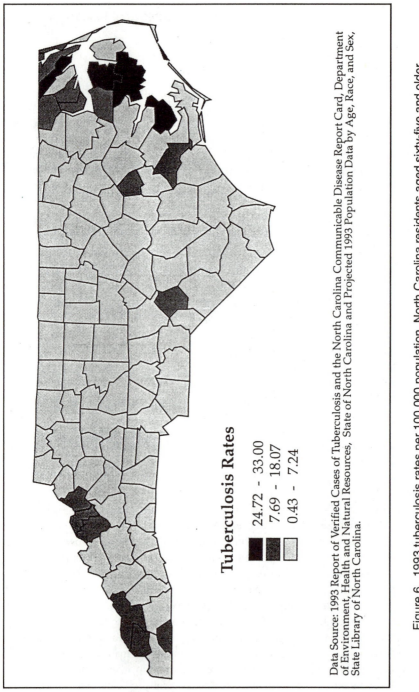

Tuberculosis Rates

24.72 - 33.00
7.69 - 18.07
0.43 - 7.24

Data Source: 1993 Report of Verified Cases of Tuberculosis and the North Carolina Communicable Disease Report Card, Department of Environment, Health and Natural Resources, State of North Carolina and Projected 1993 Population Data by Age, Race, and Sex, State Library of North Carolina.

Figure 6. 1993 tuberculosis rates per 100,000 population, North Carolina residents aged sixty-five and older.

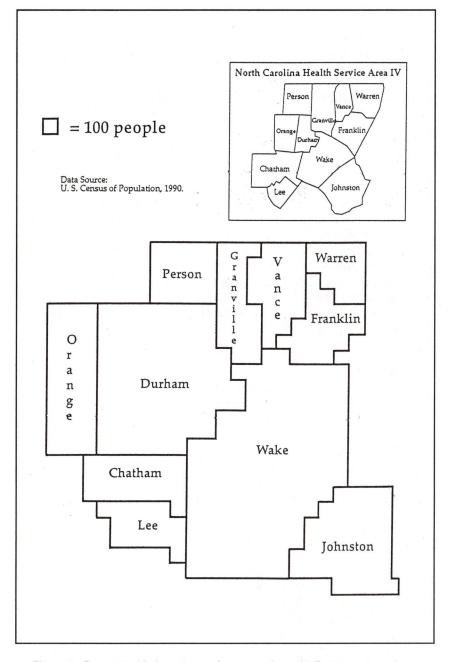

Figure 7. Demographic base map of pneumonia and influenza rates among the elderly (75+) per 100,000 population, 1985-1989.

Service Area IV of North Carolina. The size of each county is proportional to the number of persons age seventy-five and over, the "demographic base" for the map. Wake and Durham Counties, where the cities of Raleigh and Durham are located, clearly stand out in terms of size.

Availability of Health Care Resources

Where are the Facilities and Health Personnel Located
that Can Meet the Needs of Older Adults?

Health care supply is a distributional concern, so dot maps can be made for a wide range of items, including physicians with varying specialties, nurses, dentists, alternative healers, hospitals with various levels of service, specialist clinics, long-term care facilities, and social services such as meals-on-wheels and nutritional counseling. The size of the symbols can indicate such things as number of hospital beds or size of group practices. Different symbol shapes or colors could, for example, indicate levels of service—primary or specialist. Dot maps can be overlaid on infrastructure maps to indicate how closely tied health care resources are to such things as roads or schools. Three-dimensional (3-D) maps are another way of assessing supply. Choropleth maps can also be constructed that will show where absolute numbers of facilities and personnel are by geographic subunit.

Are there Geographic Inequalities in Health Care
Supplies for Older Adults?

To begin to answer this question, choropleth maps can be developed based upon facility and personnel to older population ratios. This will produce maps of, say, the number of nursing home beds per 1000 older adults or the number of oncologists per 100 older adults diagnosed with various cancers. These maps are useful in initially assessing equity in health care supply availability.

A somewhat more sophisticated choropleth map that shows the relationship between supply and demand is the *location quotient map.* Location quotients (LQs) are indices of the relative distribution of a variable of interest (e.g., number of home health nurses) in relation to a base variable such as the older population in an area. They can be calculated for each study subunit using the formula:

$$LQ(i) = \frac{A(i)/\Sigma A(i)}{P(i)/\Sigma P(i)}$$

where $A(i)$ is the value of the variable in subunit i,

$\Sigma A(i)$ is the sum or total for the variable in the entire study area,

$P(i)$ is the population in subunit i, and

$\Sigma P(i)$ is the total study population.

It can be seen from the formula that a location quotient represents a subunit's share of the variable of interest against the background of its share of the population. Thus, if a subunit has 10 percent of the hospital beds in the study area and also 10 percent of the elderly population, its LQ is one, which represents parity for that subunit in hospital beds. LQs lower than one indicate *relative* deprivation in a health care supply item; LQs greater than one indicate a *relative* oversupply. In other words, the LQ is an equity measure which has clear implications for health policy. LQs can, of course, be based on populations with particular needs or on population subdivisions. They can be ranked, categorized, and the categories given different shadings on a choropleth map. The LQ is illustrated in Figure 8 which depicts core physicians (those physicians necessary to sustain a primary medical care system in a community) relative to total population in the counties of North Carolina. There are concentrations of core physicians in counties with large hospitals, but also in some unexpected areas in the eastern and western regions of the state.

There are some disadvantages to using location quotients. If they are mapped for a large number of geographic units, they may be an inefficient form of visual summary because it is difficult for the eye to comprehend too many units at once. Also, since they are based on a single factor, they leave out many other factors that may be important, such as quality of resources, accessibility, and types of physicians. Furthermore, if geographic units are of different size, the visual impact may be misleading.

Maps can also focus on health care demand rather than on the targeted population. A common strategy used by hospitals, for example, is to delineate their *service areas*. This can be indicated by determining the proportion of each study unit's older population that went to the hospital over a certain period of time. This information can be used to make a choropleth map. Figure 9 uses imaginary data to construct a service area for a hospital in Smithfield, the county seat of Johnston County, North Carolina, based on the number of patients in the seventeen townships. The map shows clearly the phenomenon of *distance decay* (see below); that is, higher proportions of patients are seen coming from townships closer to the hospital.

As an alternative to the service area choropleth map, proportional values can be assigned to some point (usually the centroid) of each subunit and an *isopleth map* can be constructed, using appropriate computer software. Isopleth maps display contour lines at pre-determined levels (e.g., 10%, 20%, 30%, and so on). Topographic maps and weather maps showing rainfall amounts are examples of isopleth maps. The imaginary data developed for Figure 9 was used to produce Figure 10, an isopleth map.

Accessibility and Utilization

How Geographically Accessible are Health Care Services to Older Adults?

The maps that indicate the *availability* of health care resources begin to answer this question because they show the geographic relationship between

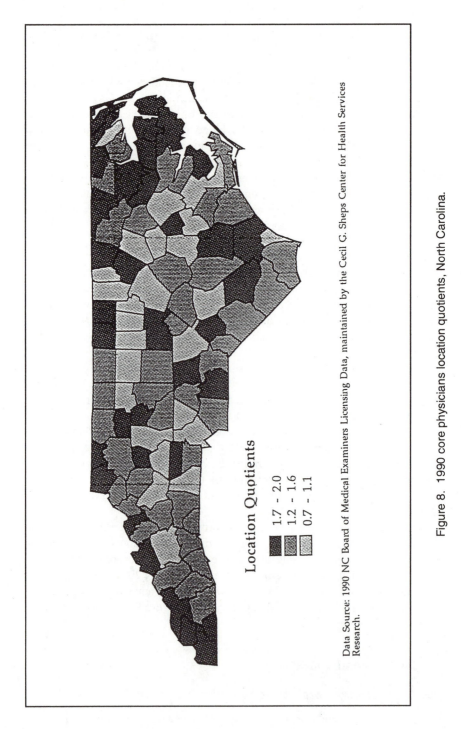

Location Quotients

■ 1.7 - 2.0
▨ 1.2 - 1.6
▧ 0.7 - 1.1

Data Source: 1990 NC Board of Medical Examiners Licensing Data, maintained by the Cecil G. Sheps Center for Health Services Research.

Figure 8. 1990 core physicians location quotients, North Carolina.

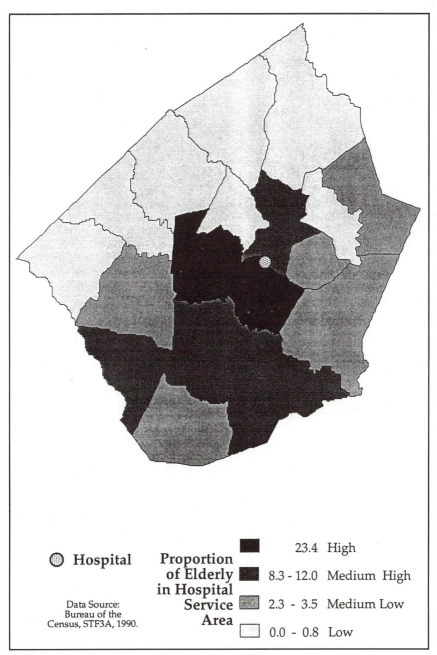

Figure 9. *A hypothetical population—*
The proportion of elderly using inpatient hospital services.

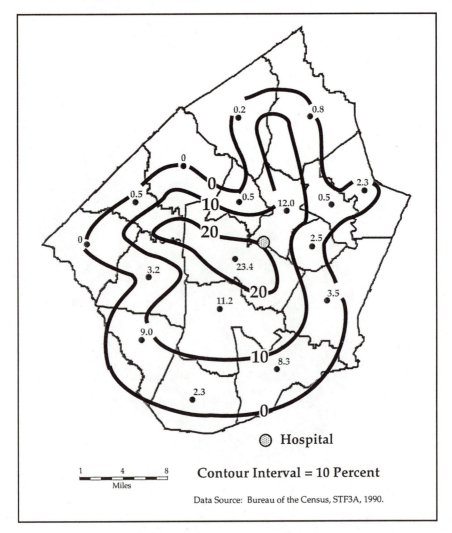

Figure 10. *A hypothetical population—*
Proportion of elderly using a community hospital's inpatient services.

older consumers and health care providers. In this section, some ways of looking more closely at accessibility or potential utilization are described.

Flow maps can be used to graphically depict patterns of movement between the homes or residential areas of older persons, and sources of care such as hospitals and physicians. The length of the arrows is a visual representation of how far older people must travel to care. The arrows can be made of varying width to indicate relative volumes of flow. Flow maps have been used to help define the service region of a single health care service center. They also can be used to define the boundaries of service regions within a large study area. The flow map shown in Figure 11 is based on the same data used for Figures 9 and 10.

Distance is often a good measure of physical accessibility, but is by no means the only one. A cartographic method for looking at the possible effect of distance is to draw radii (e.g., at 5-mile intervals) around important health care resources, count the number of older people in each distance zone, and tabulate the results. If substantial proportions of a target population are more than fifteen or twenty miles from a resource, then some remedial action may be necessary, such as providing more facilities or improving transportation for older people. If the information is available, *time distance* or *perceived distance* might be substituted for map distance.

A geographic technique that is potentially very useful, but requires a large amount of information, is the construction of *standard deviational ellipses* (SDEs). The data required are information on the *daily activity spaces* and *health care seeking spaces* of elderly consumers. More specifically, what is needed to form daily activity space ellipses are the exact locations of the places where people live, go to work, shop, and carry out other routine activities, as well as time spent at these places in a "typical" day or week. For health care seeking ellipses, information is required on where people go for health care and how long they stay there. Point locations (where the activity takes place) and activity durations (how long the activity is carried on in a place) can be used to calculate the length of the major and minor axes and the orientation of these axes of ellipses, which are a summary of where people carry on most of their health care-seeking or daily activities. The amount of overlap between daily activity and care-seeking ellipses provides another indication of geographic accessibility. SDE construction can be facilitated using a Geographic Information System or GIS (see following). We have constructed an SDE based on an imaginary population of older persons living in a small rural community and a town. Figure 12 shows where they lived (h), where they went shopping (S), where some of them worked (W), and where they visited friends and relatives (V), with all places weighted for the time spent there. Activity points are more clustered in the town than in the rural community, reflecting the higher population density of the town. The ellipse takes in around two-thirds of the activity points and is clearly oriented toward the town. It gives a rough approximation of the territory covered by a group of older adults as they carry out their routine activities. Health resources in Smithfield will be included in the "orbit" of this group of older persons, but resources outside the county will not.

What are the Health Care Utilization Patterns for Elderly People?

A common way for geographers to assess variation in utilization is to construct *distance decay curves*. These are graphs that record the numbers

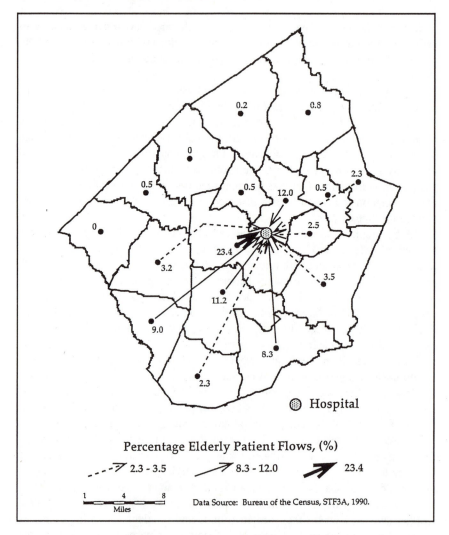

Figure 11. *A hypothetical population—*
The proportional flow of elderly hospital inpatients by township.

of people who went to a health care source from various distances. Typically, these curves have a negative slope because the tendency is for fewer people to travel to services from longer distances. The curves show how far different proportions of a target population are willing to travel to receive care. They can be constructed for different subgroups of the population, for different facilities and personnel, for different types of illness, and for different levels of

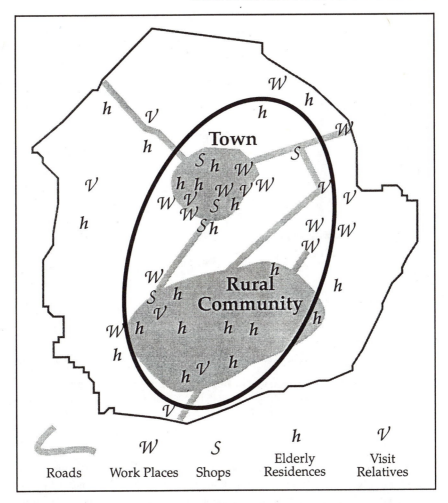

Figure 12. Using a hypothetical example, a standard deviational ellipse shows the daily activity spaces of the elderly within a county for a rural community and a nearby town.

service. As examples, travel to a hospital for certain Diagnostic Related Groups (DRGs) could be compared using HCFA Medicare data tapes. To construct Figure 13, data on an imaginary population of 200 older people were used to plot 100 dental visits and twenty-five visits to an oncologist, made over varying distances. People made more visits to the dentist, over shorter distances, compared to oncology visits.

Medical geographers are increasingly employing *Geographic Information Systems* (GIS) to aid them in their work. A GIS is a computer software system

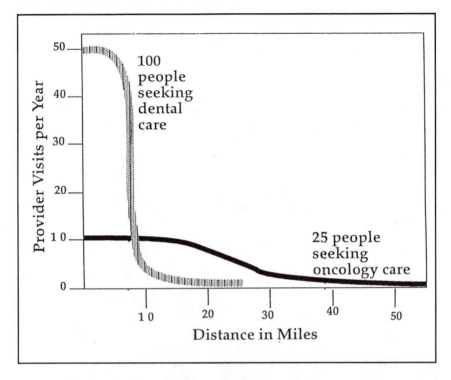

Figure 13. A hypothetical example of distance decay curves
(assuming 200 people in population).

which inputs, manages, manipulates, analyzes, and produces geographically-coded data in the form of maps and graphs. A GIS lends itself to some of the procedures discussed previously, including map overlays, flow maps, and the construction of SDEs. They can also be used in utilization studies to more precisely calculate map and road distances. A GIS could be used to help construct more complex maps overlaid with variables from the Census (such as percent nonwhite, median income) or other secondary data sources.

POLICY IMPLICATIONS OF GEOGRAPHIC TECHNIQUES

This chapter has shown how several geographic techniques can be used to provide a clearer picture of where and how older adults and health care resources are distributed and related spatially. This information can be used in several ways to improve health care delivery to older people. In other words, it is practical and policy-oriented information that visually displays complex relationships demonstrated through represented data.

Geographic analysis can help to identify subunits of a study area in which needs for older adults are not being met or are below average. Additional facilities could be set up to reach isolated or underserved older populations. Older adults without transportation can be identified and transportation alternatives suggested. Some situations can be alleviated by outreach activities or support services such as home health care. Maps and graphs might also indicate those areas that need to be targeted for intervention or tertiary care programs.

The results of geographic analysis can also be used for planning purposes to allocate or reallocate resources to provide more equitable, accessible, and cost-efficient health care services to older adults (although it is usually impossible to simultaneously fulfill all three goals). Geographic gaps in service can be identified along with redundant services that may provide a justification for regionalization efforts in areas among existing providers (e.g., alliances, networks). Geographic information, may in this manner, inform policy discussion on the use of available resources.

REFERENCES

1. R. L. Bergman, Quantum Leaps, *Hospitals & Health Networks,* pp. 28-35, October 5, 1993.
2. A. M. Davies, Epidemiology and Services for the Aged, *Public Health Reports, 103*:5, pp. 516-520, 1988.
3. P. C. Damiano, E. T. Momany, N. S. J. Foster, and H. E. McLeran, *Transportation of Rural Elders and Access to Health Care,* prepared by the University of Iowa Public Policy Center for the Midwest Transportation Center, 1994.
4. J. Van Nostrand, *Common Beliefs About the Rural Elderly: What do National Data Tell Us?* Series 3: Analytic and Epidemiologic Studies No. 28. U.S. Department of Health and Human Services, Hyattsville, Maryland, 1993.
5. Data Watch, Study: Rural Elders Living Alone at Greater Risk for Health Problems, *Hospitals & Health Networks,* p. 58, September 20, 1993.
6. A. E. Powers and V. R. Kivett, Kin Expectations and Kin Support Among Rural Older Adults, *Rural Sociology, 57*:2, pp. 194-215, 1992.
7. L. A. Wray, Health Policy and Ethnic Diversity in Older Americans: Dissonance or Harmony? *The Western Journal of Medicine,* pp. 357-361, September 1992.
8. J. M. Buckle, Severity of Illness and Resource Use Differences Among White and Black Hospitalized Elderly, *Archives of Internal Medicine, 152,* pp. 1596-1603, 1992.
9. A. E. Joseph and D. R. Phillips, *Accessibility and Utilization: Geographical Perspectives on Health Care Delivery,* Harper & Row, New York, 1984.
10. A. E. Joseph, Issues in the Provision of In-Home Health Services to the Rural Elderly: An Ontario Perspective, in *Health in Rural America: The Geography of Health Care Services and Delivery,* W. M. Gesler and T. C. Ricketts (eds.), Rutgers University Press, New Brunswick, New Jersey, 1992.

11. T. C. Ricketts, L. A. Savitz, W. M. Gesler, and D. N. Osborne, *Geographic Methods for Health Services Research: A Focus on the Rural-Urban Continuum,* University Press of America, Lanham, Maryland, 1994.
12. A. Kleinman, Concepts and a Model for the Comparison of Medical Systems as Cultural Systems, *Social Science and Medicine, 12,* pp. 85-93, 1978.
13. W. M. Gesler, *The Cultural Geography of Health Care,* University of Pittsburgh Press, Pittsburgh, Pennsylvania, 1991.

CHAPTER
4

Theoretical and Methodological Approaches to Migration Research on Rural Aging Populations

Charles F. Longino, Jr. and Mark H. Smith

INTRODUCTION

Retirees show up in such numbers in a few places that their high visibility often causes observers to overestimate the frequency of such moves. Internal migration in the United States, on the whole, however, is a youthful affair, and youthfulness is one of its enduring features. The shape of the age profile of migrants in the United States has been consistent for decades, changing only gradually over time. The younger children are, the more likely they are to migrate. The migration rate of children bottoms out in the early teens and does not increase rapidly until the late teens. More than one-third of Americans in their young adult years, ages twenty to twenty-four—the peak migration years during the life course—moved at least once between 1992 and 1993, and nearly one-half of this mobility was migratory, that is, it was across significant political boundaries, such as county or state lines. Not surprisingly, this age corresponds with college graduation and marriage for many. The increasing age of children in the home, particularly once they begin their formal schooling, dampens the attractiveness of migration for their parents. The age-specific migration rate declines slowly at first, then more steeply until age thirty-five, after which it slowly declines throughout the middle years to a life-course low point just before the retirement years. The retirement migration hump between ages sixty and seventy is small by comparison to the early adulthood migration bulge. The final increase in age-specific migration rises at the end of life and is related largely to health issues [1].

The elderly, as a broad age category, are only about one-half as mobile as the general population. Between 4 and 5 percent move across state lines in any five-year period. Indeed, roughly three-quarters of persons ages sixty and over reported having lived at the same address for at least five years during the past three censuses, making the older population residentially very stable. Nonetheless, the migration of elders has some unique features that make it worth studying, and over the past two decades, a body of descriptive demographic research has delineated many of its features [2].

Health, of course, is one reason for persons to move in their later years. Some move because they are in good health and want to enjoy those healthy years in an amenity-rich setting; others move because of declining health and an increased need for assistance and social support [3].

Rural populations are much smaller than those in urban areas. The study of the mobility patterns of rural elders, therefore, is a special piece of the large puzzle of old age mobility, with its own set of theoretical and methodological issues and dilemmas. Although this chapter will focus on mobility in rural populations, the larger context of retirement migration will often intrude because the theoretical and methodological problems of the general often also apply to the specific. Research examples, however, are usually drawn from rural settings.

THE CONCEPTUAL CONTEXT

Population Redistribution and Its Importance

Migration is the major short-term driver of age-specific population change in small areas. It is the most volatile of the population processes of birth, death, and migration. Bohland and Rowles pointed out that the proportion of the age sixty-five and over population in the United States grew by 1.4 percent between 1970 and 1980, and yet for individual counties the decadal changes ranged from −16.5 percent to +13.5 percent [4]. Population size is the central issue in demography. It is important to know how many people live in a place because these people make up markets, constituencies, and labor pools. Their needs and desires generate demand for goods and services. The characteristics of people in places are used to make important decisions by government and business planners. And the characteristics within a population change when people move in and move out. Without demographic data, therefore, including data on migration, such decisions could be made with much less confidence. Demographers like to think of themselves as the primary users of census data. However, planners including market researchers, are the ones who actually use census data the most.

Geographic Mobility from a Demographic Perspective

The study of geographic mobility within demography has been most influenced by economic issues. From a demographic perspective, migration is the major mechanism that redistributes the labor force. As local economies outgrow the local labor supply, they tend to draw in laborers from other places. And as local economies decline, poverty increases; increased poverty provides a motivation for the unemployed to seek employment opportunities in other locations. They move. As local economies change, if equilibrium is to be maintained in the economy, migration must do its work. It is assumed, therefore, that the primary motivation for migration is economic opportunity. There are many features of migration to be studied from this point of view. Important questions abound. For example, how do people find out about job opportunities in other places? What sorts of characteristics of potential migrants (and of the destination populations and their social and physical environments) encourage and discourage a move?

Geographic Mobility from a Gerontological Perspective

It is little wonder, then, that demographers were uncomfortable studying retirement migration. Most of their conceptual tools had been developed explicitly to exclude persons who were outside the labor force, unless of course, they were tagging along with a worker. Indeed, the first work on retirement migration did not appear until the mid-1970s [5] and this effort unproductively applied the usual economic formulae to older migrants.

The study of retirement migration, therefore, had to develop its own theoretical, and much of its methodological, material anew. In this sense, the study is a recent development in the demography of aging, but one that has demonstrated a good deal of creativity and excitement. The gerontological perspective on geographic mobility is concerned with the impact of migrants on the local economy, but it seeks this impact less in employment than in consumption. It examines the characteristics of the local environment, but puts more emphasis on the climate and amenities than does the general migration perspective. And it places as much emphasis on family relationships and health needs, in motivating moves, as it does on economic issues.

THE THEORETICAL CONTEXT: WHY DO OLDER PEOPLE MOVE?

The Typological Tradition and Decision Theory

It is much easier to deal with the what, where, and when questions of migration than to answer the more important inquiry, namely, why exactly do retirees move? The retiree's home represents an accumulation of a lifetime, a comfortable, secure, and familiar setting in which friends visit and to which children return for holidays; ties to the community, the neighborhood, tavern, clubs, and church are secure and socially rewarding; opportunities to indulge recreational interests and to be useful are within driving distance and plentiful enough to match the lifestyle the retiree desires in retirement; and the climate in which the retiree has lived for years poses no serious health problems. Under these circumstances, why would anyone think of moving [6]?

The earliest theoretical development on the geographical mobility of the elderly was taxonomic, delineating types of mobility [7-9]. Certain categories from these taxonomies have gained common usage in the research literature, particularly "amenity migration," which describes lifestyle-driven retirement migration [10]. There are other categories that have been applied, such as "assistance migration," which includes moves motivated by the desire to be near family members or others who could provide assistance during times of ill health. "Return migration," likewise, represents a particular type of move, one to the migrant's state of birth. The problem with the taxonomic approach is that the categories in the taxonomies overlap. Although they are useful in guiding research, their power to explain observations is limited.

A second early theoretical advancement was the development of migration decision-making theory to delineate person-environment adjustment processes by which the elderly decide whether or not to move [11, 12]. This perspective is rooted in Ravenstein's "Laws of Migration," actually the earliest attempt to make formal sense of migration in general [13]. Ravenstein wrote in terms of pushes and pulls, that is, of features of the origin or destination that repelled or attracted the migrant. The major attraction was economic opportunity. Decision-making theory when applied to the elderly, of course, featured a broader range of motivations.

The Life-Course Perspective

A more recent theoretical development has tended to make the life course of migrants its central focus, emphasizing those triggering mechanisms associated with life events and probabilities [14]. This conceptualization draws from demographic and human-development perspectives and is congenial with other concerns of gerontological research. Demographers are fond of pointing out that the migratory behavior of human beings is closely related to developmental tasks in the life course. However, prior to the development of migration research within gerontology, they had seldom explored beyond nuclear family development and career mobility [15].

Litwak and Longino [14] presented a developmental context for the patterns of elderly interstate migration commonly reported from demographic studies [16]. They argue that the nature of modern technology puts the kinship structures of older people [17] under institutional pressures to make three basic types of moves, if they move at all: one when they retire, a second type when they experience moderate forms of disability, and a third when they have major forms of chronic disability. The pressure may be slight for the first type of move, but it may increase for the second, and again for the third. The three types of moves are only sequenced on populations, not on individual persons. Many older persons will make none of these moves, or perhaps only one health-related move near the end of their lives.

The first type of move is often referred to as an "amenity move." When retirees have intact marriages, are relatively healthy, and have enough retirement income, there are social pressures for some of them to relocate for lifestyle or amenity reasons. Personal characteristics predict the expectation of migration as well as its timing, but so do ties to the current community of residence and ties to other places. As Cuba [18] demonstrated in his Cape Cod study, some retirees have planned their move for years and have vacationed at and visited their new location many times in anticipation of a move. The reasons for relocation are complex and have to do with the attractiveness of amenities, friendship network maintenance, and the ability to make a psychic move of identity from one place to another. At this stage of retirement, however, kinship functions can be managed over considerable distances, although it would be a mistake to assume that no recent retirees move closer to their children or other relatives.

The pressure for a second type of move occurs when people develop a disability that makes it difficult to carry out everyday household tasks, a situation often compounded by widowhood [19]. Migrants who move away from their children may choose to move to be near them again when they are disabled and widowed. The aggregate population profiles of migrants in the New York-to-Florida stream and the Florida-to-New York counterstream seem to fit this interpretation [14].

Limited kin resources is the motive for the third basic type of move, from more or less exclusive care by kin to institutional care [20]. Most movers of this type are not interstate migrants, but local movers.

The relevance of a developmental perspective for the geographical distribution of the elderly seems obvious. Movers of the first tend to dominate the migration streams into amenity-rich destinations in popular receiving states such as Florida, Arizona, and North Carolina. The counterstreams out of these states, although often much smaller than the migration streams, carry a much higher proportion of movers of the second type.

THE HISTORY OF GENERAL MIGRATION
IN RURAL AREAS

It is easier to discuss the geographical mobility of older rural populations if they are first put in the context of the general population. The gradual movement of young people out of rural areas to larger population concentrations is a very old pattern. Population movement in the United States has responded to many economic and political pressures. Declining economic opportunities and weakening place ties may stimulate out-migration, whereas expanding economic opportunities tend to spur in-migration. Not surprisingly, rural communities with high birthrates and regions with limited opportunities are areas of high out-migration, whereas urban, industrial regions and communities with expanding opportunities tend to have high in-migration [21]. Before 1920, a majority of U.S. citizens lived in rural areas, but since that time, the proportion in urban areas has inched up every decade, so that by 1990, 75.2 percent lived in urban areas.

Overlapping the long-standing rural-urban migration trend is a newer countertrend. One of the macro-level processes that affects geographic mobility in our time is metropolitan deconcentration. Many nonmetropolitan counties in the United States experienced a slowing of population decline in the 1960s, and in the 1970s, their net migration rates climbed above the break-even point, signaling a genuine and widespread "rural-urban turnaround."

WHAT IS KNOWN ABOUT ELDERLY MIGRATION IN THE RURAL AREAS

Place of Older Migrants in the Rural Turnaround

Older migrants are not motivated by the same constellation of pushes and pulls as younger migrants who must connect with jobs and with schools for their children. Older migrants can move to be near relatives or to engage in recreational lifestyle favored by climate and geography. For this reason, older migrants are not as constrained in their choices as others are. Because they are more flexible in destination choices, older migrants are sometimes ahead of certain migration trends.

Indeed, older migrants seem to have been in the vanguard of migration to nonmetropolitan counties, showing earlier net migration increases in such places, especially those high in climatic and recreational amenities. Much of the literature posits the 1970s as the time of the turnaround. For the elderly, the 1960s seem to have been the period in which it began [22]. Other researchers have commented on the general population shifts, especially those of the aged [23-25].

These observations were based entirely on reports of net migration rates, which may not reflect important volumes of change. For example, if a rural county with few older people gains a few more through in-migration, its net migration rate dramatically increases. A metropolitan county, however, would have to lose many more people to reduce its rate perceptibly. Thus, net migration stacks the deck in favor of growth in the least populated areas.

Longino [26] sought to further document to "forerunner of change" finding of Fuguitt and Tordella [22] using 1960 and 1970—1-in-100 samples of census microdata. The metropolitan and nonmetropolitan origins and destinations of elderly migrants in the two above-mentioned censuses were examined, and a matrix of "streams" between these types of environments was created.

About half of the migrants were moving from one metropolitan environment to another. A much smaller proportion, from one-tenth to nearly one-quarter, was moving outside metropolitan areas, thus exchanging similar nonmetropolitan environments. Among the minority (about one-third) of migrants who were moving between environmental types, evidence for the metropolitan/nonmetropolitan turnaround was compelling.

In a three-decade analysis of the same trends, Longino and his colleagues found that the metropolitan-to-nonmetropolitan turnaround identified earlier apparently continued in the 1970s [27]. The turnaround continued—not because the flow to the nonmetropolitan regions increased, as it did by 1970—but because the flow of migrants into the cities from smaller places continued to decline between 1965-1970 and 1975-1980. Another level of complexity is added to the picture when the distance of the moves between metropolitan and nonmetropolitan places is considered.

Distance of the Move

Beyond the verification of the turnaround, the 1970 and 1980 census data also point to the importance of long-distance migrants in the process. First, although the turnaround appeared to occur both among interstate and intrastate migrants, only among the interstate migrants was there an actual increase in the percentage of those who moved out of the large cities into small communities. A decline in the movement *into* metropolitan settings during the period under study accounts for the appearance of a turnaround among intrastate migrants. The proportion who left metropolitan areas for other types of settings did not increase at all. Proportionately, then, older interstate migrants came to dominate the metropolitan-to-nonmetropolitan stream during the period under study.

The implication of this finding could be of great importance to those for whom older people are either clients or represent a market. If long- and short-distance migrants tend to move for different reasons or differ greatly in their economic and social characteristics, then the shift that has been identified in this analysis could imply other unmeasured characteristics of new arrivals in a county, such as differences in health and social service needs.

The Question of Impact

The Economic Impact of Rural Amenity Migrants

Several studies reporting on the characteristics of older migrants showed that metropolitan-to-nonmetropolitan migrants, especially those moving longer distances, tend to have more income, to be married, and to live in their own homes. Lifestyle concerns, therefore, may motivate people to move to smaller places more than they would encourage moves to the city [28]. Sofranko, Fliegel, and Glasgow demonstrated that older metropolitan-origin newcomers living in the rural countryside have less access to goods and services than in-town newcomers, but that they are more satisfied and more likely to perceive new improvements over their former residences [29].

For several decades, economic development in small cities and towns has tended to emphasize only one strategy: bringing in industrial plants from larger places. Economically struggling industries, always on the lookout for new pools of accessible, nonunionized labor, were willing to be courted by these communities. Unfortunately, many of these communities are not able to compete favorably with urban areas for the plants that relocate because they simply do not have the infrastructure. And because agriculture alone is not providing the necessary diversification needed to sustain economic growth in these communities, they experience economic decline.

In this context, coaxing amenity migrants into these communities seems like an ideal answer to their economic development needs. Amenity migration is a clean industry and one that boosts the local economy largely through consumerism. When retirees move across state lines, their incomes boost the local economies at their destinations. On a statewide basis, these annual sums can be quite large [30-32].

More important, below the state level, significant economic resources are transferred to the host communities by the amenity retirement migrants. Local commerce gains new, more affluent customers. Real estate and the home construction trades benefit from the upscale tastes of the retirees. Financial institutions obtain new depositors. Local governments receive additional revenue from property and sales taxes.

A growing body of research evidence documents the positive effect of amenity migration. The Western North Carolina Retirement Migration Impact Study, for example, obtained detailed 1989 spending and financial data from 630 in-migrating retirees in the predominantly rural mountainous area [33]. The host communities' commerce captured 87 percent of the in-migrants' purchases, or over $20,000 per household in 1989. This figure did not include the average $13,299 spent on a vehicle by 38 percent of the households in the previous year. Construction and real estate industries benefited from home purchases averaging $108,884 per purchase. These items along with utilities, insurance, and health care, averaged $35,975 in expenditures during the year. Similar expenditure patterns have been documented among the migrant retirees to the New Jersey shore [34] and rural areas along the southeastern U.S. coast of the Atlantic Ocean [35].

The direct purchases are only the visible part of the economic impact. Multiplier effects applied to the retirees' expenditures in western North Carolina revealed that the economic impact was double the initial amount due to the money's circulation in the local economy. As a result, the average migrant household's overall impact on the local economy was $71,600. Measured by employment, each household's expenditures created 1.5 jobs at an average 1989 income of $14,900. Beyond spending, retirees to rural western North Carolina had additional inputs into the local economy. Retirees produced capital for local development by average deposits in local financial institutions of $22,719 per household. The minority (7%) had invested in local business ventures. Their investments averaged $45,921. Finally, retirees paid averages of $2,213 and $1,136 for state and local taxes. On both the state and local levels, these amounts are equal to the cost of the services the older migrants may require. In other words, they pay their way.

Numerous rural counties which have provided access to local recreational amenities have developed strong vacation industries and have later become, without much thought or effort, the location of a growing community of retired amenity migrants, many of whom had vacationed there for years. Recently, other rural areas have begun actively courting potential retired migrants. For example, the states of North Carolina and South Carolina produce magazines for the express purpose of attracting retirees. In addition, there are now two manuals for attracting retirees for "fun and profit" produced by Fagan [36] and Severinghaus [37].

There is always a conservative voice in rural communities that opposes attracting older migrants, which might be said to have a "gray peril" mentality [38]. Two objections are typically raised in these quarters. First, opponents suggest that retirees will vote against school initiatives because they are presumed to have no children or grandchildren in local schools. And second, opponents express some anxiety about whether the development of an amenity retirement economy will interface with other types of economic growth. Not much convincing evidence has been produced to support the first objection. However, it is reasonable to suggest that amenity migrants will tend to work against attracting smokestack industry into their own scenic paradise, thereby thwarting other economic development strategies. Such migrants tend to be on the side of the environmentalists [39, 40]. The western North Carolina study found that almost 70 percent of the employment opportunities created by the retirees were in retail sales and services, a sector of the economy with lower wages and few benefits.

The Health Care Impact of Rural In- and Out-Migration

Health is an issue that comes up frequently when retirement migration is discussed. People wonder if migrants to rural areas will find themselves in areas with relatively scarce medical resources, relative to the cities many of them moved from. And, on the other hand, some people worry that retirees will "over-burden" the local health care system. There is not much research on this topic, but what exists is very interesting [41]. The short answer to this concern is that if one gives the health care market time to work, retirement migration probably does not have a negative impact on health or health care. This topic will be discussed again later.

In and Out: The Rural-Urban Migration Cycle

In addition to expanding health care resources, within the more complex pattern of elderly migration, there is also a safety valve in rural areas to carry away excess health care demand. Census studies have shown that older persons moving out of nonmetropolitan areas indicate higher levels of dependency than those moving into these types of locations. A higher proportion, for example, were widowed and living dependently, especially with their children, at the destination of their move [42-44]. These patterns are consistent across three census decades, from 1960 to 1980 [2].

Moving to larger places, therefore, may often be motivated by health and economic concerns, especially for the old-old and the widowed. The family caretaking component of these moves cannot be studied in a very focused way using census data. As we have seen, however, the national pattern clearly points to a larger dependent older population moving up the metropolitan hierarchy than those moving in the opposite direction, and more of them are living with children or in nursing homes, implying a higher level of need for care. The particular microprocesses by which this interplay of family caregiving and residential mobility occurs, however, must be studied at the local level.

Rowles describes this process in West Virginia as moving through a sequence of six stages [45]. First, the children relocate. This is followed by a number of accommodative strategies so that loss of social and other support from children is compensated by shifts in support within the house and the surrounding community. The third stage features seasonal migration, when the parents visit their children's homes. In Rowles' sequence, a crisis requires the parents to relocate in the fourth stage, generally with or near to the child. After the crisis situation has stabilized, the fifth stage finds the parents holding onto their home and returning for visits to maintain it and to keep up network ties in the community. The sixth stage is severance, when the parents (or parent) no longer return. Older persons who have no children or younger relatives who live nearby may turn to institutional help earlier, and some may move to a metropolitan area where resources are superior.

Research supporting the Litwak-Longino model clearly applies in the Rowles scenario. When older people develop chronic disabilities that make it difficult to carry out everyday household tasks such as shopping, cooking, cleaning, and emergency first aid, they experience a push to change their living environment [46]. The disability is typically compounded when deficits from widowhood are added because the spouse who provides help and motivation for performing these tasks is no longer present [19]. In this situation, if older people live at a distance from their children's homes, they may have to move in order to get the services they need. If the children have moved earlier from rural to urban settings in search of economic and educational opportunities, the parents will tend to follow.

On the other hand, if home-delivered services are readily available, or if family and friends are nearby and eager to help, then a move may be forestalled. Would severely disabled older persons leave nonmetropolitan areas if long-term care services were more readily available locally? We think not. The family is the basic caretaker of the elderly, and institutions tend to become involved only after the physical and emotional resources and commitment of the family are exhausted [17]. The scattering of the family geographically across generations, therefore, makes the residential relocation of the severely disabled segment of the older population nearly inevitable, especially in nonmetropolitan areas.

Many methodological issues in the study of mobility in rural older populations are the same issues encountered in the study of the topic in any other population. In other words, the rural population has no monopoly on definitional and data issues. Nonetheless, it is instructive to run through the list of problems that researchers encounter in studying the mobility of the elderly.

METHODOLOGICAL ISSUES:
VITAL STATISTICS AND NET MIGRATION

Through a Glass Darkly: Assessing Underlying Assumptions, Artifacts, and Distortions

Net migration rates before 1940 were estimated using a survival-rate method, adding births and subtracting deaths in a bounded area (such as county or state) and attributing most of the resulting decade population change that is not directly due to births and deaths to migration [47]. In this way, vital statistics, rather than the census, are used to estimate migration. This is far from an ideal way of doing the job because the residual net not only includes migrants, but also errors in counting and recording deaths and births. Nonetheless, migration nets estimated from vital statistics remain a tribute to human cleverness and the power of deduction.

The 1940 census was the first to include a mobility item. (It asked where persons lived five years before.) However, the item kept changing from census to census. In 1950, after World War II, there was so much population movement that a one-year interval was substituted in the census. In 1960, the five-year mobility interval was restored and has been retained in subsequent decades. Because of these measurement changes, however, the 1960 and 1970 censuses were the first from which decade changes could be derived. It is now possible to move considerably beyond subtracting deaths from births and subtracting out-migrants from in-migrants. We can now say with much greater confidence how much a population grew or shrank because of migration during the five years before the census.

Aquatic Images: Flows and Streams

Demography always starts with documenting population size and then moves beyond it. Once the net migration measure was cleaned up, it was easy to make the next step by separating migrant inflow from outflow. In this way counties or states could be compared by their ability to attract new residents. Even Ravenstein's "laws of migration" are cloaked in aquatic images [13]. Migrants were seen as flowing from the countryside to smaller towns and from these smaller towns to the larger ones, and from those to cities, in the quest for ever-greater economic opportunity. As a rule of thumb, the term "flow" is used when one knows either the origin or destination, but not both. The term "stream" is used when both are known. Streams connect origin and destination.

Using these same concepts one can talk about flows into or out of, or streams between types of places such as metropolitan and nonmetropolitan locations. The previous discussion on the rural-urban turnaround uses exactly this frame of reference.

The Poverty of Migrant Characteristics

The printed census reports provide relatively little data on migration. The number of persons entering and leaving each state and the state's net balance is certainly recorded. In addition, there is a matrix produced each decade in a special census report that gives the number of persons in the streams between each pair of states. There is even a matrix that connects the largest metropolitan areas with one another. The state matrix is usually repeated for broad age categories. Otherwise, however, the amount of information about the migrants is extremely limited. In census tabulations, it is rare to get a glimpse of actual stream size between metropolitan and nonmetropolitan locations. Migrant characteristics are even more obscure. It would be helpful to know, for example, whether the people moving from nonmetropolitan to metropolitan places are more likely to be young men or old women, let alone whether they are married, more or less well educated, or whether they have current family incomes below or above the poverty threshold. The profiling of migrants has awaited research using census samples created for public use. Net migration studies rarely gave any characteristics of migrants.

METHODOLOGICAL ISSUES: MICRODATA'S DILEMMA

The Siren Song and Pandora's Box

Indeed, it was the promise of so much detail that attracted users to the census microdata samples in the first place. It was a siren's song that demographers with survey research background could hardly resist. As the U.S. economy grew after World War II, the Census Bureau received an increasing number of requests for custom tabulations to answer the specific questions of business and government planners. The Bureau did not have the manpower to respond to most of these requests. As a result of this pressure, the Bureau produced a sample of census records for public use in 1960. By using this sample, those with questions could answer them by creating their own custom tabulations. The Census Bureau's microdata program was born. Such samples have continued to be produced after each census since 1960 [48].

Microdata is a strange word. It evokes the intriguing image of microfilm, secret codes, and spies. Actually, the term is much more mundane in its derivation. Census data is usually reported for a number of geographic units: for the nation, states, counties, neighborhoods, or census tracts, and even for city blocks. The smallest possible unit for reporting census data, however, is the individual person. The individual, therefore, is the "micro" unit of data. A microdata sample is drawn from individual census records. Items are removed that could identify the person, such as his or her name, address, Social Security number, etc. It is the demographic do-it-yourselfer's dream. With a microdata file, one can create any information that can be derived from the samples, for any subpopulation that can be defined by the samples—from Norwegian bachelor farmers in rural Minnesota to octogenarian physicians in Manhattan. The only big problem encountered by microdata users is the danger of overgeneralizing to a population from a small sample.

Sampling Variation and Estimation

The Census Bureau always refers to the microdata program as producing "small samples" of individual records. The first samples were 1-in-100 and 1-in-1000. In 1980, a 1-in-20 sample was added. In that decade, however, the geographical codes of only half of the individual records were entered—as a cost-saving measure. The reason that this saved cost is because the geographical codes, like occupational codes, are not bubbled in; they are hand-entered and hand-coded into the dataset. As a result, microdata migration analyses from the 1980 census were based on an actual sample of 1-in-40. In 1990, for the first time, the full 5 percent sample was available for studying migration.

It is very important to note that all of the "facts" derived from census microdata about migration, or anything else for that matter, are only estimates. Samples are commonly used for making estimations. Market research, political polls, and social science surveys all estimate population parameters from samples. Polls usually make these estimates within certain confidence intervals, often stated as "give or take" a small percent. That error, called "sampling variation," is relatively larger when samples are smaller.

Consequently, estimates of a very small subpopulation from census microdata will be less certain than estimates of a large population. For example, estimates of the number of older migrants in the United States from the 5 percent sample would be very close to the total census count, off by less than 1 percent. Estimates of the number of migrants in the stream from South Dakota to Ocean County, New Jersey, however, would contain much sampling variation because the sample would be so small. Because smaller samples produce less reliable estimates than larger samples, the likelihood of missing the estimation mark is greater in the estimates from the 1960 and 1970 (1-in-100) samples, than the 1980 and 1990 (1-in-20) samples. The best estimates are from the 1990 census.

But to add another layer of complexity to the topic, most of the questions in the census are asked of only a sample of citizens (15 to 20%). The 100 percent items, as they are called, are a fairly short list. In 1980, the rural areas were oversampled, with a ratio of almost 1-in-2, but weighted down in the microdata samples. In 1990, the rural population was not oversampled, causing a fluctuation in sampling variation in rural populations between 1980 and 1990. One of the demons to escape from Pandora's box, we are convinced, is sampling variation, because it is the small geographical unit that nearly all planners are interested in, and it is detailed population characteristics that enrich planning discussions. The question: "How many angels can dance on the head of a pin?" takes the issue to an extreme, but the principle is the same.

The Census Measure of Mobility

The census contains only one item measuring residential mobility, and it appeared for the first time in the 1940 census. The question asked Americans if they lived in the same house five years before the census date, excluding children born during the interim. If the respondent did not, the census item further asked in which city or town, county and state, or country, they did live at mid-decade. In this way, detailed information was provided about who had moved where in the second half of each decade. Because persons who moved once or more in the first half of the decade would not be counted at all, and persons moving twice or more in the second half of the decade would be counted only once, the five-year question was considered as a mobility "average" for the decade. The full range of mobility choices from "none" to "from abroad" were provided on individual records from 1960 to 1980. In 1990, there was a general mobility item, indicating whether or not one moved at all, and migration origins and destinations were given for those who moved across state lines. The local movers and within-state migrants, however, could not be separated. The fickleness with which items are changed, combined, or removed from the data from one decade to the next, is a demon that plagues microdata-based migration research.

Another demographic demon to escape Pandora's box is the austerity of the mobility item because, unfortunately, it leaves many important migration issues that census data cannot address. Only the residences at the time of the census and five years earlier are recorded. One cannot tell from census data whether a person is returning to a place where he or she had lived earlier. Only one's state of birth is recorded. Further, using census data, one cannot tell how frequently a person has moved. Where, exactly, did moves originate from overseas? We know what country they moved from. But otherwise, mum's the word. Nor can one tell whether people in counterstreams (those that move in the opposite direction to the major streams) are actually returning after an earlier retirement move. Census studies of migration, therefore, do a lot with a little.

Geographical Identifiers

Census microdata geography is a world unto itself, and needs some explaining. The District of Columbia is considered as a state. Counties are not identified individually in the microdata samples. The geographical unit below the state level is an artificial one called a PUMA, the acronym standing for Public Use Microdata Area. Is that clear? These units are parts of counties, whole counties, or collections of counties, identified by state planners in each state as the most useful for state planning purposes. The only limitation placed on the PUMA by the Census Bureau is that the geographical units must have more than 100,000 people in them. There may be several PUMAs in the largest cities, and very sparsely populated counties are bundled together into units that have more than 100,000 residents. When PUMAs are not referred to directly by those who use census microdata, they are usually called "counties or county groups," which is a pretty confusing geographical unit. The PUMA is certainly from Pandora's box, too.

Finally, in 1970 and 1980 there were items that gave the metropolitan status of the migrant's residence of origin, so that it could be compared with the same type of residence at destination. In 1990, the code for origin was dropped. One cannot tell whether the movement has increased or decreased between metropolitan or nonmetropolitan types of residence. Here the fickle demon struck again in 1990.

Sample Extraction

Obviously, no survey research can work with a file as large as the 5 percent sample file, at least not for the nation as a whole. Therefore, only the census items to be used, and the individual records that are relevant to the study, are included. The others are left behind. The study sample, in other words, is extracted from the whole dataset. This is not an easy operation and is often accomplished one state or census tape at a time. It is costly in computer time.

Files are produced in what is called "hierarchical" format by the Census Bureau. The house record comes first, followed by the individual records of persons living in the house. Step one is to find the houses in which sample relevant persons live. In the case of the retirement migration study, this was "houses in which one or more persons age sixty and over were living." One pass through the data extracts only these houses.

The second step in data extraction is to rectangularize the file, making the individual, not the house, the unit of analysis. The individual records are separated and the housing record is attached to each individual record for persons living in the house. Only those persons who have moved across state lines may be selected into a smaller data file for certain analyses. This extraction process is a tedious one. Often several steps may be combined in a single run to save computer time. But at this point, mistakes are costly because of the enormous size of the original dataset. And it is important to document each step of the process so that the source of the errors can be found later if it appears that something is wrong with the data. The only demon here is the one that curses any research effort: it is a lack of care for details. Errors come back to haunt us, and if we are lucky, they can be corrected.

METHODOLOGICAL ISSUES:
AGGREGATE ANALYSIS AND MEANING

The Problems of Correlating Aggregate Statistics

For all census products *except for* microdata, the data unit is a geographical, not a human one—a block, tract, county, or state. Although research questions are often framed in terms of human social behavior, the actor is a population unit, not a person. The use of census data, in this way, creates special problems of interpretation. Sometimes the interpretation is clear. When the temperature goes up, more electricity is used for cooling. Climatic change and environmental adjustment make sense, and can be verified on the individual level.

Migration research of the past, however, that used state net migration rates as the dependent variable, often raised more questions than they answered. Aggregate data makes sense if one is studying a market. In this case, migration will be one feature of the market that may make it more or less responsive to what is sold to that market.

Research Example: Veteran Migration and Health Services

Health services research is a good example of market research that uses aggregate data appropriately. The health-motivated moves of the very old are not only of interest to state health planners, they are also of critical importance to planners in the Department of Veterans Affairs (V.A.), which operates the largest health care system in the United States. There are 172 hospitals, 233 outpatient clinics, and 119 nursing homes under the direction of the V.A. Furthermore, each year Congress allocates funds for administering the V.A. health care system based in part on the number of veterans in the area plus the number of veterans projected to move into the area. Mobility, therefore, is important in determining the public resources allocated to health care facilities in different areas of the nation.

The U.S. veteran population is currently aging primarily because of the World War II veterans. In 1970, there were nearly two million veterans over sixty-five, and three million in 1980. By 1990, there were over seven million veterans in this age category, and by the end of the century the number will approach nine million [49]. Furthermore, because the V.A. hospitals are available to all veterans regardless of health insurance, they serve a large indigent population.

Cowper and Longino examined the assumption that geographic mobility affects demand for health care by assessing, at an aggregate level of analysis, the relative importance of the migration factor in the use of V.A. health services by the older veteran population in the United States [49]. They used models in the regression analysis that measured the relative impact of demographic and social characteristics of older veterans, levels of state resources and characteristics of migrants, on admission rates of older veterans across states. They found that variation in admission rates across states is explained primarily by the characteristics of the resident non-mobile veteran population, but that the characteristics of veterans migrating to the state also explained some of the variance. The researchers concluded that demand projections should take into account the demographic, living arrangement, and socioeconomic status of the older veteran population for both the residentially stable and mobile.

METHODOLOGICAL ISSUES:
THE ADEQUACY OF NATIONAL HEALTH SURVEYS

The Secondary Data Quandary

The methodological issues examined above relate to the use of census data in studying mobility in older rural populations. Census data, however, are not the only available data for studying this topic. There are, for example, other large national studies whose data are available for analysis by researchers not connected to the original study. Often these large national studies reinterview subjects several times over standard multi-year intervals. By introducing a time dimension and linking the records of the respondents, it is theoretically possible to study some of the "causes" of mobility behavior. Increasingly, a requirement for federal funding of large projects is that the data be made available to the public through well managed archives, such as the University of Michigan's Interuniversity Consortium for Political and Social Research. The quandary in using these datasets is not their availability. Rather, the issues revolve around statistical power and content appropriateness.

Mobility and Other Transition Status

When national surveys that are not focused on mobility issues record moves, they seldom distinguish by distance of move and nearly never record the places between which the respondent moved. Furthermore, the older the respondents are, the more likely that other transitions will occur between repeated waves of the survey. Some will die, others will be institutionalized, and still others will be lost to the survey because they cannot be located or they are too ill to be interviewed. It is not surprising, therefore, that studies using such surveys have come to focus on residential mobility as only one transition. This plot shifts the focus of the research considerably.

Cranking Up the Numbers

No large national studies have interviewed only migrants. But people do move around, and especially in those studies that reinterview subjects at more than one point in time, their move is often recorded. If 5 percent of the population over sixty makes an interstate move in most recent five-year periods, how many such people will show up in a sample of three or four thousand respondents? Maybe 150 or so in 3,000, but fewer will appear if the interval between interviews is two years. Is that a large enough sample to work with? It is for some purposes and not for others. The more survey questions used in the analysis (and the more categories the items have) the lower the statistical power of the analyses will be. As a result, such a small sub-sample of mobile persons may not be appropriate for the really interesting research questions. Furthermore, samples in such national surveys are drawn in clusters. These clusters tend not to be in sparsely populated areas because the transportation and time costs would be too high, so respondents from rural locations may be underrepresented in these studies.

Research Example:
Mobility and Health Research Using LSOA Data

One current research project has explored the relationship between functional health and community-based moves, as compared with other transitional outcomes such as institutionalization and death [50]. The Longitudinal Study of Aging (LSOA), with its repeated interviews in 1984, 1986, 1988, and 1990, and with a large sample of persons age seventy and over, provided the data for the analysis. Complex statistical models were developed to explain the relationships.

The study found that because death and institutionalization take from the community those whose health declines, those who remain seem to have unusually stable functional health [51]. Furthermore, not all functional declines have the same effect on the likelihood of making a noninstitutional move within the community. Basic activities of daily living (the need for help with self-care activities, such as dressing, bathing and toileting), have a strong initial effect on the odds of moving within the community. Needing help with household activities such as housework and shopping have no effect on the likelihood of making such a move. However, a mental decline (as indicated by the need for help with managing money, telephoning, and eating), becomes significantly predictive of a move, as do lower body limitations. Living arrangements are an important factor, too. A cognitive decline increased the odds of moving (2.27 times) for those living alone over 1.42 times for) those who were living with others. A move in the previous survey interval was strongly associated with the increased odds of institutionalization and a subsequent household adjustment [52]. So shifting residence in the community when serious functional health declines occur may be only a stop-gap, deferring institutional care until later. Finally, in a preliminary analysis, health demands were examined in light of the proximity of children. Respondents are more likely to live closer to (than farther from) their nearest child *after* a decline in functional health, although about half maintain a stable proximity regardless of what happens to their functional health in the previous intervals.

METHODOLOGICAL ISSUES: THE LOCAL CENSUS

Advantages and Disadvantages

A local census is a rare event, and rarer yet when mobility issues are considered. Nonetheless, they do occur. And when they do, such data collections provide a special opportunity to examine types of mobility that are not open for observation otherwise.

Research Example: Virginia's Rural Nursing Home Census

Only one study in the United States has examined the spatial pattern of nursing home moves between metropolitan and nonmetropolitan locations in a primarily rural part of the country [53]. It took place in 1990 in southwest Virginia, the state's mountainous coal mining region. The data for this study are unique; they come from a census by the Virginia Health Department that surveyed all licensed nursing facilities in the state. Their resident populations were enumerated on May 16, 1990, recording their residence just prior to institutionalization. The state's motivation in conducting the survey was to determine the geographical need for more nursing home beds in the state. McAuley and Travis took advantage of this state planning survey to explore the nursing home mobility of elderly southwest Virginians [53].

Consistent with the census studies, McAuley and Travis found that nonmetropolitan residents of Virginia, who were in need of institutional long-term care, were more likely to travel longer distances than their metropolitan counterparts in order to enter a nursing home. Nearly half of all admissions from nonmetropolitan counties crossed county lines upon admission to a nursing home, in comparison to about one-third of the recent admissions from metropolitan areas. These findings indicate that there is a considerable amount of migration among older impaired individuals who resided in nonmetropolitan areas prior to nursing home admission. This high rate of nursing home migration is underestimated by census data that report residence five years prior. Furthermore, those who pay directly for their nursing home care are less likely to cross county boundaries to obtain a bed, than those whose care is paid for by government programs for the needy.

McAuley and Travis report that most non-city nursing home migrants are admitted to a facility in another small town. Therefore, impaired persons who must migrate to obtain institutional long-term care have a strong tendency to relocate in an environment that is similar to their home environment. Second, they also remain as close as possible to their home county when they migrate. This is not surprising since, obviously, there is a very strong place-attachment among rural elders. Arguably, those who relocate at a distance from their home, do so because they cannot afford a nearby facility that will take them. And again, as suggested by Census studies, perhaps many others relocate from rural areas or small towns to cities before the institutionalization decision is necessary, in a staged or sequenced move that eventually brings them to a nursing home from a city, rather than a country, address. One would think that increased retirement to particular destination counties would permit nursing homes to be built, or existing ones to expand, in those small town locations impacted by retirement migration. This conclusion, however, has not yet been reported in the research literature.

METHODOLOGICAL ISSUES: LOCAL SURVEYS

Generalizability and Relevance

Local surveys have a problem with their generalizability. One never knows how unique a local population is. For example, it makes a great deal of difference where the sample comes from if one is studying poverty or race. Local surveys gain credibility only through replication. If the findings hold up in dispersed locations and over time, they come to be thought of as more generally true. One local survey cannot give this result.

The Softer Landscape: Asking Why

The biggest advantage of local surveys, however, is that the researcher can ask the really relevant questions, rather than trying to make someone else's questions work for what s/he wants to study. Rather than being stuck with the census items, for example, migration history can be solicited. Using geographical images, local surveys are a softer landscape, colored not with the primary colors of behavior, but the softer hues of motivation and result. With census data, and indeed, with most large national surveys, one can describe behavior and find out statistically how the odds of it happening are changed by other characteristics of the individuals. However, figuring out why the behavior happened is a matter of inferential gymnastics. In local surveys, one can ask "Why did you do that?"

The Patchwork Quilt

Bringing together many local surveys in a meta analysis in order to define a broad subject matter, such as population mobility, is like sewing together the many cloth patches of a homemade quilt. Each patch offers a visual image, but the larger image of the whole quilt is something else. It is the "big picture," so to speak. For years, researchers have worried that migrating retirees will overburden the communities to which they move. "Overburden them with what?" is seldom answered. There is just this vague notion that they will use too much of something that is scarce. Health care is often mentioned as one of these. So, it is not surprising that local surveys are often focused on the migration impact issue when the mobility of older populations is studied.

Research Examples: Does Elderly Rural Migration Burden Rural Health Services?

Some known characteristics of older interstate migrants indicate that their health care use will be greater than that of the general population, and it will increase as they age. Cost is generally not an impediment, however, because as the aggregate socioeconomic status of interstate migrants of retirement age suggests, they generally are able to afford health care costs. Not only do they tend to have financial resources of their own, but also are very likely to be covered by Medicare and supplemental insurance coverage. Typically, they can afford to travel to the doctor and their social status suggests that they can be expected to be relatively sophisticated users of the health care system. Therefore, they can be expected to increase both the need and demand for health service in the communities where they settle. What are the consequences of this usage pattern on rural medical practices?

The only study to attempt to settle the issue chose a rural county in Florida and one in North Carolina that were the locations of sizeable influxes of retired migrants during the decade [54]. By choosing two geographically dispersed retirement locations, they hoped to increase the generalizability of their findings. In these two rural counties, Haas and Crandall surveyed all of the physicians with a brief twenty-two-item questionnaire, and over three-quarters of the doctors responded.

Not surprisingly they found that physicians decide to settle in a particular geographic area, in part, because they think the population needing services in that physician's specialty is big enough to sustain their practice. Physicians were aware that large numbers of retirees were moving into their counties. In fact, approximately three-fifths said that over half of their patients were over age sixty-five, and the same proportion said that the number of their older patients had increased due to retirement migration. The three pediatricians who saw no older patients commented that the influx of elderly people had positively affected the growth of their practices, as family and general practitioners had less time to deal with the problems of children and teens because of the needs of their older patients.

How did the increasing numbers of older patients change the practices of the physicians who served them? The proportion of acute illnesses and accidents they treated declined, and their management of chronic illnesses increased. Indeed, the average respondent reported spending two-fifths of practice time dealing with chronic problems. Haas and Crandall quoted one general practitioner as saying that he felt he was "becoming more of an internist" as a result of this change in the nature of his practice [54]. Many of the physicians asserted that their practices had become busier.

The physicians were also asked to assess the effect of elderly migrants on the local medical care system as a whole. The most frequent change they noted was an increase in the number of physicians in the county, in particular, internists, internal medicine sub-specialists, and surgical specialists associated with the treatment of older individuals. In addition, they indicated there had been an increase in demand for inpatient care. It was becoming more difficult, according to these doctors, to place patients in nursing homes. Furthermore, since hospitalization in the community had also risen, this had created enough new demand so that hospitals had added critical care beds and sophisticated diagnostic equipment. Where is the negative impact on health care delivery if the concentration of immigrating retirees creates the market demand that expands health care resources in the area?

Research Example: What Health Care Strategies Do International Elderly Seasonal Migrants Use?

In 1986, the Canadian Embassy in Washington, in cooperation with the International Exchange Center on Gerontology (IECG), commissioned a study of Canadian winter residents of Florida. A team of Canadian and Florida gerontologists designed a mail survey to focus, among other things, on the use of health care in Florida while Canadians were wintering there. Because tourism data indicate that over 60 percent of Canadian visitors to Florida are from Ontario, most of whom are English-speaking, a Florida-based weekly newspaper (*Canada News*) was used to provide the names and addresses of 4,500 English-reading seasonal migrants on their subscription list. The number responding to this English-speaking Canadian survey was 2,728 [55, 56]. Canadian seasonal migrants to Florida present an unusual opportunity to canvas opinions about two national health care systems, with a group of "privileged informants" experienced in both systems.

Almost all seasonal migrants preceded their trip with a visit to their Canadian family doctor. Perhaps because of Canadian drug-benefit plans (such as the Ontario Drug Benefits Program), which provided free or low cost drugs to seniors, they tended to fill prescriptions and stock up on medications prior to leaving Canada. Also, the vast majority had taken out health insurance for Canadians traveling abroad, in order to cover any differential between Canadian medicare reimbursement levels and Florida cost, and also to facilitate payment in the event of an emergency. Less frequently, but still quite often, instructions had been given to relatives about what to do in the event of a medical emergency, and travel arrangements had been made (such as the purchase of "open" return tickets) to facilitate sudden return visits to Canada.

These behaviors suggest a sensitivity to health concerns in this population that increases both with age and in relation to decreased health status. Anticipating such a pattern, the researchers examined precautionary behavior in relation to health status and found individuals with poorer self-reported health more likely to report precautionary behavior. The ultimate precautionary behavior, of course, is to cease seasonal migration when concern for health increases, in order to decrease the financial risks of seeking care outside Canada, and to remain where one feels comfortable [57]. As with any aged population, the health behavior of these seasonal migrants is strategic, insofar as it is intentional and oriented to contingencies.

Migration selectivity among permanent migrants tends to favor those who are younger, healthier, more often married and residentially-independent persons, at least in long distance streams [58]. Migration selectivity, however, has a double meaning for "snowbirds." Not only does dual community residence tend to select participants with the positive characteristics as it does among permanent migrants, but as the health of those twice-annual migrants declines, a second selection occurs. In other words, among those whose health declines, there is a decrease in their winter sojourns to Florida. Canadian "snowbirds" in Florida apparently place few demands on the health care system; they pay their way and they stop coming when they reach the state at which their demands on the system might increase.

METHODOLOGICAL ISSUES:
THE GRAND ALLIANCE OF MACRO AND MICRO

The Truth is in the Cracks

Sometimes we feel that disciplinary academics get so used to viewing the world through their particular lenses that they forget that one academic discipline is only one perspective, one take, on the puzzles of the world. Reality cannot be contained in one discipline, as valuable as that discipline may be to generating knowledge on a subject. The truth is always in the cracks. It lies between the disciplines. This is just as true of methodologies. No one research methodology can generate information on the whole of reality. It is therefore very important to respect several methodologies, several kinds of information and data, and to piece it together creatively to look into the cracks and get a peek at reality.

Collage: The Art of Using Several Types of Data

In this world of specialization, it is not an easy sell to say that we should know and respect several types of research, but that is indeed what is being said. The kinds of research that will authentically contribute to knowledge about reality, whatever the subject of that reality may be, will not come from technicians, but from broadly educated critical thinkers, who solve the puzzles by bringing to bear a range of investigative approaches. These are men and women who can answer the "how many" question, and proceed to the "where," "when," "who," and "what" of the matter. Their interest in theory pushes them to go the final step and to ask, "why" raising the puzzle to the level of a mystery. Puzzles can be solved, mysteries cannot. We never know all of the answers to the "why" question. The following research example is an attempt to bring together two methodologies and two types of data to understand a broader research question. This case also illustrates some of the frustrations in making such an attempt.

Research Example: On the Nesting of Snowbirds

There may be an important relationship between permanent and seasonal migration that helps to explain the social integration of older seasonal migrants. Permanent migrants from the same origin may provide for seasonal migrants a socially receptive place to "nest" for the winter. What would constitute minimal evidence for the influence of permanent migration on seasonal migration? Migrants of both types from the same origin would have to have settled in the same destination. Only then could the potential exist for a type of network recruitment in which permanent residents encourage seasonal migration. This level of evidence would be necessary, but not sufficient to demonstrate such a proposition.

Such minimal evidence is not available in census data alone because seasonal migration is not recorded. However, it is available in the two parts of the study of Canadian snowbirds in Florida: the survey of snowbirds and the census analysis of permanent Florida residents who were born in Canada. Marshall and Longino found in the survey data some indirect evidence of network recruitment [59]. Of older English-speaking Canadian snowbirds in Florida, 2 percent had one or more children who lived permanently in Florida, within fifty miles of their parents' wintering home. This seems like an unimportant matter, but the story continues. Eight percent reported that at least one of their siblings was a permanent resident of Florida and lived closer than fifty miles. Finally, 8 percent said that they had another relative, other than children and siblings, who lived nearby and permanently in Florida. Depending on the degree of overlap between these categories, from 8 to 18 percent of the Canadian snowbirds had family members living permanently in Florida—close enough to be an important part of their social environment. The contact with permanent-resident family members by seasonal migrants is certainly a suggestive finding. Another is that 70 percent of the retired snowbirds from Canada had friends who were permanent residents of Florida; half of them had six or more friends in Florida and nearly a fifth had eleven or more.

Many Canadian snowbirds say that they have family members or friends who live year-round in Florida. Is there any evidence from other data sources that such Canadian permanent migrants do reside in Florida? If so, did some of these Canadian permanent migrants serve as an unofficial reception committee and were they an important part of the social networks of Canadian visitors? To examine this second piece of the puzzle, Longino et al. extracted from the 1-in-40 census microdata migrant file the records of all persons born in Canada who, in 1980, were permanent residents of the United States [60].

In 1980, fewer than a million (833,920) native-born Canadians lived in the United States. Most (84%) of these migrants had become naturalized U.S. citizens; 39 percent were sixty years or older. Florida is the only distant state from the Canadian border on the East Coast that attracts native-born Canadians in large numbers. In 1980, there were an estimated 70,540 persons of all ages living in Florida who had been born in Canada. Furthermore, the researchers found that Florida is even more attractive to persons born in Canada who are in their sixties or older; nearly half of the native-born Canadians who live in Florida are in that age group. On April 1, 1980, there were 34,700 Canadians over age sixty in Florida.

The survey of Canadian seasonal migrants does not "prove" that permanent Canadian-born migrants to Florida function to recruit snowbirds or to make them more comfortable once they come. Unfortunately, no direct questions were asked in the interview that would firmly establish this point. A minority of them are in contact with family members who migrated permanently. A much larger part of the Canadian snowbirds have friends among year-round Florida residents. If many of these friends were Canadian by birth, then the research proposition would be supported. One could speculate that many of the Florida friends that Canadian winter visitors mentioned are also Canadians, considering that Florida has over 70,000 permanent residents who were born in Canada, and that a high proportion of them live in mobile homes and condominiums, the favored type of residence for Canadian seasonal migrants. Nevertheless, this evidence is only circumstantial. Direct evidence from another survey would be necessary to turn this speculation into a finding. The piecing together of evidence from two or three types of data to make one story is not easy to accomplish, unless it is carefully designed ahead of time.

THE FUTURE DEVELOPMENT OF MIGRATION RESEARCH ON RURAL AGING POPULATIONS

Further Research is Needed Using Census Data

The census microdata for 1990 contains an item attempting to establish a continuum from highly urban to highly rural. The categories are ordered as follows: central city, or a part of it; the highly urbanized suburban ring, or a part of it; the entire Metropolitan Statistical Area (MSA) combining the central city and suburbs; an MSA county combined with one or more adjacent nonMSA counties; clusters of adjacent counties that are nonmetropolitan entirely.

There was no attempt in 1990 to construct a similar scale for residence in 1985. Therefore, there is no way of telling whether a person moved up or down the metropolitan hierarchy between 1985 and 1990. Nonetheless, the characteristics of migrants who moved into the various type of community environments could be profiled and compared.

Further Research is Needed Using Large Secondary Datasets

Large secondary datasets for aging research tend to focus on issues of policy importance such as income maintenance, supportive relationships and services, living arrangements and health. The demographic characteristics tend to be sparse and limited to age, gender, race, ethnicity, marital status, education, and income. Mobility measures often are limited to whether or not the person has changed his address in the past two years or since the last interview. The destination of the move is often not available, let alone the origin.

Furthermore, because of the cluster samples on which major datasets tend to be built, these studies do not attempt to be representative of all populations up and down the metropolitan hierarchy; coverage at the rural end is often not representative at all. The use of large national studies, therefore, are a real challenge to rural aging research, particularly if mobility is important. In this kind of research environment, nearly anything would be considered an advance.

Further Research is Needed Using Local Surveys

Local surveys may provide more information on the mobility of rural populations than any other kind of research. The generalizability of the findings of these studies will gain credibility through the replication process.

CONCLUSION

This chapter has attempted to survey the theoretical and methodological approaches to migration research on rural aging populations. The topic is one that has generated a good deal of interest because of its relationship to rural economic development. Because of this interest, there is likely to be continued research. We have argued in the pages above that there are problems inherent in any methodological approach to the study of older movers to, or from, rural settings, and, therefore, it is important to begin comparing studies with different approaches and methodologies to leverage the insights out of the "cracks" between them. No one approach is likely to be adequate.

REFERENCES

1. C. F. Longino, Jr., Internal Migration, in *Encyclopedia of Sociology*, E. F. Borgatta and M. L. Borgatta (eds.), Macmillan, New York, pp. 974-980, 1992.
2. C. F. Longino, Jr., Geographical Distribution and Migration, in *Handbook of Aging and the Social Sciences* (3rd Edition), R. H. Binstock and L. K. George (eds.), Harcourt Brace Jovanovich, San Diego, California, pp. 45-59, 1990.
3. C. H. Patrick, Health and Migration of the Elderly, *Research on Aging, 2,* pp. 233-241, 1980.
4. J. R. Bohland and G. D. Rowles, The Significance of Elderly Migration to Changes in Elderly Population Concentration in the United States: 1960-1980, *Journal of Gerontology: Social Sciences, 43,* pp. S145-S152, 1988.
5. S. Barsby and D. R. Cox, *Interstate Migration of the Elderly,* Heath, Lexington, Massachusetts, 1975.
6. C. F. Longino, Jr., Where Retirees Prefer to Live: The Geographical Distribution and Migratory Patterns of Retirees, in *The Columbia Retirement Handbook,* A. Monk (ed.), Columbia University Press, New York, pp. 405-416, 1994.
7. F. A. Cribier, European Assessment of Aged Migration, *Research on Aging, 2,* pp. 225-270, 1980.
8. T. O. Graff and R. F. Wiseman, Changing Concentration of Older Americans, *Geographical Review, 68,* pp. 379-393, 1978.
9. R. F. Wiseman and C. C. Roseman, A Typology of Elderly Migration Based on the Decision Making Process, *Economic Geography, 55,* pp. 324-337, 1979.
10. A. Speare, Jr. and J. W. Meyer, Types of Elderly Residential Mobility and Their Determinants, *Journal of Gerontology: Social Sciences, 43,* pp. S74-S81, 1988.
11. P. Gober and L. E. Zonn, Kin and Elderly Amenity Migration, *The Gerontologist, 23,* pp. 288-294, 1983.
12. F. Wiseman, Why Older People Move: Theoretical Issues, *Research on Aging, 2,* pp. 141-154, 1980.
13. E. G. Ravenstein, The Laws of Migration, *Journal of the Royal Statistical Society, 52,* pp. 241-301, 1989.
14. E. Litwak and C. F. Longino, Jr., Migrating Patterns Among the Elderly: A Developmental Perspective, *The Gerontologist, 27,* pp. 266-272, 1987.
15. W. J. McAuley and C. Nutty, Residential Preferences and Moving Behavior: A Family Life-Cycle Analysis, *Journal of Marriage and the Family, 44,* pp. 301-309, 1982.
16. W. J. Serow, Why the Elderly Move, *Research on Aging, 9:*4, pp. 582-597, 1987.
17. E. Litwak, *Helping the Elderly,* Guilford, New York, 1985.

18. L. J. Cuba, From Visitor to Resident: Retiring to Vacationland, *Generations, 13*:2, pp. 63-67, 1989.
19. J. E. Bradsher, C. F. Longino, Jr., D. J. Jackson, and R. S. Zimmerman, Health and Geographic Mobility Among the Recently Widowed, *Journal of Gerontology: Social Sciences, 47,* pp. S261-S268, 1992.
20. A. Speare, R. Avery, and L. Lawton, Disability, Residential Mobility and Changes in Living Arrangements, *Journal of Gerontology: Social Sciences, 46,* pp. S133-S142, 1991.
21. C. F. Longino, Jr. and W. H. Haas, III, Migration and the Elderly, in *Aging in Rural America*, C. N. Bull (ed.), Sage Publications, Newbury Park, California, pp. 7-29, 1993.
22. G. V. Fuguitt and S. J. Tordella, Elderly Net Migration: The New Trend of Non-metropolitan Population Change, *Research on Aging, 2,* pp. 191-204, 1980.
23. S. M. Golant, G. Rudzitis, and S. Daiches, Elderly from United States Central Cities, *Growth and Change, 9,* pp. 30-35, 1978.
24. D. T. Lichter, G. V. Fuguitt, T. B. Heaton, and W. B. Clifford, Components of Change in the Residential Concentrations of the Elderly Population: 1950-1975, *Journal of Gerontology, 36,* pp. 480-489, 1981.
25. L. H. Long and D. DeAre, *Migration to Nonmetropolitan Areas: Appraising the Trends and Reasons for Moving,* Special Demographic Analyses, CDS-80-2, Bureau of the Census, Washington, D.C., 1980.
26. C. F. Longino, Jr., Changing Aged Nonmetropolitan Migration Patterns, 1955 to 1960 and 1965 to 1970, *Journal of Gerontology, 37,* pp. 228-234, 1982.
27. C. F. Longino, Jr., R. F. Wiseman, J. C. Biggar, and C. B. Flynn, Aged Non-metropolitan Migration Patterns Over Three Census Decades, *Journal of Gerontology, 39,* pp. 721-729, 1984.
28. N. Glasgow and C. L. Beale, Rural Elderly in Demographic Perspective, *Rural Development Perspectives, 2,* pp. 22-26, 1985.
29. A. J. Sofranko, F. C. Fliegel, and N. Glasgow, Older Urban Migrants in Rural Settings: Problems and Prospects, *International Journal of Aging and Human Development, 16,* pp. 297-309, 1983.
30. N. Glasgow, Attracting Retirees as a Community Development Option, *Journal of the Community Development Society, 21*:1, pp. 102-114, 1990.
31. C. F. Longino, Jr. and W. H. Crown, The Migration of Old Money, *American Demographics, 11,* pp. 28-31, 1989.
32. C. F. Longino, Jr. and W. H. Crown, Retirement Migration and Interstate Income Transfers, *The Gerontologist, 30,* pp. 784-789, 1990.
33. W. J. Serow and W. H. Haas, Measuring the Economic Impact of Retirement Migration: The Case of Western North Carolina, *Journal of Applied Gerontology, 11*:2, pp. 200-215, 1992.
34. K. M. Heintz, *Retirement Communities: For Adults Only,* The State University Press of New Jersey, New Brunswick, New Jersey, 1976.
35. D. G. Bennett, *The Impact of Elderly In-Migration on Private and Public Economic Development Efforts in Predominantly Rural Areas Along the South Atlantic Coast,* U.S. Department of Commerce, Economic Development Administration Project No. 9-07-1373, 1990.

36. M. Fagan, *Attracting Retirees for Economic Development,* Center for Economic Development, Jacksonville State University, Jacksonville, Alabama, 1988.

37. Severinghaus, *Economic Expansion Using Retiree Income: A Workbook for Rural Washington Communities,* Rural Economic Assistance Program, Washington State University, Pullman, Washington, 1989.

38. C. F. Longino, Jr., The Gray Peril Mentality and the Impact of Retirement Migration, *Journal of Applied Gerontology, 7,* pp. 448-455, 1988.

39. R. H. Aday and L. A. Miles, Long-Term Impacts of Rural Migration of the Elderly: Implications for Research, *The Gerontologist, 22,* pp. 331-336, 1982.

40. W. H. Haas, *The Influence of Retirement In-Migration on Local Economic Development,* Appalachian Regional Commission Contract 89-48 NC-10269-89-I-302-0327, 1990.

41. C. F. Longino, Jr. and I. M. Taplin, How Does the Mobility of the Elderly Affect Health Care in the U.S.A.? *Aging: Clinical and Experimental Research 6*:6, pp. 399-409, 1994.

42. W. B. Clifford, T. Heaton, and G. V. Fuguitt, Residential Mobility and Living Arrangements Among the Elderly: Changing Patterns in Metropolitan and Nonmetropolitan Areas, *International Journal of Aging and Human Development, 14*:2, pp. 139-156, 1982.

43. N. Glasgow, The Older Metropolitan Migrant as a Factor in Rural Population Growth, in *Rebirth of Rural America: Rural Migration in the Midwest,* A. J. Sofranco and J. D. Williams (eds.), Iowa State University, North Central Regional Center for Rural Development, Ames, Iowa, 1980.

44. C. F. Longino, Jr., Residential Relocation of Older People: Metropolitan and Non-Metropolitan, *Research on Aging, 2,* pp. 205-216, 1980.

45. G. D. Rowles, Between Worlds: A Relocation Dilemma for the Appalachian Elderly, *International Journal of Aging and Human Development, 17,* pp. 301-331, 1983.

46. D. J. Jackson, C. F. Longino, Jr., R. S. Zimmerman, and J. E. Bradsher, Environmental Adjustments to Declining Functional Ability: Residential Mobility and Living Arrangements, *Research on Aging, 13,* pp. 289-309, 1991.

47. D. J. Bogue and C. L. Beale, *Economic Areas of the United States,* Free Press, New York, 1961.

48. C. F. Longino, Jr., *Retirement Migration in America,* Vacation Publications, Houston, Texas, 1995.

49. D. C. Cowper and C. F. Longino, Jr., Veteran Interstate Migration and VA Health Service Use, *The Gerontologist, 32,* pp. 44-50, 1992.

50. C. F. Longino, Jr., M. Miller, R. T. Anderson, M. K. James, and A. S. Worley, *Changes in Functional Status and the Risks of a Subsequent Community-Based Move. A Final Report to the National Institute on Aging,* Reynolda Gerontology Program of Wake Forest University, Winston-Salem, North Carolina, 1996.

51. R. T. Anderson, M. K. James, M. Miller, A. S. Worley, and C. F. Longino, Jr., *The Timing of Change: Patterns in Functional Status,* paper presented at the 49th Annual Scientific Meeting of the Gerontological Society of America, 1996.

52. C. F. Longino, Jr., M. Miller, R. Anderson, and M. K. James, *Functional Health and Geographic Mobility in Old Age: A Final Report to the National Institute on Aging,*

Reynolda Gerontology Program of Wake Forest University, Winston-Salem, North Carolina, 1996.

53. W. J. McAuley and S. S. Travis, *The Nursing Home Moves of Metropolitan and Non-Metropolitan Elders: An Examination of Distance Moved,* Gerontological Society of America Annual Scientific Meeting, San Francisco, California, 1991.

54. W. H. Haas and L. A. Crandall, Physician's Views of Retirement Migrants' Impact on Rural Medical Practice, *The Gerontologist, 28,* pp. 663-666, 1988.

55. L. C. Mullins and R. D. Tucker, *Snowbirds in the Sun Belt: Older Canadians in Florida,* International Exchange Center on Gerontology, University of South Florida, Tampa, Florida, 1988.

56. R. D. Tucker, V. W. Marshall, C. F. Longino, Jr., and L. C. Mullins, Older Anglophone Canadians in Florida: A Descriptive Profile, *Canadian Journal of Aging, 7,* pp. 218-232, 1988.

57. J. Daciuk and V. W. Marshall, Health Concerns as a Deterrent to Seasonal Migration of Elderly Canadians, *Social Indicators Research, 22,* pp. 181-197, 1987.

58. C. F. Flynn, C. F. Longino, Jr., R. F. Wiseman, and J. C. Biggar, The Redistribution of America's Older Population: Major National Migration Patterns for Three Census Decades, 1960-1980, *Gerontologist, 25,* pp. 292-296, 1985.

59. V. W. Marshall and C. F. Longino, Jr., Older Canadians in Florida: The Social Networks of International Season Migrants, *Comprehensive Gerontology, 2,* pp. 63-68, 1988.

60. C. F. Longino, Jr., V. W. Marshall, L. C. Mullins, and R. D. Tucker, On the Nesting of Snowbirds: A Question About Seasonal and Permanent Migrants, *Journal of Applied Gerontology, 10*:1, pp. 157-168, 1991.

CHAPTER
5

The Community-Based Laboratory Approach to the Development of Collaborative Rural Health and Aging Research and Demonstrations

Harold L. Cook and Gordon H. DeFriese

In the fields of applied social science and health policy analysis, academic institutions have often sought to develop community/population-based research enterprises which would facilitate the process of research question clarification, guide the development stages of research design and project implementation, and increase the relevance of research findings to the "real world" lives of those who have experienced the problems studied. Much of the early history of American social science was developed through such arrangements, particularly in large cities such as Chicago, Detroit, New York; in small communities like Candor, New York [1]; Dansville, New York [2], Beech Creek, Kentucky [3]; Claxton, Georgia [4]; or Asheville, North Carolina [5].

More recent examples of these kinds of community-based research laboratories are the long-term epidemiological studies in Framingham, Massachusetts [6] and Pawtucket, Rhode Island [7]. In most of these now-famous study sites, the thing that distinguished the method and product of these studies was the close relationships that developed over a number of years between an interdisciplinary group of university researchers and a local citizenry. Except for the case of *Small Town in Mass Society* [1], in most of these circumstances, the way in which the problems were selected for study and the way these studies were done gave local community groups a feeling that, through their participation in such research, their collective interests would be well served. At the same time, mutual commitments emerged between academic and local community leaders to making the research conducted in these settings as useful and relevant as possible to a broad spectrum of other communities facing similar problems and concerns in other locales.

For their part, universities have always had difficulties in establishing such relationships, and in maintaining them once they were developed. University faculty have rarely had the experience of working in collaboration with lay or citizen groups, even in their own communities and neighborhoods. Moreover, there is a feeling of apprehension and distrust between the two parties to such relationships, in no small measure due to the way in which many academic researchers have tended to operate in relation to local community groups. The feeling of lay and community groups that they are usually asked to serve as research "subjects," or as human "guinea pigs," but are rarely asked to contribute to the formulation of the questions and the issues, much less the methods used to carry out these studies, has contributed to these feelings. In many cases, no one in the community studied is ever given an opportunity to read or hear the results of the research before it is shared widely with academic peers, even though identity of the site of the research may be clearly discernible from these reports.

Lay and community groups, on the other hand, have their own problems with such collaborations. There is a certain level of modesty, if not embarrassment, on the part of some local citizens in offering their own statement of a researchable question. Without an understanding of the technical and analytical capacities of visiting academic researchers, who come with "fancy titles" and positions at distant institutions many local citizens will never even visit, there is an understandable reticence in even making suggestions regarding the rewording or rephrasing of a research question or proposed study design. Then there are the feelings that, whatever is proposed or undertaken, the local resources to support lay participation are meager, even though the in-kind resources available through lay or citizen groups are often of inestimable value to the academic researchers who have tried to do research in other communities without such cooperation.

In two other chapters of this book, by Hunter et al. [8] and by Hogue [9], descriptions are provided of two efforts over more than a decade to develop such community-based laboratories in two separate rural areas of eastern North Carolina. In each of these settings, significant research in the field of rural health and aging has served a useful role in strengthening programmatic efforts to address the problems of older adults. In this chapter, we will refer to these developments in order to highlight the different approaches that have been taken in each setting. In one of these settings, the approach was defined by a series of social science and epidemiological research questions, in combination with a commitment to define new approaches to community-level health services and program interventions likely to benefit the people of this rural county. In the other, the approach was defined by a program of geriatric clinical services and interdisciplinary health professional education, all of which had the potential for leading to new research on rural health and aging. In both cases, the interests of individual academic faculty members, which happened to intersect with the interests and needs of local citizens or health service providers, proved to be the focal point for these collaborative research developments.

In each of these two community settings, different groups of university researchers used somewhat diverse methods to explore similar sets of issues related to the health beliefs and practices of older adults living in rural areas. For example, the chapter by Arcury, Gaylord, and Cook [10] in this volume describes the similarities and differences in approach to the study of multiethnic health beliefs and attitudes employed in these two communities. In their chapter, these researchers who worked separately, jointly author a synthesis of their separate findings from these different research milieux. Though similar questions drove the research in each of these communities, the source of the questions guiding the research and the methods chosen were different. In each case, however, a partnership between local community and university faculty was critical to the success of these endeavors. From these two university-community partnerships it is possible to derive important lessons regarding the utility of community-based collaborative efforts for the field of rural health and aging research and policy development.

THE JOHNSTON COUNTY RURAL HEALTH RESEARCH CENTER: BUILDING ON A UNIVERSITY-BASED EDUCATIONAL PROGRAM REQUIRING "REAL WORLD" LEARNING EXPERIENCES FOR STUDENTS

Our involvements in Johnston County in rural eastern North Carolina began from the effort of a single UNC-Chapel Hill (UNC-CH) faculty member to find a community within which to train public health education and social science graduate students in the skills necessary for observing and studying the impact of racial/ethnic and cultural forces on health beliefs, behavior, and morbidity. Dr. Tony L. Whitehead,[1] an African-American social anthropologist and member of the faculty of the Department of Health Behavior and Health Education within the UNC-CH School of Public Health, was seeking an ethnically-diverse and culturally-interesting community or county within reasonable driving distance from Chapel Hill as a training and research location for himself and his students. Smithfield, the county seat of Johnston County, at one time in the early 1970s had a reputation of having uneasy relations between the African-American and the

---

[1] Dr. Whitehead is now Professor and Chairman, Department of Anthropology, University of Maryland.

white populations. Yet, by the time Whitehead became involved in Johnston County, there were several local activities which suggested a renewal and sense of opportunity for people of both ethnic groups in this setting.

Whitehead immersed himself completely in the day-to-day life of the county, especially among its non-white population. By attending as many neighborhood and community events as possible (church and revival services, weddings, funerals and wakes, church homecomings, family reunions, river baptisms, home dedications, and "hog killings"), he established a relationship among community residents based on familiarity, common interest, and mutual concern for a number of issues related to health. Among the first studies undertaken by Whitehead was a project supported by the National Heart, Lung and Blood Institute (NIH) on how the social events within the African-American rural community tend to influence food choices and eating habits, their intergenerational transmission, and patterns of cardiovascular disease [11].

Among the topics of interest to local citizens, particularly the African-American older adult members of the Johnston County Citizens Association, was the prevalence and severity of arthritis. Whitehead was asked if assistance could be arranged from colleagues at UNC-Chapel Hill for a study of this set of conditions, with the hope that some kind of intervention program might be arranged to address the problems likely to be documented through the study. Whitehead turned to one of his former students, Dr. Harold Cook, who was then affiliated with the UNC-CH Thurston Arthritis Research Center, to help design such a study. Funding was eventually arranged through the National Institute on Arthritis, Musculoskeletal and Skin Diseases (NIAMS) of the National Institutes of Health (through the UNC-CH Thurston Arthritis Research Center) for a study of this problem in Johnston County.

When the NIAMS funding arrived, it was considered important to have some local organization designated to have fiscal responsibility for the administration of at least some portion of the funds. This was considered important as a way of ensuring long-term local commitment to the project and at the same time, a way of emphasizing the collaborative nature of the venture between the University and the local community. For this purpose, the Johnston County Council on Aging (COA) proved to be a useful local agency to fulfill this fiscal and administrative function. The project involved the hiring of local personnel to conduct the interviews with Johnston County residents in several small towns and communities. Funds were channeled through the COA to interviewers for this purpose. In addition, the COA was responsible for the recruitment (but not the training) of interviewers, meetings of the local project advisory committee, and maintaining close relationships with local health care providers, county commissioners and other elected officials, and local service agencies serving older adults. University personnel took primary responsibility for managing the data collected via this project, as well as the preparation of reports of findings from the study.

In the mid-to-late 1980s it became clear that the range and volume of potential research activities involving University faculty and local citizen groups was such that a more formal organizational base within Johnston County made sense. With funds from the UNC-CH Center for Health Promotion and Disease Prevention, a new office to coordinate such studies was opened in 1989 under the name of the Johnston County Center for Rural Health Research. A county resident was hired as office manager, two advisory committees were formed, and Dr. Cook was appointed the full-time director of the Center, moving his residence to Smithfield within a year or so of the Center's creation. In order to assure that local citizens would have easy access to the activities and research endeavors of the new Center, a local Community Leaders' Advisory Committee was formed, in addition to a Professional Advisory Committee, including representatives of local medical, health professional, and education interests.

Among its first efforts toward the development of a community-oriented agenda for research and demonstration in Johnston County, the Center for Rural Health Research sponsored a series of forty-eight focus group interviews with the general public, and an additional sixteen focus group discussions with local physicians, hospital and health department employees, social service professionals, business leaders, adolescents and farm families. Out of these discussions came insights and perspectives helpful in developing the research agenda for the Center.

In 1990, the Centers for Disease Control and Prevention (CDC) awarded a contract to the UNC-CH School of Public Health, in conjunction with the Association of Schools of Public Health, for a prospective cohort study of osteoarthritis (OA) of the hip and knee (the so-called "OA Project"). This multi-year, longitudinal study of OA incidence, has enabled the Johnston County Center to launch a number of corollary projects, such as a study of the disabling effects of OA on work and activities of daily living among older adults in this rural county. In addition, research by faculty from the UNC-CH Department of Geography has focused on patterns of spatial mobility in search of medical care by persons living in different areas of Johnston County. This set of arthritis-related research investigations became a major part of the Johnston County Center's participation in the North Carolina Rural Aging Program at the Cecil G. Sheps Center for Health Services Research at UNC-CH, funded by the National Institute on Aging.

In 1992, local citizen leaders affiliated with the Center began consideration of the long-run financial structure of the Johnston County program and proposed that the Center be reconfigured as a private, non-profit corporation, with a local Johnston County board of directors. Therefore, in that year, a new organizational entity, Rural Health Research, Incorporated (RHR), was formed with a five-member local citizen board. In order to oversee the University relations with the new non-profit corporation, UNC-CH formed a special Advisory Committee on Johnston Rural Health Research, consisting of senior faculty, research center directors, and chaired by an Associate Vice Chancellor for Health Affairs.

Since this time, additional research projects have been piloted in Johnston County, using the facilities and staff of RHR, and have subsequently been funded as investigator-initiated research projects. It is the policy of RHR that, wherever possible, Johnston County residents will be hired to staff projects taking place under its umbrella. Specific research projects have usually been funded to UNC-CH faculty, with provisions for subcontracting the day-to-day field operations of these projects to RHR. Scientific expertise for these projects continues to reside on the University campus among faculty who are regularly on-site in Johnston County (about an hour's drive from Chapel Hill). Local facilities, such as physicians' offices, the local hospital, local churches, senior citizens' centers, etc., have been used for medical examinations and testing, as well as other types of interventions under investigation by UNC-CH faculty. These arrangements have provided income for some of these facilities, study participants have been able to encounter familiar faces at the data collection sites, and local people have gained experience with the research process and in working with academic research personnel.

After several years, there is a local citizenry with a substantial degree of acceptance of research and its potential contributions to the health and life of the community, especially research on health and aging issues. Many community residents have been involved as research staff, far more have served as study subjects, and several of the projects have led to important interventions (e.g., school-based programs to reduce the frequency of student-carried firearms, exercise programs for rural elderly persons, and educational/clinical intervention programs to provide assistance to the sufferers of osteoarthritis). RHR staff and University colleagues have assisted other local groups with the preparation and submission of grant proposals for other types of projects and there has developed a close working relationship with the Office of the County Manager and all other relevant activities of the County Government.

University faculty find it easy to move in and around the County in connection with their research. RHR staff have facilitated necessary connections with local citizen groups and the regular interview staff of RHR are well-known to most local citizens. Students from UNC-CH have been welcomed in Johnston County, as participants in RHR-affiliated research, or as part of their on-site observational assignments as part of coursework in Chapel Hill. University faculty and staff are learning that they can carry out creditable community-based research without compromising their other academic activities or standards, while Johnston County citizens can gain a greater level of confidence that they can turn to the University with concrete problems needing careful research and analysis by faculty who are willing to invest time and energy in these collaborative efforts.

THE NORTHAMPTON-HALIFAX COUNTY RESEARCH LABORATORY: BUILDING FROM A STRONG CLINICAL RELATIONSHIP BETWEEN UNIVERSITY AND COMMUNITY PROGRAMS

The chapter by Hunter et al. in this volume offers a detailed description of how the partnership emerged between the faculty of the University of North Carolina with interests in the field of aging, and a local health care delivery system serving two of the more remote and low-income counties of the state [7]. Whereas in Johnston County, the initial contact between the University and the local population was through the effort of a single faculty member to find a suitable site for UNC-Chapel Hill graduate students to observe and learn about rural health and illness behavior, in Northampton and Halifax Counties. Initial contact started in connection with the effort to bring to these rural counties university-based clinical consultant and continuing educational services from geriatric specialists in medicine, dentistry, nursing, physical therapy, and pharmacy. Though the Johnston County effort grew from an approach of University faculty to the local citizenry, the opportunities for research collaboration in Northampton and Halifax Counties grew from a program of service and clinical teaching initiated at the request of local health care and social service providers.

In Northampton and Halifax Counties, the focus of activity revolved around service and teaching in a clinical setting. Hence, it was the questions of primary concern to health care providers that determined the basic framework for University-community collaboration in aging research. First, there were concerns raised about the impact of interdisciplinary team consultation to the nursing home, leading to a plan to collect both baseline and follow-up measures of nursing home resident outcomes in the areas of functional health status and goal attainment. This project met with several difficulties, most notably the inability of some nursing home residents to complete important clinical outcome measures, particularly measures of cognitive and sensory impairments. Adaptations of the approach to measurement led to useful information about the progress of individual patients, and the nursing home population as a whole, enabling care plan modifications for some patients to be made.

The second project taking place in Northampton and Halifax Counties involved a qualitative study of health beliefs and practices in this multicultural eastern North Carolina community. Using two-to-three-hour interviews as the principal data collection modality, this study sought to identify principal dimensions of local customs and attitudes toward health. The results were used to inform health program staff with regard to views of patients and their families about such subjects as the way in which "health" and "illness" were defined, perceptions of the factors which determined health status and outcomes, and self-reported previous efforts to seek formal medical care in the event of acute or chronic illness.

Both of these studies were requested and seen by staff of Rural Health Group, Inc. (an existing health care delivery organization, and its affiliated nursing homes, senior centers, and other programs) as benefiting older rural residents of these two counties. But a central feature of all of the aging-related research that has taken place in Northampton and Halifax Counties is the nexus between the research enterprise itself and the scope of responsibility felt by Rural Health Group, Inc. for the design and implementation of a broad set of clinical and social service programs serving the people of its target area. Research is seen as instrumental to this function and the value of the enterprise is defined by the utility to be derived from research-based information. If the potential results are not likely to be useful in program development or management, then the effort to host research in this venue is not likely to be seen as worthwhile.

LESSONS FROM TWO COMMUNITY-BASED RESEARCH LABORATORY EXPERIENCES

One of the first and most important lessons from these efforts is that there is no one "best way" of developing these community-based research laboratories. Moreover, as university relationships develop in relation to specific communities in connection with educational programs, clinical practice or research, it is likely that the initiative for a more intensive effort in research and program evaluation will come from community organizations as well as from the university. A thorough opportunistic approach on the part of the university is warranted. The chance to carry out research can often come from a relationship established for other purposes, not from relationships established for the primary purpose of initiating research.

Second, while not every community is particularly well suited to this type of intervention, not every faculty member is interested in (or well suited for) this type of relationship. There is value for both teaching and research in a community-university joint venture of this kind, but the match between the interests of particular faculty members and particular communities is critical to the success of the joint venture. Some communities and local health care provider organizations are naturally suspicious of university faculty motives in seeking entry to do research and program evaluation in their surroundings. The time it would take to establish a basis for a trusting relationship and a meaningful collaboration, as demonstrated by Professor Tony Whitehead in Johnston County, is simply too great for some (particularly young) faculty who have career pressures to extract high quality scholarly products from every endeavor. When the match between a host community and a group of university faculty seems mutually beneficial, this can lay the foundation for a number of productive research endeavors likely to enable the field of health and aging to advance.

Third, the "managerial" aspects of collaborative research endeavors involving universities and community-based populations and/or provider groups can be viewed as having at least two separate facets. First, those aspects having to do with the scientific and measurement issues germane to the research itself are rarely ones where laypersons from the studied community either expect or want to have a major role. Yet, local citizen groups and health care providers often have insights of relevance to a research endeavor. These insights can prove useful if employed in the process of instrument design and the planning of fieldwork parts of community-based research endeavors. Second, those aspects having to do with the assurance of access to study respondents, and the feedback of research results to local audiences, are areas where community representatives can often be especially helpful and assume a primary responsibility.

Fourth, community-based research laboratory arrangements can benefit from infrastructural arrangements which visibly give local community groups the sense that a tangible investment has been made by a "distant" university with a greater-than-short-term interest in the health and well-being of local citizens. In the Johnston County experience, this type of infrastructural investment was exemplified by the opening of a formal research office financed by funds from the University of North Carolina and by the establishment of a local citizen advisory board. In Northampton and Halifax Counties, infrastructural supports for the emerging research program were closely tied to the overall program of an existing health care delivery organization, Rural Health Group, Inc. In both cases, the activities of research were seen as substantial investments having local public benefit, and not transient activities of persons from outside the community who held their own interests in the highest priority.

In essence, the idea of *partnership* for research must be mutually beneficial. It cannot benefit one partner more than the other. Given the fact that the activity of focal importance to these relationships is *research,* it is not surprising that university faculty often have a tendency to see their own role as most important in these relationships. But the promise of a longer term relationship for purposes of research with a local community requires a mutual understanding of the potential value of such relationships, and a commitment on each side to the conduct of research having a clear public benefit. Rural communities have a great deal to gain from an ongoing presence established by university research faculty they trust, and with whom they share basic understandings of the local cultural and environmental influences on health and disease. These relationships can help assure the validity of the findings of research, and therefore enhance the scientific quality of the work of university faculty. With so much to gain, partnerships of this kind appear to offer great promise for further work in the field of rural health and aging research.

REFERENCES

1. A. J. Vidich and J. Bensman, *Small Town in Mass Society: Class, Power and Religion in a Rural Community*, Princeton University Press, New Jersey, 1958.
2. E. L. Koos, *The Health of Regionville: What the People Thought and Did About It*, Columbia University Press, New York, 1954.
3. J. S. Brown, *Beech Creek: A Study of a Kentucky Mountain Neighborhood*, Berea College Press, Kentucky, 1988.
4. C. G. Hames and K. J. Greenlund, Ethnicity and Cardiovascular Disease: The Evans County Heart Study, *American Journal of Medical Sciences, 311*:3, pp. 130-134, March 1966.
5. J. C. Cassel, Factors Involving Sociocultural Incongruity and Change: Appraisal and Implications for Theoretical Development, *Milbank Memorial Fund Quarterly/Health and Society, 45*:2, pp. 41-48, 1967.
6. W. B. Kannel, Clinical Misconceptions Dispelled by Epidemiological Research, *Circulation, 92*:11, pp. 3350-3360, 1995.
7. R. A. Carleton, T. M. Lasater, A. R. Assaf, H. A. Feldman, and S. McKinlay, The Pawtucket Heart Health Program: Community Changes in Cardiovascular Risk Factors and Projected Disease Risk, *American Journal of Public Health, 85*:6, pp. 777-785, 1995.
8. R. H. Hunter, M. E. Williams, J. McCaleb, and W. Remmes, *The Potential of Community Service and Research Partnerships: The Geriatric Team Consultation Project*, Chapter 7, pp. 127-147 [this volume].
9. C. C. Hogue, *Methodologic Rigor and Therapeutic Obligation: The Dialectic in Community Research*, Chapter 10, pp. 199-208 [this volume].
10. T. A. Arcury, S. Gaylord, and H. L. Cook, Incorporating Qualitative Methods Into the Study of Health Beliefs and Health Behaviors of Rural Older Adults, Chapter 6, pp. 109-126 [this volume].
11. H. L. Cook, J. Goeppinger, S. E. Brunk, L. J. Price, T. L. Whitehead, and S. V. H. Sauter, A Reexamination of Community Participation in Health: Lessons from Three Community Health Projects, *Family and Community Health, 11*:2, pp. 1-13, 1988.

PART TWO

Measuring the Health and Well-Being of Rural People

CHAPTER
6

Incorporating Qualitative Methods Into the Study of Health Beliefs and Health Behaviors of Rural Older Adults

Thomas A. Arcury, Susan A. Gaylord,
and Harold L. Cook

There is a strong tradition of qualitative research in gerontology [1-3], and qualitative investigations have been an important element in our developing knowledge of the social life of the rural elderly [e.g., 4-7]. However, there has been little effort by gerontologists to apply qualitative methods to the investigation of the health beliefs and health behaviors of rural older adults. Our objective in this chapter is to illustrate how qualitative research methods can provide empirically-based information describing the health beliefs and health behaviors of rural older adults by presenting results from our research in rural North Carolina.

We begin this chapter with a brief review of the qualitative research methods literature in gerontology, emphasizing the variety in data collection methods. We then examine the results of the extant published qualitative rural aging research literature. This review highlights the limited amount of qualitative rural aging research that has examined health beliefs and health behaviors. We next present results from research conducted in collaboration with the North Carolina Rural Aging Program to illustrate how two qualitative research methods, focus group interviews, and in-depth personal interviews, can be used to study the health beliefs and behaviors of rural older adults. The focus group interviews were used to investigate general health beliefs, as well as health beliefs specific to arthritis, cancer, heart disease, and injuries. The in-depth personal interviews were used to examine general health beliefs, beliefs about longevity, and how these beliefs affect self-described health behavior. Finally, we present general conclusions and recommendations for conducting qualitative research on the health beliefs and behaviors of rural older adults.

QUALITATIVE RESEARCH METHODS IN GERONTOLOGY

Those wishing to conduct qualitative gerontological research are fortunate to have a plethora of contemporary works discussing both the philosophy and pragmatics of qualitative methodologies [e.g., 8-10]. Equally important, recent volumes edited by Reinhartz and Rowles [2], and Gubrium and Sankar [3] specifically discuss the use of qualitative methods in gerontology. With the availability of these detailed methodological works, we are limiting our remarks to a general discussion of the distinctive nature of qualitative research, the variety of ways in which qualitative data can be collected, and the benefits and disadvantages of using a qualitative methodology.

The Distinctive Nature of Qualitative Research

Qualitative research is a distinct research methodology. Qualitative research in gerontology, or in any other domain of scientific inquiry, can produce empirical results from which general statements about human behavior, beliefs, and organization can be made. These empirical results can be descriptive or they can be analytical statements reporting relationships among different factors. These results are also used to test hypotheses about the relationships among different variables. Qualitative research is especially well-suited for the explication of the meaning of events and beliefs among actors, of social process, and of decision making.

Qualitative research is neither the precursor to the "real science" of a quantitative investigation, nor is it simply a hand-maiden that supplies interesting quotes to soften hard numbers. Gubrium states this best.

> Qualitative research is not primarily a precursor to quantification. It is a separate and distinct tradition with its own standards of procedural rigor. The rigor is more analytic than technical, and thus may be deceptively captivating for the enthusiastic but untrained. Its aim is not to explore blindly, to muddle through, as it were, before ostensibly rigorous scientific practice takes over. Rather, it systematically and carefully attends to the organization of meaning in its various guises and venues, in relation to meaning's manifold contingencies [11, p. 581].

It is important to emphasize Gubrium's statement that qualitative research is systematic. For qualitative research to maintain the standards of empirical investigation, preparation for data collection (selecting subjects, designing interview guides), data collection (interviewing, observation, note taking), and data analysis (transcription, coding, interpretation) must be completed in a documented, systematic manner.

Qualitative methods can be integrated into multimethod project designs that include quantitative approaches. This methodological integration has produced very rewarding results, as the publication by Keith and colleagues dramatically illustrates [12]. Unfortunately, many studies which include a qualitative component do not well integrate this method into the design, using the qualitative research only as a lead into the quantitative component.

The data produced in qualitative research are text; that is, narrative statements in the form of transcribed interviews, field notes, or statements written by subjects, as well as photographs and other artifacts. Qualitative data are therefore readily amenable to humanistic as well as scientific interpretation. The possibility of humanistic interpretation has attracted many scholars to the use of qualitative methodology. However, this dualism does not lessen the scientific value of these data when approached in an empirical, systematic manner.

Qualitative Methods

While the data of qualitative research are text, there is no single "right" way to collect and analyze these textual data. Patton notes that there are three basic types of qualitative data collection: observation, interview, and document review [13]. The specific methods that fall within each of these basic types are extremely varied. Observation includes structured observation of behavior and more informal observation as in the participant observation of "just hanging out" of ethnography. Qualitative interviews can be conducted at different levels of formality: passing conversations, unstructured key informant interviews, oral history interviews, structured in-depth interviews, short-response open-ended interviews, and focus group interviews. Interview records may be in the form of interviewer notes or tape-recorded transcripts. There are subject-initiated documents such as personal correspondence, diaries and journals, family photographs, movies, and video recordings. Researcher-initiated documents include research diaries, open-ended questions on survey questionnaires, photographs, and cognitive and memory maps.

Several approaches are also available for the analysis of qualitative data. These data can be analyzed using older approaches dependent on note cards and manual sorts. The last decade has seen the rise of many different computer-assisted text analysis programs (see [14] for a review of computer-assisted text analysis programs).

Those wishing to use qualitative methodology should become familiar with a range of collection and analysis methods so that they can select the best method for their particular research problem. More detailed information about specific methods is available in such works as *Handbook of Qualitative Research* [9], *Qualitative Research Methods for Health Professionals* [15], *Research Methods in Anthropology* [16], and *Systematic Fieldwork* [17, 18].

Benefits and Disadvantages

There are several benefits to a qualitative study of health beliefs and health behaviors of older adults. Qualitative research is conducted at a human scale. The field worker has the opportunity to become familiar with the subjects and to know more about their lives than the narrow segment which is the focus of the research. Qualitative research provides the opportunity for subjects to present themselves in their own words, and for the investigator to learn the detailed meanings that subjects attach to behaviors, beliefs, and events. Qualitative research enables the investigator to document the range and variability of beliefs and behaviors, as well as the central tendencies, and to use this knowledge of variability to better analyze the phenomena being considered. The intimacy of qualitative research can provide a window for documenting the causal path of everyday events, such as how health care decisions are made, or how siblings negotiate the care of aged parents. The long-term involvement of some qualitative field studies allows the investigation of the causality of long-term processes, such as the decision to enter a nursing home or the compliance with a treatment plan. Finally, although the investigator is systematic in collecting qualitative data, there is the flexibility to follow insights that arise during the data collection process.

There are also important disadvantages in the use of qualitative methods to study the health beliefs and behaviors of older rural adults. Because qualitative samples are often small and purposively selected, there are always questions about the generalizability of study results. Because of the largely non-number character of qualitative results, their reporting often sounds imprecise. Qualitative research is extremely time consuming. The time needed to prepare for a qualitative study and to analyze qualitative data is equal to that of quantitative studies. In addition, while a qualitative researcher may be part of a team or use research assistants in the field, she/he must also commit significant time to the actual gathering of data. Finally, at face value, qualitative research appears to be an easy undertaking, so many untrained individuals try to do it, but end up doing it poorly.

QUALITATIVE RESEARCH OF RURAL AGING

While significant in its contribution, the total body of qualitative rural aging research is limited in size and in topics considered. The majority of this research examines aspects of social aging among rural older adults. A handful of qualitative studies investigate the involvement of rural elders in formal organizations (senior centers, nursing homes), their nutrition, or their health beliefs and health behaviors.

Qualitative studies of social aging focus largely on issues of the social relations and social support of rural elders, or on the importance of place for their psycho-emotional well-being. Graham Rowles' ethnographic study of "Colton," West Virginia, is the most extensive and diverse set of analyses [5, 6, 19-22]. His analyses bridge the domains of social support, and the meaning and use of space and place. Norris-Baker and Schiedt use open-ended interviews, supplemented with observation, informal interviews and photography to examine environmental stress and meaning of place among elders living in declining rural Kansas towns [23, 24].

Lozier and Althouse, using an ethnographic approach in a West Virginia community, examine the integration of elders into the community and the social resources of these elders in maintaining community support [4, 25]. Van Willigen uses ethnographic and structured interview data to investigate both historical and life-course changes in the social networks of the elderly in a Kentucky county [26]. Shenk uses life history and in-depth structured interviews, along with social network profiles, to investigate the types and sources of social support used by older women in central Minnesota [27].

Groger uses ethnography to investigate the relationship between the resources—particularly land ownership—the social support they receive, and the exchange relationships among African- and European-American elders in a rural North Carolina community [28-30]. Salber [7] and Carlton-LaNey [31] use oral history interviews to study African Americans in different rural North Carolina communities. Salber presents verbatim portions of these interviews which address such topics as loneliness and social support without interpretation. Carlton-LaNey analyzes the information provided by the elderly women she interviewed to explicate the extraordinary problems faced by these women due to their declining health, continuing care-giving responsibilities, and lack of resources.

Qualitative studies focusing on the involvement of rural older adults in formal organizations are very much an extension of the social relations and social support literature. Yearwood and Dressel use participant observation and in-depth interviews to examine race relations and integration in a senior center in rural Georgia [32]. Rowles uses ethnography to study the integration of a nursing home into a rural Appalachian Kentucky community [33, 34]. Longhofer examines differences in household formation and resulting community structure to explain differences in the use of nursing homes among Hutterites, Amish, and Mennonites [35]. Nye uses "life stories" to examine the importance of religion in the aging process of African Americans in rural Virginia [36].

Projects examining nutritional issues among the rural elderly examine different issues with different methods. Crockett et al. use focus groups to elicit information for the development of a nutrition education program in North Dakota [37]. Quandt and colleagues use a multimethod approach that integrates in-depth interviews with personal survey interviews to examine the food acquisition (gardening) and meal patterns in two Appalachian Kentucky counties [38-40].

Rowles draws on his extensive ethnographic understanding to discuss issues of general health beliefs and behaviors among community dwelling Appalachian (West Virginia) elders [41]. These health beliefs and behaviors include the use of self-treatment, folk medicine and local remedies, the reliance on family during times of illness, and the lack of emphasis on preventive care. Rowles also notes that generational change in traditional health beliefs is occurring as younger cohorts, including the young-old, have more experience with formal health services and higher educational attainment.

Davis et al. offer another example of a qualitative investigation of the health beliefs of rural older adults [42]. Using in-depth interviews, they find that elders in a six-county area of southeast Alabama equate health with feeling good and being independent. To maintain their health, these elders maintain a balanced diet, exercise, and take their medications. In addition, they try to remain active and keep a positive attitude. Unfortunately, Davis and colleagues do not delve further into the meaning these behaviors have for their subjects.

Fifer uses key-informant interviews within an ethnographic study to elucidate Native American perceptions of the caring behaviors of health care providers [43]. The in-depth interviews with twelve Southwestern reservation residents allow her to differentiate perceived caring from non-caring behavior for nine dimensions: touch, voice, attitude, visibility, availability, presence, respect, visiting, and time perception. For example, in terms of respect, a health care provider is perceived to be caring when he or she treats elders with respect and reverence, and indicates that he or she can learn from the elder. In terms of visibility, a caring health care provider is seen at community functions, not just in the clinic or hospital setting.

Finally, Griffin addresses the health beliefs of rural older adults from a contrasting perspective through her analysis of elder abuse among rural African Americans [44]. Eight service delivery themes emerge from her case-study-based investigation of ten abused African-American elders who reside in a rural North Carolina community. These themes indicate that poverty, isolation, and dependence of abused and abuser are important determinants of abuse.

This literature has several characteristics. Research has only begun to address the health beliefs and behaviors of the rural elderly. Few studies have directly applied qualitative methods to the study of rural elderly health beliefs or behaviors [41, 42]. Quandt and colleagues [38, 39] have used these methods to investigate food beliefs and behaviors, and Crockett and colleagues [37] have used these methods as the basis of a nutrition education program. A wide variety of qualitative methods have been used by researchers investigating the rural elderly, but most of these have centered on ethnography. A few of the researchers have used a design that integrates qualitative and quantitative methods [e.g., 26]. Many of the studies, and most of the publications, have focused on distinct rural ethnic groups, largely Appalachians and African Americans. The great majority of these studies have also been completed in Southeastern communities, specifically communities in Kentucky, North Carolina, and West Virginia.

OUR EXPERIENCES IN USING QUALITATIVE METHODS TO STUDY THE HEALTH BELIEFS AND BEHAVIORS OF RURAL OLDER ADULTS

Research supported by the North Carolina Rural Aging Program (NC•RAP) is making a significant contribution to the investigation of the health beliefs and health behaviors of rural older adults using qualitative methodology. Investigators in two NC•RAP projects with qualitative designs are investigating the health beliefs and behaviors of rural older adults. Each study is being conducted in one of the rural counties in which NC•RAP has established one of its community-based laboratories (see Chapter 5). The study in Johnston County uses focus group interviews to investigate general health beliefs, as well as health beliefs specific to arthritis, cancer, and heart disease. The study in Northampton and Halifax Counties uses semi-structured, in-depth personal interviews to examine general health beliefs, focusing particularly on beliefs about longevity and health status, and the ways these beliefs affect health behavior. Results from our research highlight the value of these qualitative methods in the study of the health beliefs and behaviors of rural older adults.

Health Beliefs and Chronic Disease:
Focus Group Interviews in a Diverse Rural Population

Group interviews are a standard qualitative approach in health research as well as other research domains [45]. Focus group interviews are conducted with a group of subjects who are asked to discuss topics with an investigator who poses questions and acts as a moderator [46, 47]. Krueger defines a focus group "as a carefully planned discussion designed to obtain perceptions on a defined area of interest in a permissive, non-threatening environment," in which "group members influence each other by responding to ideas and comments in the discussion" [46]. Specific strengths of the focus group interview can be used to elucidate the health beliefs and health behaviors of rural older adults. The focus group interview results discussed here are one component of a comprehensive health promotion and disease prevention initiative conducted in Johnston County, North Carolina.

Johnston County is an ethnically diverse rural community of 80,000 residents. The goal of this study was to provide a comprehensive and systematic understanding of the health beliefs among country residents. With the diverse population of this county, it was necessary to complete a large number of focus groups. We completed forty-eight focus group interviews, with each group being relatively homogeneous in ethnicity (African American and European American); income (less than $10,000 per year, and more than $10,000 per year); age (18-49 years, and 50 plus years); and place of residence within the county (Kenly, Smithfield, Benson areas).

Each group included approximately eight participants, with a total of 365 county residents participating. Individuals were selected using a purposive sample design. Well-placed individuals throughout the county provided lists of potential participants who were offered transportation to and from the focus group site, refreshments, and $10 for attending.

Each focus group interview had several components. Interviews began with a series of general questions about life in the county, followed by questions concerning general health beliefs. Examples of the general health belief questions were: "What causes someone to be sick?" "What causes someone to be healthy?" and "What can people do to stay healthy?" In addition to these general health belief questions, each group received a series of disease-specific questions about their beliefs on the causes and prevention of arthritis, heart disease, or cancer. Examples of these questions were: "How does someone get arthritis (get cancer; get heart disease)?" "What can you do to prevent getting arthritis (cancer; heart disease)?" and "What can you do once you have arthritis (cancer; heart disease)?"

Our approach to the study of health beliefs among older rural adults illustrates six important attributes of the focus group interview method. These attributes include the potential to compare beliefs about different chronic diseases, the importance of group interaction to help reveal varying notions about a disease, participants discussing diseases in their own terms and using their own concepts, variation in the ways participants define the same action, culturally shared metaphors of the participants, and the moral tone participants apply to health conditions. Each of these attributes is discussed below.

The sample design (focus groups that varied by age, gender, ethnicity, and residence) and the content of the different focus groups (general health beliefs, and health beliefs about arthritis, cancer, or heart disease) allowed this study to be comparative. For example, in answering the general health belief questions, every focus group mentioned that people can stay healthy by taking preventative measures such as "eating right" (staying away from fats and sweets were the most common ideas expressed), exercising, and "taking care of yourself." From these responses we might conclude that these rural residents hold an activist attitude toward illness [48]. However, the disease-specific questions suggest a varying sense of power regarding the causes and consequences of difference diseases. Group members expressed belief in an activist role in the prevention and control of heart disease. They also saw themselves as having an active, though somewhat limited control, over exposure to carcinogens, but expressed a high to moderate degree of fatalism regarding the outcome of contracted cases. Group members had an accurate appraisal of their lack of power in arthritis prevention and treatment. For example:

Speaker 1: You know, different things happen (to people when they get arthritis), they can't walk, they can't feed theirselves. They get, they's a real bad crippling kind that people really gets down with that stuff, real bad.

Speaker 2: You can't cure arthritis no how even if you go to a doctor.

Speaker 3: People can't make themselves feel better.

Interaction among group members reveals their varying notions about the topic at hand. Many of these ideas would have gone untapped with individual interviews. An example of this phenomenon can be seen in the following comments made when respondents in one group were asked what happens to people when they get arthritis.

Speaker 1: Get lazy. They get lazy cause they can't do nothing.

Speaker 2: I was lazy before I had arthritis. That ain't true.

Speaker 3: My brother works. He stays up on his legs. They hurt. They really hurt. They get him down sometimes, but he just do that—that he just gon' have to deal with it. And he just keep on.

Speaker 4: Sometime you ache so bad you have to lay down.

Speaker 3: . . . he [speaker's brother] don't let that interfere with . . .

Speaker 4: I can't help it cause when I get of aching, I got to quit.

Speaker 5: My husband has [a] cousin. His wife has poly-arthritis. I don't know if you've heard of it or not. A lot of people in Johnston County hadn't never heard of it or Raleigh. And hers is just so bad sometime, They have to put her in the hospital in Chapel Hill. And she have to stay there for about two months and takes treatment every day. Every day they have to draw everything out her body and replace it. She has it in her legs. And every week she have to go to Chapel Hill and has this medication in, through the IV.

Another benefit of the open-ended format is that it allows respondents to use their own terms and concepts in their discussion. In this way, open-ended questions are able to capture the social, historical, cultural, and interpersonal context of what people say.

Speaker 1: My mama used to tell me that I would have arthritis. When I lived in Mount Vernon, New York, I walked to work and I'd sit on the job a half a day and my knees and legs would be numb. She used to tell me, "If you don't stop doing it, you're gonna have trouble." And, God knows, she's sleeping today, but I'm feeling the effects.

Speaker 2: I've heard my old aunt say being exposed to—your body—to cold weather over a period of time. Expose your pores, not your body, but your pores. I heard them say that now. And air conditioning is good, but I believe being exposed to air conditioning, going out in the heat and returning can really upset your bones.

Speaker 3: The old people used to say it would be cold weather setting in.

Speaker 4: I know when I worked the swing shift in a cold, wet environment. When I would stay out in that a lot it would bother me and I think most of the people that I know of that have been in that cold wet environment for years are suffering now.

Speaker 5: When I was in the hospital having these steel plates put in, there was a old man. He was probably about eighty year old. When he said, "son, you're in for something when you get a little age on you." He said, with those steel plates, and where they took these discs out, he said it's a good place for arthritis to really set up and work on you. So, you know, I feel like where they worked on my back and took disks out and put steel plates in, I've got something to look forward to on that. So far, I haven't got it yet.

Speaker 6: I heard Jimmy Dixon's father say he got it from staying out in the cold somewhere.

The group interview format also makes it possible to get some insight into an important part of interpersonal relations—the ways in which various parties in the situations define or interpret the same actions. When asked what happens to people after they get arthritis, the following responses were given:

Speaker 1: Become less active.

Speaker 2: Beome less active. I got it.

Speaker 3: Ain't nothing else they can do. They can't get comfortable. Can't sit comfortable, the ones I know about. Ain't nothing humble about it. Some of them don't never get over it.

In contrast, a different view is suggested in the following exchange:

Speaker 1: Some of them just give up.

Speaker 2: They sit right down.

Speaker 3: Then they get still, it gets worse. Joints freeze up. Can't move them. Big knots come.

The open-ended format allows people to talk with culturally shared metaphors. For example, when asked what things can give a person arthritis, many respondents mentioned "the cold" in their answers:

Speaker 1: I think the climates can cause this disease.

Speaker 2: One man told me he caught it from the cold.

Speaker 3: I think working in that cold your muscles draw up and you stretch your joints. You know, you stretch them doing physical labor. And once you go out, you kinda cool down, you know, you done some damage.

Finally, responses of some group members reveal a moral tone about getting arthritis. Thus, when asked about the causes of arthritis, the following comments were made:

Speaker 1: . . . bad living.
Speaker 2: Not taking care of your self when you are young.
Speaker 3: If that's the case [arthritis can be caught from the cold], you should see what they [young people] wear out here.
Speaker 4: I believe you can keep from getting arthritis. As I say, if you take care of yourself . . . and overstrain can cause it to come on you. As I say, that cold settles in betwixt them bones.
Speaker 5: You got children—one year olds—that's got it [arthritis]. It's more or less how you stay out in the cold that causes it.

In summary, the six focus group attributes that we have discussed corroborate the value of this qualitative method for the investigation of the health beliefs of rural older adults. At the same time, our ability to effectively use these focus group interview data in an empirical study of health beliefs is based on the systematic application of this method. The study sample was of sufficient size to represent the variation in the population along four dimensions which might affect individual beliefs and behavior (age, gender, ethnicity, and locale), and to have groups that were homogeneous for each dimension. This was not a random sample, but it was a representative sample. The issues raised and discussed in each of the focus groups were also presented in a systematic manner. Question order and probes varied among the groups, but each issue was asked of every group. Only with the orderly selection of respondents and presentation of questions can focus group interviews have the attributes which make them a valuable tool in the study of the health beliefs and behaviors of older rural adults.

Beliefs About Health and Longevity in a Multicultural Population of Rural Elders: The Value of In-Depth Personal Interviews

In-depth personal interviews have been a mainstay of behavioral science research since the beginning of the field work tradition. These open-ended, probing discussions with the people who are the subjects of our study take many forms including the ethnographic interview, the oral history interview, and the journalistic interview. The semi-structured in-depth interview method can be an extremely important tool in the study of older adult health beliefs when the investigator must insure that a set of specific topics are discussed in each interview. Our examination of the beliefs about expected and desired longevity, as well as present and future health, among older European Americans, African Americans, and Native Americans living in rural Halifax and Northampton Counties, North Carolina, illustrate the value of the semi-structured, in-depth interview method in studies of health beliefs.

Halifax and Northampton Counties together have a population of 77,000 residents, about 15 percent of them sixty-five years of age and older. Approximately 42 percent of the older population is African American, 56 percent is European American, and 2 percent is Native American. Almost one-third (31%) of these older residents are poor, 34 percent have less than an eighth-grade education, and 34 percent live in substandard housing. Functional impairment rates exceed those of the state as a whole, as do the rates for severe cognitive impairment and mental illness.

We completed semi-structured, in-depth interviews with forty-two community-dwelling older people aged sixty-two to ninety-seven. The convenience sample included eighteen African Americans (7 male, 11 female), thirteen European Americans (6 male, 7 female), and ten Native Americans (5 male, 5 female). Selection of respondents was based on referrals from health care providers and other knowledgeable local people, and was designed to capture a wide range of ages, socioeconomic strata, and health conditions.

The interviews explored a number of areas in which health beliefs and health practices appear to affect quality of life, likelihood of morbidity, and life expectancy. Most important for this illustration, a set of questions asked about the respondents' beliefs, expectations, and desires for longevity. Expectations represent projections based on selective perception of past or present performance (e.g., ages of death of parents and other significant others; perceived course of an illness). Expectations often differed qualitatively from desires, which are based on the fundamental hope to live a good and full life, and which are tempered with the desire for continued independence. Taken together, an individual's expectations and hopes may allow room for negotiation of life span, and may provide the conceptual space in which health-promotional interventions may occur.

The open-ended and probing nature of the in-depth interview encourages respondents to discuss issues in their own words, to elaborate on their responses, and to explain terms which have special meanings to them. For example, to the question, "How long do you expect to live?" most respondents answered in terms of a numerical figure. However, many also discussed their expectations in non-numerical terms, often with elaborate responses. Two major themes reflecting the respondents' beliefs arose from the analysis of these narrative responses. The first theme was that of life-span estimates, which were based on personally significant social reference points, including the ages-at-death of close relatives and the age-at-death of peers. The second theme was that the time of death is outside of personal control, and that it is controlled by, and known only to, the Lord. Lesser themes related numerical life-span estimates to the time-course of an illness, physical function, a physician's comment about projected longevity, or intuition. A few people would not directly address their personal longevity, indicating that it was impossible to determine or that it was better to avoid thinking about death. In longer dialogues, respondents' answers often reflected more than one theme.

The in-depth interview encourages the investigator to probe for complexity and subtlety in responses. This subtlety may provide the key to understanding the cognitive or behavioral processes involved. For example, Mr. Oakley (this and all other names are pseudonyms), a sixty-nine-year-old European American, gave what might seem to be a typical response in which life expectancy was estimated by considering the ages of death of both parents.

> I expect to live to at least 80 years old, another 10 years. . . . My mother lived in her 80s and my father was 70, and I'm a great believer that would give me a 75 average. I'm a stickler for technical situations.

Looking closely at such statements reveals a richness beyond the surface "answer." Although Mr. Oakley's response implies that he was using a straight-forward averaging technique, in fact it exemplifies a common phenomenon of specifying an age range, from "a 75 average" to "at least 80." In a variation of this response, Mrs. Davis, a sixty-five-year-old European American, used an averaging technique but drew a somewhat general conclusion: "My mother died at 78. My father died at 87. I'd say in the 80s, I hope." Use of qualifying terminology such as the phrases "I hope," "Lord willing," "if I'm lucky," and "I don't know" serve to modify and soften statements of expectation, indicating respondents' uncertainty or unwillingness to speculate on something so unforeseen as one's own date with death.

In-depth interviews provide the information needed to help uncover the cognitive processes of respondents' selective highlighting of certain information and ignoring information that is unwanted. Respondents' statements about life-expectancy often involved selection of one reference point for death from among other potential social reference points. Often the age of death of only one parent—almost always the longer lived and almost always the mother—is used as the reference point. Respondents' justification for excluding the death age of the shorter-lived parent from the calculation process was usually that the parent suffered unnatural or premature circumstances of death, such as disease or accident, and thus did not live out a normal life course. This is illustrated by Mrs. Ray, a seventy-year-old Native American. She described her expectations of living at least until her mother's age of death, while bracketing her father's early demise, which was presumed to have resulted from witchcraft.

> Well, I expect to live 15 or 20 more years. My mama lived to be 85. My daddy had a young death. He was 51. He had what they called dropsy . . . He just went down gradually . . . They say there was a spell on him.

The in-depth personal interview allows the investigator to better examine the sociocultural context of individuals' responses, appreciating how the responses reflect that which is meaningful and valuable in their lives. For example, although one or both parents are often mentioned, in some cases parents are omitted entirely, and long-lived aunts and uncles or siblings are mentioned instead. In other cases, unrelated peer groups, an important biblical figure, or a disease process were used as longevity signposts.

Detailed examination of subjects' responses revealed how the language of uncertainty might facilitate adaptation to changing circumstances. For example, in the dialogues on expected longevity, respondents combine selected social and other reference points with the vagueness of age estimates, hedging language, and the ultimate control of the Lord over life-span, to reflect their uncertainty in speculating about longevity. While such hedging guards against the perceived danger of tempting fate by making a bold assertion about life expectancy, such uncertainty also reflects openness to changing circumstances. Such openness is an indication of flexibility, necessary in the process of individual adaptation. In a parallel manner, statements about desired life-span, which contained conditional requirements, a shifting concept of function, selective reference points of long-lived people, and the open-endedness of being at the Lord's will, also allow for adaptive processes and continued life.

Finally, viewing a subject's responses holistically brings additional insights. In comparing an individual's responses to questions about expectations versus desires for longevity, we noted the dynamic tension between expectations and hopes for longevity.

Like the focus group interviews, the in-depth personal interview process has important attributes for the investigation of the health beliefs of rural older adults. The in-depth personal interview encourages respondents to discuss issues in their own words and to present the meanings they ascribe to these issues. This interview method encourages the investigator to probe the complexity and subtlety of the respondent's discussion. In soliciting the respondent's meaning, and probing the complexity of responses, these qualitative interview data can lead to the discovery of cognitive processes used by the respondent. Finally, the in-depth interview method places the respondent in a sociocultural context and provides the investigator with a holistic frame within which to evaluate interview data.

DISCUSSION AND CONCLUSIONS

Qualitative research has made a significant contribution to our knowledge of the social life of rural elderly. However, little qualitative research has attended directly to issues of the health beliefs, health behaviors, or medical care of rural older adults. This chapter illustrates the viability and the value of qualitative methodology for the investigation of the health beliefs and health behaviors of rural older adults. Qualitative methods uniquely can elicit and probe people's perceptions, rationales, and feelings about sensitive topics such as health beliefs. Qualitative methods permit the emergence and investigation of unanticipated questions and patterns in these beliefs during the research process. These methods are amenable to the investigation of groups with diverse cultural backgrounds, such as those groups found among the rural elderly. Finally, qualitative investigation has the capacity to illuminate the complex psychological processes underlying beliefs, to search for patterns, to identify relevant explanatory variables, to explore the mechanisms by which explanatory variables shape perspective, to uncover and conceptualize unexpected phenomena, and to generate propositions for further testing.

The two methods we used in our research also demonstrate that while qualitative methods are similar in some attributes, they differ in others. Both focus group and in-depth personal interviews are intended to discover the language and meaning that the respondents attach to a phenomenon. However, data collected from focus group interviews benefit from the synergistic effect of group interaction not available in the in-depth personal interview. The in-depth interview provides more holistic understanding of the individual respondent than can be collected in a focus group. Investigators who wish to conduct qualitative research, whether this is research on rural elderly health beliefs and behaviors or other problems, should become familiar with several different qualitative methods. They will then be able to select the best method for the specific problem they need to address.

Our research on rural older adult health beliefs and behaviors should be extended. This qualitative research will illuminate the variation in health beliefs and behaviors of rural elders, and elucidate the importance of these beliefs and behaviors for providing appropriate care to this segment of the population. Methods in addition to in-depth and focus group interviews should be used to investigate other aspects of health beliefs, health behaviors, and health care. An ethnographic study examining the use of various health care services by rural older adults; and in-depth interview study of beliefs about the causes and treatment of cancer among rural elderly of different ethnicities; or a multimethod personal interview and diary investigation of the use of formal and alternative health care in the daily lives of rural elders, are all examples of the types of qualitative investigations that can be pursued.

REFERENCES

1. C. L. Fry and J. Keith (eds.), *New Methods for Old Age Research: Strategies for Studying Diversity,* Bergin & Garvey, Massachusetts, 1986.
2. S. Reinharz and G. D. Rowles (eds.), *Qualitative Gerontology,* Springer, New York, 1988.
3. J. F. Gubrium and A. Sankar (eds.), *Qualitative Methods in Aging Research,* Sage, Thousand Oaks, California, 1994.

4. J. Lozier and R. Althouse, Social Enforcement of Behavior Toward Elders in an Appalachian Mountain Settlement, *The Gerontologist, 14*:1, pp. 69-80, 1974.
5. G. D. Rowles, Growing Old 'Inside': Aging and Attachment to Place in an Appalachian Community, in *Transitions of Aging,* N. Datan and N. Lohmann (eds.), Academic Press, New York, 1980.
6. G. D. Rowles, Place and Personal Identity in Old Age: Observations from Appalachia, *Journal of Environmental Psychology, 3,* pp. 299-313, 1983.
7. E. Salber, *Don't Send Me Flowers When I'm Dead: Voices of Rural Elderly,* Duke University Press, Durham, North Carolina, 1983.
8. A. Strauss and J. Corbin, *Basics of Qualitative Research: Grounded Theory Procedures and Techniques,* Sage, Newbury Park, California, 1990.
9. N. K. Denzin and Y. S. Lincoln (eds.), *Handbook of Qualitative Research,* Sage, Thousand Oaks, California, 1994.
10. M. B. Miles and A. M. Huberman, *Qualitative Data Analysis: An Expanded Sourcebook,* Sage, Thousand Oaks, California, 1994.
11. J. F. Gubrium, Qualitative Research Comes of Age in Gerontology, *The Gerontologist, 32*:5, pp. 581-582, 1992.
12. J. Keith, C. L. Fry, A. P. Glascock, C. Ikels, J. Dickerson-Putman, H. C. Harpending, and P. Draper, *The Aging Experience: Diversity and Commonality Across Cultures,* Sage, Thousand Oaks, California, 1994.
13. M. Q. Patton, *Qualitative Evaluation and Research Methods,* Sage, Thousand Oaks, California, 1990.
14. E. A. Weitzman and M. B. Miles, *Computer Programs for Qualitative Data Analysis: A Software Sourcebook,* Sage, Thousand Oaks, California, 1995.
15. J. M. Morse and P. A. Field, *Qualitative Research Methods for Health Professionals* (2nd Edition), Sage, Thousand Oaks, California, 1995.
16. H. R. Bernard, *Research Methods in Anthropology: Qualitative and Quantitative Approaches* (2nd Edition), Sage, Thousand Oaks, California, 1994.
17. O. Werner and G. M. Schoepfle, *Systematic Fieldwork. Volume 1: Foundations of Ethnography and Interviewing,* Sage, Newbury Park, California, 1987.
18. O. Werner and G. M. Schoepfle, *Systematic Fieldwork. Volume 2: Ethnographic Analysis and Data Management,* Sage, Newbury Park, California, 1987.
19. G. D. Rowles, The Surveillance Zone as Meaningful Space for the Aged, *The Gerontologist, 21*:3, pp. 304-311, 1981.
20. G. D. Rowles, Between Worlds: A Relocation Dilemma for the Appalachian Elderly, *International Journal of Aging and Human Development, 17*:4, pp. 301-314, 1983.
21. G. D. Rowles, Geographical Dimensions of Social Support in Rural Appalachia, in *Aging and Milieu: Environmental Perspectives on Growing Old,* G. D. Rowles and R. J. Ohta (eds.), Academic Press, New York, 1983.
22. G. D. Rowles, The Rural Elderly and the Church, *Journal of Religion and Aging, 22,* pp. 79-98, 1986.
23. C. Norris-Baker and R. J. Scheidt, From 'Our Town' to 'Ghost Town'?: The Changing Context of Home for Rural Elders, *International Journal of Aging and Human Development, 38*:3, pp. 181-202, 1994.

24. R. J. Scheidt and C. Norris-Baker, A Transactional Approach to Environmental Stress Among Older Residents of Rural Communities: An Introduction to a Special Issue, *Journal of Community Psychology, 11*:1, pp. 5-30, 1990.

25. J. Lozier and R. Althouse, Retirement to the Porch in Rural Appalachia, *International Journal of Aging and Human Development, 6*:1, pp. 7-15, 1975.

26. J. van Willigen, *Gettin' Some Age on Me: Social Organization of Older People in a Rural American Community,* University Press of Kentucky, Lexington, 1989.

27. D. Shenk, Older Rural Women as Recipients and Providers of Social Support, *Journal of Aging Studies, 5*:4, pp. 347-358, 1991.

28. B. L. Groger, Growing Old With or Without It: The Meaning of Land in a Southern Rural Community, *Research on Aging, 5,* pp. 511-526, 1983.

29. B. L. Groger, Tied to Each Other Through Ties to the Land: Informal Support of Black Elders in a Southern U.S. Community, *Journal of Cross-Cultural Gerontology, 7,* pp. 205-220, 1992.

30. L. Groger and S. Kunkel, Aging and Exchange: Differences Between Black and White Elders, *Journal of Cross-Cultural Gerontology, 10,* pp. 269-287, 1995.

31. I. Carlton-LaNey, Black Farm Workers: A Population at Risk, *Social Work, 37*:3, pp. 517-523, 1992.

32. A. Yearwood and P. Dressel, Interracial Dynamics in a Southern Rural Senior Center, *The Gerontologist, 23*:5, pp. 512-517, 1983.

33. G. D. Rowles, *Nursing Homes in the Rural Long-Term Care Continuum,* presented at "Long-Term Care for the Rural Elderly," Third National Biennial Conference on Rural Aging, University of Kentucky, Sanders-Brown Center on Aging, Lexington, Kentucky, September 23-24, 1994.

34. G. D. Rowles, J. Concotelli, and D. M. High, Community Integration of a Rural Nursing Home, *Journal of Applied Gerontology, 15*:2, pp. 188-201, 1996.

35. J. Longhofer, Nursing Home Utilization: A Comparative Study of Hutterian Brethren, the Old Order Amish, and the Mennonites, *Journal of Aging Studies, 8*:1, pp. 95-120, 1994.

36. W. P. Nye, Amazing Grace: Religion and Identity among Elderly Black Individuals, *International Journal of Aging and Human Development, 36*:2, pp. 103-114, 1993.

37. S. J. Crockett, K. E. Heller, J. M. Merkel, and J. M. Peterson, Assessing Beliefs of Older Rural Americans About Nutrition Education: Use of the Focus Group Approach, *Journal of the American Dietetics Association, 90*:4, pp. 563-567, 1990.

38. S. A. Quandt, J. B. Popyach, and K. M. DeWalt, Home Gardening and Food Preservation Practices of the Elderly in Rural Kentucky, *Ecology of Food and Nutrition, 331,* pp. 183-199, 1994.

39. S. A. Quandt, M. Z. Vitolins, K. M. DeWalt, and G. M. Roos, Meal Patterns of Older Adults in Rural Communities: Life Course Analysis and Implications for Undernutrition, *Journal of Applied Gerontology, 16,* pp. 152-171, 1997.

40. G. Roos, S. A. Quandt, and K. M. DeWalt, Meal Patterns of the Elderly in Rural Kentucky, *Appetite, 21,* pp. 295-298, 1993.

41. G. D. Rowles, Changing Health Culture in Rural Appalachia: Implications for Serving the Elderly, *Journal of Aging Studies, 5*:4, pp. 375-389, 1991.

42. D. C. Davis, M. C. Henderson, A. Boothe, M. Douglass, S. Faria, D. Kennedy, E. Kitchens, and M. Weaver, An Interactive Perspective on the Health Beliefs & Practices of Rural Elders, *Journal of Gerontological Nursing, 17*:5, pp. 11-16, 1991.

43. S. Fifer, Perceptions of Caring Behaviors in Health Providers, *The IHS Primary Care Provider, 21*:7, pp. 89-95, 1996.

44. L. W. Griffin, Elder Maltreatment Among Rural African-Americans, *Journal of Elder Abuse & Neglect, 6*:1, pp. 1-27, 1994.

45. J. Coreil, Group Interview Methods in Community Health Research, *Medical Anthropology, 16*, pp. 193-210, 1995.

46. R. A. Krueger, *Focus Groups: A Practical Guide for Applied Research,* Sage, Thousand Oaks, California, 1994.

47. D. L. Morgan (ed.), *Successful Focus Groups: Advancing the State of the Art,* Sage, Newbury Park, California, 1993.

48. T. Parsons, *The Social System,* Free Press, New York, 1951.

CHAPTER
7

The Potential of Community Service and Research Partnerships: The Geriatric Team Consultation Project

Rebecca H. Hunter, Mark E. Williams,
Jane H. McCaleb, and William D. Remmes

Community-based research has particular merit for addressing questions pertaining to the health and well-being of older persons living in rural areas. To conduct community-based research, researchers are clearly dependent upon the good will and support of the rural community or communities in which they seek to study. Moreover, they must develop an appreciation for the perspectives of the members of the rural community who will be their subjects, hosts, fellow investigators, and/or advocates. These may be citizens, program administrators, physicians and/or other health care providers, opinion leaders, and/or employees and volunteers in senior-serving agencies. Failure to take into account these diverse perspectives may result in closed doors, data of questionable validity, and lack of cooperation for follow-up studies.

In studies pertaining to the health and well-being of rural, older people, careful attention must be directed to the process of planning and implementation as well as to the selection of specific methods. A variety of approaches, ranging from single-subject case studies, to large-scale surveys, to complex intervention studies, have been successfully used to address many important questions pertinent to the health and well-being of rural older people. Each type of approach poses particular demands upon researchers and participants relative to issues such as time involvement, trust, and communication. There are also variations in the extent to which the rural community is involved in shaping the research agenda, design, and methods, and in the extent to which the community realizes some benefit from the research.

Partnerships for service and research have significant potential for generating answers to important research questions while addressing real problems in rural communities. Such partnerships meet immediate community needs while involving researchers in the community at a deeper, more active level than would otherwise be the case. Collaborative service and research foster durable relationships and may stimulate additional joint efforts.

The goals of this chapter are to sensitize researchers to the potential impact of divergent needs and views of research within rural communities, and to outline a process for building effective partnerships with communities, drawing upon the experience of the Geriatric Team Consultation Project, a collaborative effort among several health programs in North Carolina. The Project involves monthly visitations by a university-based geriatric assessment team to primary and long-term care settings in a rural community. Through this process, university and rural practitioners formed a strong, active partnership focused on the needs of frail elderly persons which yielded joint problem-solving efforts in clinical, research, and educational arenas. The history of the program will be presented; basic objectives and overall philosophy will be reviewed; current staffing and roles of staff members will be outlined; and the implications for the integration of service and research in future collaborations will be presented. First, however, we provide a context for the project by briefly highlighting some of the imperatives for rural health research, in particular, research pertaining to older persons. In addition, perspectives important to the conduct of research in rural areas are discussed.

A LIMITED UNDERSTANDING

At present, our information about the health and well-being of older rural people is incomplete and fragmented. We know, for instance, that older women in rural areas are more likely to die of breast cancer than women in metropolitan areas, and that the women in rural areas are less likely to be screened for breast cancer [1]. Unfortunately, we don't know *why* this is the case, or exactly what to do about it. Is this an issue of, for example, access to primary care, availability and cost of mammography, health beliefs, provider attitudes and practices, health-seeking behavior, or environmental influences? How do these possible contributing factors play out in a given geographical area or areas? How can we design and integrate a variety of approaches from small-scale qualitative interviews to community education demonstrations to develop a fuller understanding of this significant problem?

Data on older minority populations, the poor, and the uneducated are severely limited [2], while the health status of these groups is severely compromised. People of color in rural areas are often distrustful of research given its tainted history. Paying special attention to entry and relationship development is therefore of critical importance. Educational level and cultural background must be taken into consideration in instrument design, and studies must be conducted with respect for the dignity of those who lack material resources.

A limited understanding is also evident in our very focus on "illness" and on problems when we use the word "health." As Kaiser and Camp have suggested, much remains to be learned from an alternative paradigm of aging focusing on productivity and resilience [3]. Without a broad understanding of factors contributing to health and well-being, we remain prisoners of the biomedical model, unable to develop and test effective preventive strategies.

Indeed, the need for efficacious disability and disease prevention strategies is increasingly an imperative with elderly citizens who are the fastest growing segment of the rural population. There has been tremendous growth in health-promotion programs for older adults and an accompanying increase in participation [4]. As has been the case with workplace wellness programs, however, the typical participant in these programs is urban, relatively well-educated, and already favorably disposed to health-promoting behavior [5]. Rural elderly persons typically receive less preventive care, although there is evidence that rural hospitals are becoming more active in this area [6].

White and Maloney write of the "hard-to-reach" Americans—the disadvantaged, minorities, and others—for whom there are personal, cultural, or economic barriers to engagement in positive health practices [7]. In a market research study of groups of the "hard to reach," these authors identified a "chasm between awareness and practice" [7, p. 277] suggesting a limited understanding of relationships between health status and behavior, and specific health practices, for example, most participants believed that positive health behavior would decrease risk of acute but not chronic illness; the latter they attributed to heredity and fate. Community-based research can provide direction for bridging this "chasm."

Our understanding of the most effective ways to overcome barriers and to deliver health and health-related care in rural areas is also limited. Yawn, Busby, and Yawn note that medical practice in rural areas is different from in metropolitan areas [8]. Physicians must respond to a vast array of patient and community problems while lacking the technological and consultative resources of their urban peers. Few have received specialized training to prepare them for the particular challenges of rural practice such as high caseloads of elderly patients, stabilization of accident victims, and diagnosis and treatment of psychiatric disorders. Similarly, most are unprepared for the new roles they will be asked to assume, for example, as nursing home medical director.

A major issue in rural health care is the scarcity of health and health-related professionals. Some professions, notably allied health, social work, and psychiatry, may lack a sufficient client base for rural practice [9], while others, such as medicine, simply gravitate toward the urban settings in which practitioners are predominantly trained and where they will receive greater monetary rewards.

Rural health professionals work long hours, have limited peer support, and deliver care that is often compromised by the familiar problems of distance, economics, and understaffed service settings. While health professionals experience great satisfaction in playing a pivotal role in providing ongoing care and in intervening during acute illness, their satisfaction is eroded by bureaucratic complexity, a rapidly expanding information base, and an increasing sense of being "out of touch." Documentation and other paper work requirements are staggering. In addition, few health professionals have received training in effective collaboration with other disciplines.

A full continuum of service for elderly persons in rural areas typically is impossible. Moreover, there is a "noticeable lack of geriatric programs, skilled personnel, and resources . . . to treat complex geriatric conditions" [10, p. 109].

The delivery of rural long-term care is another area demanding attention. In general, there has been extensive documentation of problems in nursing home care. Among the most significant problems are inappropriate prescribing and utilization of medications [11], high prevalence of mental health problems among residents [12, 13], and a host of obstacles to effective care delivery including inadequate staff incentives, high staff turnover, poor preparation for physically and emotionally demanding caregiving roles, and lack of medical staff training in geriatrics.

Long-term care settings in rural areas share the complex problems of their urban counterparts while also struggling with difficulties such as limited resources and geographic isolation that are largely a function of their rurality. Such difficulties potentially limit resident access to medical, psychiatric, and rehabilitative care as well as other specialty care. Staff and administration also feel the effects of isolation, frequently lacking support, feedback, and education to enhance their capacity to function effectively [14]. "Burnout" is a significant problem.

Numerous strategies have been utilized to address the complex problems in nursing home care. Regulatory strategies and training of frontline caregivers have been extended to rural settings [15]; of particular interest is a geriatric mental health training program for rural nursing personnel developed by Smith and colleagues [16]. Pharmacy consultants now routinely provide oversight with the goal of reducing inappropriate medication prescribing and utilization [17], geropsychiatric consultation-liaison teams have been mobilized [18, 19], and electronic consultation to nursing homes has been proposed, but is not yet widely implemented [20]. The potential of geriatric assessment teams as consultants to nursing homes has received less attention. However, outcomes of a study in which sixty-three nursing home residents were randomly assigned either to team or to usual-care conditions suggest that team assessment has a favorable effect on quality of care [21].

DIVERGENT PERSPECTIVES

Rural Citizens and Researchers

The perspectives of researchers and those of rural persons whom they hope to study are generally quite different, and are based upon differences in expectations as well as personal factors such as cultural background and education. An appreciation of these differences can be valuable to researchers as they plan and negotiate with members of the rural community. Moreover, researchers cannot operate in a vacuum, but must understand how the research is perceived and understood in order to have confidence in the responses that are offered.

Researchers vary in their understanding of rural settings and rural people which they bring to their work. Researchers typically are affiliated with universities and live comfortable middle-class lives in metropolitan areas. They may or may not have direct personal experience with rural life. Contingent on their experiences, they may cherish romantic stereotypes of rural living, or alternatively, be poorly prepared to deal with poverty or the unfamiliar life experiences of those with very different educational and cultural backgrounds.

In simply offering to rural citizens the opportunity to participate in a study, the researcher has an awesome responsibility. For better or worse, the tendency of an older citizen is to say "yes" generally out of respect for the mission of the academic institution or because they do not fully realize that their participation is voluntary [22]. Too often, people say "yes" without a full understanding of the research and of their right to say "no" without qualification. If the research topic is at all sensitive, the consentee may subsequently have regrets about his or her involvement.

Our rural colleagues note that researchers can be subtly condescending or controlling in their encounters with poor or uneducated, rural people. Perhaps because of educational and socioeconomic differences, they fail to recognize that although older rural people may be uneducated, they are nonetheless capable and intelligent. Older rural people are also able to shape their own destinies. Recognition of this fact is essential in designing intervention programs. The tendency of the researcher or program developer is to take over, or attempt to solve problems *for* rather than *with* people.

Like journalists, researchers pursue knowledge and share concern about the plight of the poor and the disenfranchised. However, they must also be sensitive to the ways in which information about rural communities of interest is communicated. Older rural people typically have pride no matter what their circumstances.

In one illustrative situation, local people recoiled from a regional newspaper's depiction of their community as "impoverished."

The importance of communication—understanding the expectations, perceptions, and values of those you seek to help or to study—cannot be underestimated. Rowles notes that there is variation in the degree to which elderly people in different rural settings accept modern health care values and practices [23]. Their attitudes are tempered by the views of families, neighbors, and clergy, while peer persuasion and community values are powerful sources of influence. While there has been a media-induced homogenization of American culture, differences still are evident in rural settings which can greatly influence clarity of communication, and subtly influence the outcome of research. Careful pilot testing is essential. For example, in studies of health and health-related factors among older people, it is common to ask, "How many times per week do you exercise?" However, the term *exercise* may have markedly different meaning to older rural respondents than it does to a researcher who is interested in physical activity among older people. For example, a study by White and Maloney found that older people defined exercise as a "sweat-producing" activity, and would not include exercise, such as gardening or walking, in responding to such a question [7].

At the simplest level, the approaches selected for a particular study must not only address the question being posed, but be acceptable in methods and understandable in language and purpose to participants. Researchers must be aware that their motives, trustworthiness, and commitment are under scrutiny. Initially, they are likely to be viewed as outsiders and provided with what has been termed "front stage" as opposed to "back stage" information [24]. For example, a "one-shot" telephone survey conducted from a remote location is likely to generate "front stage" responses, i.e., those which are superficial and/or socially acceptable in nature. To obtain the "back stage" answers to the difficult questions in rural aging, researchers must be willing to invest time and energy to develop trust and engage their subjects and the community in the process.

Rural Service Providers and Researchers

Research pertaining to the health and well-being of older rural people is often conducted in rural health and human service settings. Choice of service settings such as research sites is advantageous in service delivery and intervention studies and allows researchers to "borrow" upon the trust and rapport that service settings have developed with the community. While offering these obvious advantages, research in service settings also poses several challenges. Unlike universities, service settings typically do not embrace research as a primary part of their mission, although sites utilizing a community-oriented primary care model clearly include an evaluative component. The conduct of research by rural service settings therefore represents a stretch of monies, personnel, and oftentimes, philosophy.

Time and money are of critical importance to rural service settings, a fact which is often underappreciated by researchers from academic settings. Rural service providers labor under heavy caseloads, and they can ill afford to conduct time-intensive protocols. Moreover, rural settings usually lack working capital and have little, if any, monetary cushion. Accordingly, researchers should recognize that grant funds must be allocated to participating service settings to compensate staff for their time and for the potential loss of revenue that may be entailed in giving time to research endeavors.

The values of service providers and the settings they represent are also of importance. With few exceptions, service providers are in the business of service because they have a strong helping ethic. Accordingly, they may be impatient with research that lacks social utility or relatively immediate application. Often, there also exists a distinct tension between the requirements of research and provision of service. In intervention, for example, service providers are accustomed to providing what they perceive to be the "treatment of choice." Accordingly, in an intervention study, they may perceive a real conflict between their instincts and the need to test an alternative intervention through random assignment to different treatment conditions.

It is clearly imperative that service providers be fully involved in problem formulation and methods development to assure their ownership and the feasibility of the study's operations. Researchers and service providers alike must recognize, nonetheless, that conduct of research in a rural service setting is difficult:

> The imposition of research discipline on a service-giving field staff expectably generates ambivalent reactions. . . . On the one hand, sensing the national and local significance of the research, many local personnel are stimulated, commit themselves to the project, and expect personal growth benefits. On the other hand, small over-extended rural service staffs soon find that the extra time per patient, the rigors of extra record keeping, and the constrictions of choices imposed by a research design become a burden that slowly erodes the best of commitments [25].

Given the intrinsic hurdles to be overcome, the development of viable collaborative research efforts are dependent upon researcher sensitivity to the perspectives of service providers and community members and commitment to addressing local needs.

BRIDGING THE GAP: RESEARCH PARTNERSHIPS WITH COMMUNITIES AND SERVICE SETTINGS

Hatch and colleagues have defined four levels of community-based research [26]. In the first level, advice is obtained primarily from service providers in the community, but the target community has no real input into the focus or design of the project. In the second level, support is solicited from a broader group of community leaders, such as ministers and leaders of civic groups, but the researcher still maintains control of the project. At the third level, community leaders have greater involvement, helping to select local project staff and interpreting the research to the community as a whole. Nonetheless, the role of community is still limited and the researcher retains significant control. The fourth level both involves and engages the community as collaborator in the research, in defining the problem, in exploring pertinent factors, and in designing acceptable goals and methods for the conduct of the study. Hatch and colleagues identify such community-research partnerships as essential to the responsible conduct of research pertaining to minorities. Partnerships increase the likelihood of true community support and benefit to the community, including continuation of programs developed as a result of research.

Empowerment is another key concept in conceptualizing research, especially intervention studies. Fostering a sense of competence and control, and enabling elderly persons and communities to draw upon their strengths, are essential. Programs developed and conducted with attention to these goals should enhance community ownership, the viability of program strategies, and the continuation of the program over time. Among the key components of the empowerment model are involvement of community stakeholders in the planning process, a fundamental belief in the basic capacity of people to help themselves, and good community organizing [27].

Partnerships with service settings as integral parts of communities are also important vehicles for conducting the research. Such partnerships are conducive to collaborative research with strong community ownership. Moreover, they foster continuation of programs by building local institutional support. We now turn to a detailed description of one such partnership and an introduction to the communities and sites involved.

PARTICIPATING RURAL PRACTICE SITES

The rural practice sites participating in the project are located in Northampton County, economically one of the poorest rural counties in North Carolina. The population of 20,732 had a per capita income of $14,306 in 1991, with a poverty rate of 26.2 percent, and an unemployment rate of 8.7 percent. African Americans make up 50 percent of the population and a disproportionate share of the poor. Seventeen percent of the population is sixty-five years of age and over. Twenty-eight percent of those over sixty-five, and 38 percent of those over seventy-five years of age, exist below the poverty level. Educational levels are low: in 1980, 40 percent of the population older than twenty-five had completed less than nine years of school and only 36 percent had earned a high school diploma.

As in most rural areas, physician recruitment and retention are extremely difficult; there are less than two physicians per 1,000 residents over sixty-five, compared to nearly thirteen per 1,000 over sixty-five in North Carolina as a whole. Other health professionals, such as physician assistants, nurse practitioners, pharmacists, and physical therapists, are also in short supply. For nurses, the rate is less than six per 1,000 residents over sixty-five, compared to fifty-four per 1,000 in North Carolina as a whole [28].

In the minds of most county residents, health care in Northampton has become synonymous with Rural Health Group, Inc., an association of primary care and long-term care settings based in Northampton County and including Roanoke Amaranth Community Health Group, Inc., home base for the current project. The history and development of Rural Health Group, Inc. reflects the growth in rural health policy during and subsequent to the 1970s. During the 1970s, several national initiatives were launched to stimulate health care in underserved areas and to train additional health care practitioners for rural service. Among these initiatives were manpower training, federal grants, and outreach and educational programs such as Area Health Education Centers (AHECs), as well as financing mechanisms, for example, the Rural Clinics Act. Roanoke Amaranth Community Health Group, Inc., was formed in 1978, with the support of the North Carolina Office of Rural Health Services. It was one of the thirteen Rural Practice Projects funded by the Robert Wood Johnson Foundation that year and, subsequently, became a National Health Services Corps training site [29].

In the 1980s, Rural Health Group, Inc., was initiated, as clinics in Northampton and Halifax, including Roanoke Amaranth, joined to share physician call and administrative services. Eventually, five clinics became associated in this fashion. Each entity has enjoyed tremendous community support and functioned in the spirit of community-oriented primary care, looking for creative ways to respond to the needs of its community.

In Northampton County, the diverse needs of the rapidly growing numbers of older people led, over time, to the creation of a number of innovative services. During the late 1980s and early 1990s, Rural Health Group conceived and built the Hampton Woods Senior Campus, including a nursing home, senior center, and assisted living [30]. Just after the nursing home opened in 1990, the leaders of Rural Health Group cultivated external relationships to bring a program of geriatric interdisciplinary consultation to the community.

THE DEVELOPMENT OF THE GERIATRIC TEAM CONSULTATION PROJECT

Joining the Rural Health Group in planning and conducting the geriatric interdisciplinary consultation were the Program on Aging of the University of North Carolina at Chapel Hill School of Medicine (UNC-CH) and the Area L

Area Health Education Center (AHEC). Goals of the collaboration were to directly enhance the quality of care provided to older rural residents, to complement the expertise of rural generalists with that of geriatric specialists, to enhance training opportunities for health professions students, and to foster research collaboration.

Basic to the approach is a monthly consultation by a university-based interdisciplinary geriatric assessment team in rural primary and long-term care settings, including the Roanoke Amaranth clinic and the Hampton Woods Senior Campus. The consulting team joins local practitioners from various organizations, such as home health, social services, mental health, and pharmacy, to assess elderly patients with complex problems. This service component has come to be known as the Interdisciplinary Geriatric Evaluation Clinic (IGEC). Essential to the IGEC process is the empowerment of the local interdisciplinary team, support and respect for the individuals involved, and an appreciation for the complexities of care in rural settings. The program is an acknowledgment of the need for a new model to enrich clinical decision making by focusing on teamwork, and by facilitating management of identified medical and social problems through increased access to relevant information and expertise. Health professions student training and research have been integral parts of the program. Team visits began in September 1990 and have been in continuous operation since that time.

Prior to the initial consultation visit and periodically thereafter, University, AHEC, and rural community personnel met together to share perspectives and to jointly develop goals for the process. University staff visited community practitioners in their work settings to learn about the realities of their practices, their perception of problems, and their personal and professional goals for the visitation program. University staff also accompanied local practitioners on home visits and rounds, and observed meetings to learn about the challenges facing elderly residents, and about the informal and formal resources available. These visits were essential to initial relationship development (and subsequently to maintenance of established relationships) and to a thorough understanding of community perceptions and preferences.

On an ongoing basis, three additional strategies helped ensure good communication between partners in the multiple endeavors. One strategy was the designation of a liaison person from the university whose role it was to maintain communication with the many participants, proactively planning and troubleshooting as necessary. Process evaluations, which included all of the partners, also took place annually on a formal basis, and periodically on an informal basis. These evaluations tapped: 1) perceptions of the utility of the team consultation, 2) the effects of the team consultation on role perceptions and local interdisciplinary teamwork, 3) the effects relative to reduction of barriers to care and enhancement of quality of care, and 4) ideas for ongoing collaboration.

The IGEC service component was in operation for a full year prior to the initiation of any research. During that first year, university and local team relationships were solidly established and intervention procedures and processes were refined. The trust and rapport which had developed between community practitioners and university researchers were invaluable in designing, implementing, and conducting subsequent research. Community practitioners brainstormed acceptable phrasing of questions, introduced researchers to community residents for pilot testing, and ensured that protocols were feasible for their staff to carry out. They also carefully scrutinized proposed measures and called attention to those which they regarded as of questionable utility or impractical. Similarly, researchers, who had already had the benefit of several months to acquire an appreciation for community norms and service setting operations, were much more aware of key factors that needed to be taken into consideration in project planning. They recognized, for example, the crucial need to tie the protocol and measures as closely as possible to existing staff practices to minimize disruption of established routines.

Two small scale studies were undertaken during the second year of collaboration, including a qualitative study of the health beliefs of community residents and a study of the outcomes of the IGEC. Both proved useful beyond their scientific purpose, complementing the service component, providing feedback on outcomes, and augmenting understanding of the community.

IGEC Outcomes in the Nursing Home

To examine the outcome and process of the team consultation to the nursing home, a simple one-group pretest-posttest with follow-up at one and three months was employed. The primary outcomes of interest were nursing home resident functional status and goal attainment.

The seventeen residents consenting to data collection ranged in age from fifty-one to ninety-five (mean = 77), 29 percent were white; 71 percent African American; 71 percent were female. About half required extensive Activities of Daily Living assistance; 41 percent were incontinent on a daily basis. Residents averaged 2.79 chronic disease diagnoses, and 5.8 prescribed medications (range 1 to 17). "Change in functional status" and "mental health/behavioral problems" were the factors most often precipitating requests for team consultation.

Cognitive and sensory impairments greatly complicated the measurement of resident outcomes. Less than one-fourth of the residents were able to complete the Timed Manual Performance test while only one-half were able to respond to the Dartmouth COOP charts. However, a simple goal attainment measure proved to be quite productive, providing information about the residents' wishes and concerns of value for both planning and evaluative purposes. Responses varied greatly; e.g., "to be able to walk and go home," "to play my guitar," "to cuddle a baby." Even residents with significant cognitive impairment were generally able to respond in a meaningful, and often clinically relevant, way. For example, a demented woman with frequent anxiety attacks said, "I don't want to be frightened." Two-thirds of those residents who were able to state a goal reported "some" to "much" progress toward achievement of their goals while one resident fully achieved her goal of regaining mobility and returning home.

Change in resident functional status was also rated by nursing home staff at follow-up with 47.1 percent of residents judged to be "generally improved"; 29.4 percent "about the same"; and 23.5 percent, "generally worse."

Health Beliefs Study

The purpose of this qualitative pilot project was to explore the associations among health-related beliefs and values, expectations and desires for length of life, attitudes and beliefs about aging and growing older, self-reported health, self-care, and help-seeking behaviors in a multicultural population of rural elderly people. Informants were forty-two older men and women, including African Americans, Euro Americans, and Native Americans, who resided in Northampton and Halifax counties. Selection of respondents into a convenience sample was based on referrals from health-care providers and other knowledgeable local people, and was designed to capture a wide range of ages, socioeconomic strata, and health conditions.

Two- to three-hour interviews took place either in the home of the older person or in conjunction with a clinic visit. The interviews explored areas in which health beliefs and health practices appear to have an impact on quality of life, likelihood of morbidity, and life expectancy. Interview questions covered topics, such as: 1) respondents' own definitions of health and sickness, 2) perceived major influences on health, and 3) retrospective accounts of help-seeking behaviors for selected chronic conditions. Respondents were encouraged to answer in their own words, to elaborate on their responses, and to explain terms that they employed with a specialized meaning.

Key findings included a prevailing attitude of fatalism toward illness and a prevailing view of health as ability to carry out normal activities of daily life.

Both studies served to inform the service component, enhancing understanding of prevailing views and issues in the community and yielding data for on-course readjustments in the IGEC process. We now turn to a detailed description of the IGEC.

PURPOSE OF THE INTERDISCIPLINARY GERIATRIC EVALUATION CLINIC

The immediate goal of the IGEC is to respond in a comprehensive way to older persons and their families living in rural communities who are facing a crisis. Usually these problems include complex medical, functional, and social circumstances that have reached such urgent proportions that additional assistance is needed for management and ongoing care. The team evaluation is designed to determine the care and types of services needed by the older person to maintain his or her independence and to help in the initiation and coordination of these services. In this respect, the IGEC fills a service gap on the local continuum of care.

Through the IGEC process, geriatric case consultation is provided to local practitioners to augment their effectiveness in providing care to older persons, while also supporting the development of local interdisciplinary team care. Increased focus upon interdisciplinary care has been advanced as a sound strategy for enhancing quality of care in rural areas through greater service integration, and for improving practitioner recruitment and promoting retention through enhanced peer support.

The consulting team's approach is a blend of client-centered case consultation and consultee-centered case consultation. Caplan has identified the former as the traditional type of consultation provided by medical specialists in which the objectives are expert case assessment and specific recommendations to the consultee [31]. While these objectives are embraced by the team, there is also a goal of enabling the consultee—in this case, the nursing home staff or the local primary care team—to function more effectively. Therefore, the consultation is also "consultee-centered" with goals to increase staff knowledge and skills, enhance confidence, and augment judgment and objectivity. From time to time, there is also spill-over into more program-oriented consultation through recognition that the identified needs of an individual generalize to a larger group or issue.

In their combined training mission, the university and local teams seek to develop in participating health professions students an appreciation of the resources and strategies for geriatric problem-solving available through cooperation among health professionals from different disciplines, and to stimulate student interest in rural practice. In addition, university-based faculty enhance their understanding of the problems faced by rural community practitioners.

THE STRUCTURE AND PROCESS OF THE IGEC

Each of the collaborating organizations lends financial and other support to the project. AHEC has a central organizational role, in addition to coordinating the involvement of health professions students in the rural training experience. AHEC also bears the expense of transporting university faculty and students to the facility. Consistent with its mission of service, particularly to underserved communities, and of preparation of students for rural practice, UNC-CH contributes faculty time to the project. Rural Health Group, Inc., frees staff time for participation, and carries responsibility for selection, preparation, and follow-up relative to elderly persons to be presented, inviting family and others who are involved in caregiving to participate. While program costs are generally absorbed by the collaborators, there are some offsets in patient billing and training grants.

The geriatric assessment team from UNC-CH is an experienced interdisciplinary team that includes a fellowship-trained geriatrician, two nurse-practitioners, a social worker, and a physical therapist. From time to time, persons from other disciplines, notably geropsychiatry, pharmacy, and dentistry are represented on the team. For example, a geropsychiatrist may attend in the case of concern about probable depression or dementia.

Three community-based teams—primary care, interagency, and nursing home—participate in the process. The teams have overlapping membership and reconfigure themselves as needed around the needs of specific patients. The university team joins with local team members, for example, physicians from the Roanoke Amaranth Clinic, nurses, nursing assistants, social workers from the adjacent Department of Social Services or Hampton Woods, and persons from other community health care settings such as Home Health and Public Health.

Cases for team consultation are selected by local practitioners generally because of changes in functional status or concerns about appropriate management of complex medical, social, and psychological problems. Consent to be seen by the team and to have data collected for evaluative purposes is secured from the patient and family by local staff. Persons who do not wish to have data collected may still take part in the consultation process.

A typical visitation is organized in two segments. In the morning, team members (both local and consulting) see an elderly person and his or her family in the clinic or on a home visit to broadly evaluate functional, mental, and physical status and specific needs for care. Commencing the consultation is a meeting between the teams to share staff concerns and pertinent patient data. Subsequently, various team and staff members interview the patient (conducting a limited physical examination as indicated) and whenever possible, meet with family members.

The IGEC assessment process is adapted from a geriatric evaluation model developed by Dr. Williams. Physician team members typically conduct a comprehensive medical history and relevant physical examination, evaluate mental status and mood, review and suggest laboratory tests, monitor medical therapy, and then communicate with others involved regarding any medical issues of the care plan.

Nursing team members address functional activity, psychosocial functioning, coping and adaptation patterns to illness, and behavioral issues. The functional evaluation includes vision, hearing, communication skills, performance of basic activities of daily living, mobility status, and instrumental activities of daily living such as performing housework and taking medication. Basic nutritional status is covered as are hobbies and special interests, sleep/rest patterns, potential for physical or verbal abuse, and other behavioral characteristics.

Social work members typically assess family dynamics and the nature and extent of the support system. The social worker also serves as an advocate for the person's family, and may assess the resources available to the patient, financial and otherwise. Important information obtained by social workers includes the type and location of the usual living arrangements of a particular older person, any significant losses he or she has experienced, the individual's former occupation, retirement age, and other relevant psychosocial data.

Students from various health care backgrounds participate in the day's activities. When feasible, students are also involved in activities prior to and after the team visitation. For example, medical students may make a preliminary home visit and, subsequently, present a summary to the team to begin the assessment process. Pharmacy students may complete a comprehensive medication review.

An evaluation and planning conference concludes the morning session. All team members meet to discuss and agree upon an appropriate care plan for each individual that reflects the concerns and goals of the individual, community practitioners, and the family. This interaction provides significant opportunity for sharing ideas, informal teaching, and modeling of team work, while utilizing an approach to patients that focuses on maximizing their independence and functioning. The conference blends the various assessment perspectives, providing a composite picture of the elderly person and the problems he or she faces. A plan of care is specifically tailored to meet the needs of the individual and his or her family, and is subsequently carried out by the local team in cooperation with the patient and family.

The afternoon segment consists of consultation with the staff of the Hampton Woods long-term care facility. As in the morning segment, one or more patients are seen and discussed. In this setting, deliberations about the needs of a specific patient often lead to discussion of broad issues of importance to staff in long-term care settings. Among these are coping with end of life issues, management of demanding or difficult patients, and enhancing communication among staff, patients, and families. Also acknowledged and appreciated is the fact that commitment to quality of life in a nursing home is a complex and elusive goal that often forces difficult choices for patients and providers alike. The ground work for this project was established at a time when Hampton Woods began operation. Therefore, the consulting team has had the unique opportunity to witness and support the staff in their individual and professional development as well as in their development as a team.

Discussions take place in a spirit of mutual collaboration and respect. The consulting team seeks to model effective interdisciplinary communication and teamwork and to fully support the local team members as individuals, as professionals, as caregivers, and as a team. This attitude of acceptance and support fosters honest interchange and facilitates discussion of difficult issues which are emotionally charged. Key consulting activities that occur to a variable degree from session to session include:

1. *teaching,* for example, reviewing the course and management of Parkinson's disease, negative effects of certain drug combinations, or the relationship between cognitive impairment and anxiety;
2. *reinforcing staff capabilities and problem-solving,* for example, underlining the importance of contributions of different staff;
3. *facilitating understanding of resident, staff, and family interactions,* for example, helping staff understand the complex web of feelings associated with end-of-life issues; and
4. *providing support and reassurance,* for example, acknowledging that staff are often doing all that can be done in very trying and difficult situations and reinforcing their capacity to support one another.

Follow-up on the recommendations for care are carried out by local staff. For those persons who have consented to data collection, measures are repeated at one-month and three-months post-consultations. Progress is also formally reviewed during consultation visits at the same intervals. This is an important strategy in light of studies which suggest that consultant recommendations are not necessarily acted upon [32].

PROBLEMS ENCOUNTERED

The geographic distance between the university and the rural community has posed problems from time to time. When bad weather has forced AHEC planes to the ground, the IGEC has been canceled creating substantial frustration among rural practitioners who have allocated time for the visitation and gone to great lengths to schedule other participants. Since 1995, the establishment of a fiber optic telecommunications link between the university and the rural community has provided valuable backup in case of travel complications.

The time commitment necessary on the part of rural practitioners to participate in the IGEC, in teaching and in research, also has been a major challenge to the collaboration. The time of community practitioners is decidedly precious, and accordingly, constant care must be taken to insure that activities do in fact benefit them and the older people in the community. University consultants and researchers must be sensitive to the needs of their collaborators, making adjustments to processes and procedures as necessary to assure their continuing utility and efficiency.

The research component of the project initially included no monies for the collaborating service settings. This was immediately recognized as serious strategic error, and steps were taken to remedy the situation to the extent that was feasible after funding had already been allocated. In subsequent projects undertaken by the university and rural community, personnel time and other resources have always been made available to the rural participants.

Initially university and local service setting staff gathered data for research purposes. Again time and distance conspired to present barriers to timely and consistent data collection. After the first year, monies were allocated to hire a member of the local community to work with staff and study participants to gather data, thereby reducing the burden on staff and increasing adherence to the protocols. While promoting staff ownership of the project is of the utmost importance, there must also be someone who coordinates their efforts locally and offsets the cost to the setting of staff involvement in the collaboration.

Finding appropriate measures was yet another problem of significant proportions. The older population of the community is culturally and educationally diverse and many are of low literacy. Established measures of health and functional status, with excellent track records in research with urban, relatively well-educated persons, were frequently of little use. Considerable and time-consuming adaptation and revision were often necessary.

OUTCOMES

Project activities are highly valued by the community participants. Collaborative interdisciplinary teamwork effectively reduces the isolation that is so often problematic for rural professionals, more fully utilizes the skills of all, and leverages scarce resources. An increased emphasis on interdisciplinary teamwork has been evident within the service settings, and within the larger senior-serving community which has organized a local interagency geriatric team. Change is also evident in a greater sense of mastery in confronting patient situations that are complex from both a medical and ethical perspective. The overall knowledge base in geriatrics has been augmented, as is evident in practices such as more conservative use of multiple medications.

Moreover, the team consultation has provided a forum for addressing many of the issues that are most difficult in nursing home care. Among these are medication reduction, coping with the "troubled" and the "troubling," and dealing with the often conflicting values and needs of staff, residents, and family at times of crisis. However, implementing consistent approaches, especially in the area of behavior management, and working through difficult problems is extraordinarily demanding. There were many instances in which staff needed ongoing support on a more frequent basis than just monthly contact in order to be successful. In this regard, the IGEC heightened awareness of the severe limitation in mental health resources in rural areas and the consequent unmet needs for counseling and medication optimization.

A favorable impact on patient functional outcomes and patient care has also been achieved. Improvement has been most often noted in the attainment of the patient's own goal for change, and in the overall outcome assessment by staff. Family perceptions have been favorable, and the consultation has often spared patients from long trips to see specialists.

The team visitation has been heavily utilized by the Area L AHEC for interdisciplinary health professions education. Over forty students have taken part in IGEC sessions each year, and others have participated in site-based rotations at the local sites, learning clinical care in a rural context, conducting research, or addressing community problems. These experience are greatly valued by the students. Many of them reported that it was the first time they had experienced interdisciplinary teamwork or seen individuals from their professions function as part of a team, approaching problems in a holistic fashion.

Throughout the project, service, training, and research components have constantly informed one another, serving to strengthen the program and augmenting its overall efficiency. There have been several notable outgrowths of this program. In April 1995, for example, UNC-CH and the rural community were linked by fiber optic cable through the North Carolina Information Highway. This has significantly expanded the potential of the relationship for ongoing and efficient interaction. Also, the community has begun an excellent frontline caregiver staff development program, the consulting team has expanded its service to other rural long-term care settings, and new research initiatives have been designed and implemented.

APPROACHES AND OPPORTUNITIES FOR RESEARCH IN RURAL AGING

This program illustrates the potential for integration of outreach and collaborative research to help address the needs of rural elderly people. While directly responsive to many human problems in the rural community, the program is also consistent with the research mission of the university. Moreover, the shared teamwork that is integral to the collaboration of university and community practitioners provides a solid foundation for research activities. Given that the clinical environment is not always hospitable to research, the solidification of working relationships in complementary activities is of significance. The creative interaction of university and rural participants has the potential to identify and effectively problem-solve ways to increase understanding of many of the issues at the front lines of rural health care; for example, of belief systems that promote independence but oftentimes delay help-seeking or preventive care activities. Joint problem solving increases understanding that informs teaching at the institutional level and may stimulate social advocacy. While visiting faculty members consult, they also learn about real issues in rural health and aging and develop new research ideas in concert with the rural community.

There are several factors that collectively contribute to the program. Perhaps the most important is the truly collaborative spirit in which the program is approached. There is a sense of a shared mission to serve older people and to research innovations of health care delivery. In addition, there is the recognition of the unique contribution to problem resolution that is made by each person and by each discipline participating. The importance of these solid working relationships cannot be understated.

For others who may wish to develop such a program or to do research in a rural setting, we recommend that collaborators enter into a relationship with mutual respect and a shared sense of commitment and responsibility. A strong investment by community leaders is critical because they must free staff to be involved in planning and program operations. A clear focus on the needs (and constraints) of all involved will facilitate effective collaboration.

Keeping the process simple is of utmost importance. Such a program involves very busy people with multiple and often conflicting responsibilities. As a result, data selected for research purposes must be clinically relevant and kept to the minimum. Traditional research methods involving lengthy questionnaires or extensive interviews may be quite problematic in busy rural service settings.

Developing community relationships and attending to the oftentimes conflicting needs of participants, pay rich dividends not only in terms of enhanced service delivery, but also in innovative research projects and comprehensive educational initiatives. With such approaches, strategies can ultimately be developed to foster the health and independence of older rural residents and to maximize their productivity, creativity, well-being, and happiness. These goals are relevant not only for the present generation of rural elderly people, but for the many yet to come.

ACKNOWLEDGMENTS

This project was funded in part by the National Institute on Aging through a Rural Health and Aging Exploratory Research Center Grant (AG09648-05) to the Cecil G. Sheps Center for Health Services Research, University of North Carolina at Chapel Hill, and by the Area L Area Health Education Center, Rocky Mount, North Carolina.

REFERENCES

1. J. F. Van Nostrand, Common Beliefs about the Rural Elderly: What Do National Data Tell Us? *Vital Health Statistics, 3*:28, National Center for Health Statistics, Hyattsville, Maryland, 1993.
2. C. N. Bull (ed.), *Aging in Rural America,* Sage, Newbury Park, California, 1993.
3. M. A. Kaiser and H. Camp, The Rural Aged: Beneficiaries and Contributors to Rural Community and Economic Development, in *Aging in Rural America,* C. N. Bull (ed.), Sage, Newbury Park, California, pp. 45-58, 1993.
4. D. L. Smith, Health Promotion for Older Adults, *Health Values, 12*:5, pp 46-51, 1988.

5. J. J. Simmons, E. Nelson, E. Roberts, Z. T. Salisbury et al., A Health Promotion Program: Staying Health after Fifty, *Health Education Quarterly, 16*:4, pp. 461-472, 1989.
6. M. S. Hendryx, Rural Hospital Health Promotion: Programs, Methods, Resource Limitations, *Journal of Community Health, 18*:4, pp. 241-250, 1993.
7. S. L. White and S. K. Maloney, Promoting Health Diets and Active Lives to Hard-to-Reach Groups: Market Research Study, *Public Health Reports, 105*:3, pp. 224-231, 1990.
8. B. P. Yawn, A. Busby, and R. A. Yawn (eds.), *Exploring Rural Medicine: Current Issues and Concepts,* Sage, Thousand Oaks, California, 1994.
9. R. T. Coward, D. K. McLaughlin, R. P. Duncan, and C. N. Bull, An Overview of Health and Aging in Rural America, in *Health Services for Rural Elders,* R. T. Coward, C. N. Bull, G. Kukulka, and J. M. Galliher (eds.), Springer Publishing Company, New York, pp. 1-32, 1994.
10. R. B. Wallace and P. L. Colsher, Improving Ambulatory and Acute Care Services for the Rural Elderly: Current Solutions, Research, and Policy Directions, in *Health Services for Rural Elders,* R. T. Coward, C. N. Bull, G. Kukulka, and J. M. Galliher (eds.), Springer Publishing Company, New York, pp. 108-126, 1994.
11. M. H. Beers, J. G. Ouslander, S. F. Fingold, H. Morgenstern, D. B. Reuben, W. Rogers, M. J. Zeffren, and J. C. Beck, Inappropriate Medication Prescribing in Skilled-Nursing Facilities, *Annals of Internal Medicine, 117*:8, pp. 685-689, 1992.
12. M. Smith, K. C. Buckwalter, and M. Albanese, Geropsychiatric Education Programs: Providing Skills and Understanding, *Journal of Psychosocial Nursing, 28*:12, pp. 8-12, 1990.
13. T. T. Phan and B. V. Reifler, Psychiatric Disorder Among Nursing Home Residents: Depression, Anxiety, and Paranoia, *Clinics in Geriatric Medicine, 4*:3, pp. 601-612, 1988.
14. J. E. Beaulieu and D. E. Berry, *Rural Health Services: A Management Perspective,* AUPHA Press, Ann Arbor, Michigan, 1994.
15. M. Smyer, D. Brandon, and M. Cohn, Improving Nursing Home Care Through Training and Job Redesign, *The Gerontologist, 32*:3, pp. 327-333, 1992.
16. M. Smith, K. C. Buckwalter, L. Garand, S. Mitchell, M. Albanese, and C. Kreiter, Evaluation of a Geriatric Mental Health Training Program for Nursing Personnel in Rural Long-Term Care Facilities, *Issues in Mental Health Nursing, 15*:2, pp. 149-168, 1994.
17. M. H. Beers, S. F. Fingold, and J. G. Ouslander, A Computerized System for Identifying and Informing Physicians about Problematic Drug Use in Nursing Home, *Journal of Medical Systems, 16*:6, pp. 237-245, 1992.
18. K. M. Sakauye and C. J. Camp, Introducing Psychiatric Care into Nursing Homes, *The Gerontologist, 32*:6, pp. 849-852, 1992.
19. L. S. Goldman and A. Klugman, Psychiatric Consultation in a Teaching Nursing Home, *Psychosomatics, 31*:3, pp. 277-281, 1990.
20. L. J. Haywood, C. K. Francis, L. L. Cregler, M. D. Freed, and D. J. Skorton, Task Force 1: The Underserved, *Journal of the American College of Cardiology, 24*:2, pp. 282-290, 1994.

21. T. A. Cavalieri, A. Chopra, D. Gray-Miceli, S. Shreve, H. Waxman, and L. J. Forman, Geriatric Assessment Teams in Nursing Homes: Do They Work? *Journal of the American Osteopathic Association, 93*:12, pp. 1269-1272, 1993.
22. S. Williams, How Do the Elderly and Their Families Feel about Research Participation? *Geriatric Nursing, 14*:1, pp. 11-14, 1993.
23. G. D. Rowles, Changing Health Culture in Rural Appalachia: Implications for Serving the Elderly, *Journal of Aging Services, 5*:4, pp. 375-389, 1991.
24. M. M. Leininger, *Qualitative Research Methods in Nursing,* Grune & Stratton, Inc., New York, 1985.
25. W. G. Hollister, J. W. Edgerton, and R. H. Hunter, *Alternative Services in Community Mental Health: Programs and Processes,* The University of North Carolina Press, Chapel Hill, 1985.
26. J. Hatch, N. Moss, and A. Saran, Community Research: Partnership in Black Communities, *American Journal of Preventive Medicine, 9,* pp. 27-31, 1993.
27. J. M. Iutcovich, Assessing the Needs of Rural Elderly: An Empowerment Model, *Evaluation and Program Planning, 16,* pp. 95-107, 1993.
28. Center for Aging Research and Educational Services, *North Carolina Comes of Age: County Profiles in Aging,* North Carolina Division of Aging, Raleigh, 1990.
29. M. E. Williams, D. J. Rabiner, and R. H. Hunter, The Interdisciplinary Geriatric Team Evaluation Project: A New Approach to the Delivery of Geriatric Medicine in Geographically Remote Locations, *North Carolina Medical Journal, 56*:10, pp. 502-505, 1995.
30. K. G. Reeb, Jr., and W. Remmes, *Community Health Centers: Engines for Economic Growth,* National Association of Community Health Centers, Inc., Washington, 1994.
31. G. Caplan, *The Theory and Practice of Mental Health Consultation,* Basic Books, New York, 1970.
32. R. C. Abrams, J. A. Teresi, and D. N. Butin, Depression in Nursing Home Residents, *Clinics in Geriatric Medicine, 8*:2, pp. 309-322, 1992.

PART THREE

Measuring Health Practices and the Use of Formal and Informal Health Care

CHAPTER 8

Research in Rural Minority Aging in the Southeast U.S.: Results and Directions

Thomas A. Arcury, Ronny A. Bell,
and Iris B. Carlton-LaNey

The impact of minority status for the processes and outcomes of aging has gained wide acceptance [1]. Minority status often results in differential treatment by society across the entire life course. For minority groups which have been the subject of prejudice or racism, this status influences the social, health, and financial resources that individuals bring into old age. Ethnicity influences how the group feels about and acts toward the elderly, acceptable roles for elders in the group, and the availability and strength of social support networks. While ethnicity and minority status are known to be important influences on the lives and well-being of elders, little aging research has considered the ethnicity and minority status of rural elders. In this chapter we address rural minority aging through an examination of the research literature and consideration of methodological issues for research dealing with rural minority elders in the southeast United States. We limit our discussion to this region so that we can maintain control of the literature and because it is the region with which we have direct minority aging research experience.

African Americans are the predominant rural elder minority group in the southeast United States. In a few limited areas (e.g., Robeson County, North Carolina) there are significant numbers of elderly Native Americans. The

Hispanic population continues to increase in many states within the Southeast; however, the rural segment of this population is relatively young.

This chapter has three objectives. First, we review the current research literature on rural minority aging in the southeast United States, emphasizing health and social services use and needs. Second, we discuss special circumstances and issues that must be considered in the design and conduct of research on rural minority elders. Finally, we suggest areas of particular importance for future research on the health and social service needs of rural minority elders. Before we address these three objectives, we define the population we are considering in this chapter in terms of region, residence, and minority and ethnic status. We also report some demographic information from the 1990 U.S. Census of Population and Housing to document the number of minority elders in the southeast United States and their intra-regional distribution.

RURAL MINORITY ELDERS
IN THE SOUTHEAST UNITED STATES

It is extremely important to define the population when researching rural minority elders. What constitutes rural and what constitutes a minority group and ethnic status are issues of considerable debate. We must also define the geographic area we are including in the southeast United States. After we have defined the population of interest, we present some data on the number and distribution of rural minority elders in the Southeast.

Defining the Population

We are defining the southeast United States as the thirteen-state area bounded on the north by the Mason-Dixon Line, and on the west by the Ohio and the Mississippi Rivers (Figure 1). These states are Alabama, Delaware, Florida, Georgia, Kentucky, Louisiana, Maryland, Mississippi, North Carolina, South Carolina, Tennessee, Virginia, and West Virginia. When we compare rural and urban elders, the urban population includes Washington, D.C.

Substantial literature on the definition of rural has been written [2], and we do not add more to this literature here. For our purposes, the rural area of the Southeast includes all nonmetropolitan or non-SMA (non-Standard Metropolitan Areas) counties in 1990. In 1990, there were 741 nonmetropolitan counties in the thirteen-state Southeast region on which we are focused, as well as 278 metropolitan or SMA counties.

The debate over definitions of race, ethnic group, and minority group continues among researchers and policy makers [e.g., see 3, 4]. In the section of this chapter on research design issues, we discuss the key points in this debate. In our analysis of the demographic data and in our literature review, we use the ethnic or racial groups used in the materials reviewed. For the research literature, the

Figure 1. Southeast United States showing state and
county boundaries.

minority groups include Blacks or African Americans, Native Americans or American Indians, and Hispanics. The U.S. Census data uses five races (White, Black, American Indian or Alaskan Native, Asian or Pacific Islander, and Other), and two ethnic groups (Hispanic Origin and Non-Hispanic Origin). Those races which are not White, and that ethnic group which is Hispanic Origin, constitute what are referred to as minority groups in the United States. The way in which these data are reported by the Census makes it impossible to obtain a total minority count for age-specific segments of the population, as Hispanic Origin individuals can be included in any of the five race groups. Therefore, in our analysis we can only include a total non-white category.

Population Characteristics

Black elders are the predominant minority group in Southeast non-SMA counties in 1990 (Table 1). Blacks comprise 97.5 percent of the non-SMA, non-white population aged sixty-five and older; Blacks comprise 84.1 percent of the SMA, non-white population. There are about 10,000 Hispanic Origin elders in Southeast non-SMA counties, whereas there are 190,000 Hispanic Origin elders in Southeast SMA counties. There are fewer than 10,000 Native American elders, and about 2,000 Asian elders residing in Southeastern non-SMA counties.

Examining state-by-state variation in the number of non-SMA minority elders (Table 2) indicates that there are few rural Black elders in several states: Delaware, Florida, Kentucky, Maryland, Tennessee, and West Virginia. States with large numbers of Black non-SMA elders are Alabama, Georgia, Louisiana, Mississippi, North Carolina, South Carolina, and Virginia. The only state with substantially more than 1,000 non-SMA Hispanic Origin elders is Florida, which has 1,531 males and 1,835 females. This is 35.3 percent of non-SMA Hispanic Origin elders in the Southeast. There are few non-SMA Native American elders in this region, and most of these live in North Carolina. There are 1,858 male and 2,670 female non-SMA Native American elders residing in North Carolina; this is 56.6 percent of all those living in the Southeast.

A comparison of the number of males and females by age group for each race or ethnic group for the Southeastern non-SMA counties shows no surprises (Table 3). The number of persons in each gender-race or -ethnic group declines with increasing age. The number of females in each age group for each race or ethnic group is larger than the number of males (with one exception, "Other"). The proportion of males to females in the seventy-five and older cohort for Whites, Blacks, those of Hispanic Origin, and American Indians is within a

Table 1. Population Aged Sixty-Five and Older by Gender and Race/Ethnicity for Non-SMA and SMA Counties in the Southeast United States, 1990

Race/Ethnicity	Gender:	Non-SMA		SMA	
		Male	Female	Male	Female
Black		160,209	261,914	275,453	459,741
American Indian		3,450	4,543	2,863	3,954
Asian/Pacific Island American		800	1,251	10,029	13,865
Other		470	491	6,202	9,461
Total Non-White		164,929	268,199	294,547	487,021
Hispanic Origin		3,960	5,511	76,474	114,292
White		917,008	1,334,955	1,918,780	2,836,638

Table 2. Minority Non-SMA Population Aged Sixty-Five and
Older by Gender and Race/Ethnicity for States in
the Southeast United States, 1990

	Black	American Indian	Asian/ Pacific Islander	Other	Total Non-White	Hispanic Origin
Alabama						
Females	25,200	198	62	8	25,468	210
Males	15,417	160	50	32	15,389	136
Delaware						
Females	2,048	108	32	2	2,190	61
Males	1,339	135	47	2	1,523	50
Florida						
Females	8,567	291	246	211	9,315	1,835
Males	5,939	258	154	245	6,596	1,531
Georgia						
Females	36,449	179	93	45	36,766	483
Males	20,542	93	80	23	20,738	258
Kentucky						
Females	5,403	159	76	19	5,657	311
Males	3,329	151	39	15	3,534	207
Louisiana						
Females	23,969	171	101	71	24,312	689
Males	15,282	228	48	50	15,608	423
Maryland						
Females	4,482	34	16	7	4,539	57
Males	3,082	20	2	9	3,113	39
Mississippi						
Females	43,974	185	133	8	44,300	364
Males	27,543	123	110	10	27,786	125
North Carolina						
Females	48,337	2,670	191	55	51,258	437
Males	28,364	1,858	96	20	30,340	366
South Carolina						
Females	31,702	110	95	18	31,295	243
Males	18,295	90	34	8	18,427	171
Tennessee						
Females	8,819	166	47	9	9,041	247
Males	5,675	101	11	34	5,821	213
Virginia						
Females	19,207	165	79	30	19,481	276
Males	13,400	170	63	20	13,658	234
West Virginia						
Females	3,757	107	80	8	3,952	298
Males	2,272	63	64	2	2,401	157

Table 3. Population by Age Group and Gender for Race and Ethnicity Groups in the Southeast United States Non-SMA Counties, 1990

Age Group:	55 to 64		65 to 74		75 and Older	
Race/Ethnicity	Male	Female	Male	Female	Male	Female
Black	111,000	151,670	94,601	143,635	65,608	118,279
American Indian	3,514	4,039	2,431	2,804	1,019	1,739
Asian/Pacific Island American	1,240	2,592	599	958	201	293
Other	909	749	318	296	152	195
Total Non-White	116,663	159,050	97,949	147,693	66,980	120,506
Hispanic Origin	4,755	4,964	2,625	3,176	1,335	2,335
White	704,164	784,650	593,423	741,061	323,585	593,894

narrow range, 0.54 for Whites, 0.55 for Blacks, 0.57 for Hispanic Origin, and 0.58 for Native American.

Of the 741 non-SMA counties in these thirteen Southeastern states, eighty-six (11.6%) have over 39 percent of their elderly populations being non-white (Table 4) (non-white is not total minority, it does not include white Hispanic Origin individuals). An additional 149 (20.1%) of these counties have 25 percent to 39 percent of their elderly populations being non-white. These large elderly non-white population counties are not evenly distributed across the region. Delaware, Kentucky, and West Virginia have no counties with an elderly population at least 25 percent non-white. Florida, Maryland, and Tennessee have eight such counties among them. The states with the greatest number and highest proportion of non-SMA counties with elderly populations over 39 percent minority are Alabama (11 total non-SMA counties, 23.4% of all non-SMA counties), Georgia (16, 13.2%), Mississippi (21, 28.0%), and South Carolina (15, 44%).

The geographic distribution of counties with proportionately large non-white populations is illustrated in Figure 2. There is a clear continuous geographic concentration in the region referred to as the Black Belt [5]. This crescent shaped region begins in southeastern Virginia, sweeps through eastern North Carolina, into eastern and central South Carolina, southwest through central Georgia to southeastern Alabama, turns northwest through Alabama and crosses Mississippi into Louisiana, and north into southwest Tennessee.

Black elders are the poorest non-SMA group, with 46.1 percent being below the poverty level (Table 5). By comparison, 19.6 percent of white non-SMA elders fall below the poverty line. The fewest poor non-SMA elders (15.5%) are Asians, but there are very few persons in this group. The percentages of poor non-SMA Native American elders (36.9%) and Hispanic Origin elders (25.8%) are still quite high, but are substantially below the Black percentage.

Table 4. Number of Non-SMA and SMA Counties in Each
Southeast United States State by Proportion of Sixty-Five and Older
Population That is Minority

	Non-SMA Counties			SMA Counties		
Percentage of those 65+ that is Minority	<25%	25-39%	>39%	<25%	25-39%	>39%
Alabama	24	12	10	17	4	0
Delaware	2	0	0	1	0	0
Florida	2	0	0	31	0	0
Georgia	32	37	16	26	10	2
Kentucky	101	0	0	19	0	0
Louisiana	20	19	6	12	6	1
Maryland	8	1	0	13	1	1
Mississippi	29	25	21	5	1	1
North Carolina	40	27	8	22	3	0
South Carolina	11	8	15	7	5	0
Tennessee	64	2	2	26	1	0
Virginia	62	15	8	37	10	4
West Virginia	45	0	0	10	0	0
Washington, D.C.	0	0	0	0	0	1
Total	506	149	86	226	41	11

There is significant variation among the thirteen Southeastern states in the absolute numbers of poor Black elders, and in the percentage of the Black elders who are poor. In Alabama, Louisiana, and Mississippi, over one-half of Black elders are poor. Mississippi also has the largest absolute number of poor Black elders—36,777. Mississippi is followed by North Carolina with 30,734 poor Black elders, Georgia with 25,698, South Carolina with 22,150, Alabama with 20,107, Louisiana with 19,772, and Virginia with 10,861. The percentage of poor Black elders is similar to the regional proportion in Kentucky and Tennessee, but the absolute number of rural Black elders is small. In Delaware, Maryland, and West Virginia the percentage of poor Black elders is below 40 percent, and the absolute number is also very small.

In summary, these demographic data show that the rural elderly minority population in the southeast United States is predominantly Black. The Hispanic Origin and Native American elderly populations are small and concentrated in Florida and North Carolina, respectively. There are large areas in the rural portions of states from North and South Carolina, through Georgia, Alabama, and Mississippi in which minorities constitute a very large (40% or more) part of the elderly population. This rural elderly minority population is very poor—

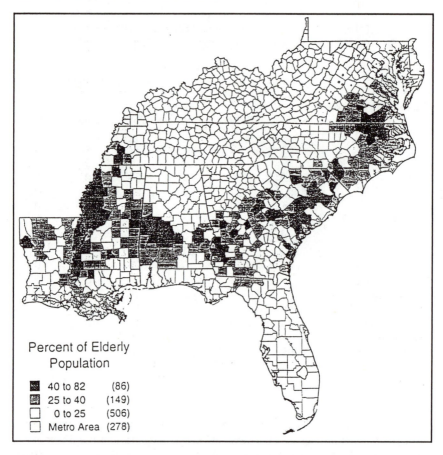

Percent of Elderly Population

- 40 to 82   (86)
- 25 to 40   (149)
- 0 to 25   (506)
- Metro Area (278)

Figure 2. Non-SMA southeast United States counties by proportion of population aged sixty-five and older that is non-white.

46.1 percent of the Black rural Southeast elders were below the poverty line in 1990. The number and proportion of rural Black elders who are poor is not evenly distributed among the thirteen states in this region. In Alabama, Louisiana, and Mississippi over half of the rural Black elders are poor. There are over 20,000 poor minority elders each in Alabama, Louisiana, Mississippi, North Carolina, and South Carolina.

CURRENT RESEARCH LITERATURE

The number of minority elders in many Southeastern rural counties is substantial, as is the overall number of rural minority elders. However, the research literature that attempts to describe and explain the social and cultural lives of

Table 5. Percent of the Non-SMA Population Sixty-Five and Older in the Southeast United States Below Poverty Line by Race/Ethnicity, and for Blacks by State, 1990

	Number Below Poverty	Percent Below Poverty
Black Total	185,568	45.1
Alabama	20,107	55.5
Delaware	1,057	33.6
Florida	5,787	42.5
Georgia	24,698	46.0
Kentucky	3,310	41.6
Louisiana	19,772	53.9
Maryland	2,705	37.9
Mississippi	36,777	53.1
North Carolina	30,734	42.2
South Carolina	22,150	45.4
Tennessee	6,023	43.8
Virginia	10,861	35.4
West Virginia	1,587	27.6
American Indian	2,870	36.9
Asian and Pacific Islander	307	15.5
Other	356	38.4
Total Non-White	189,101	45.8
Hispanic Origin	2,325	25.8
White	419,047	19.6

these rural minority elders, their health status, and their health service needs is limited. Virtually all of this literature for the rural Southeast examines Black elders. We conducted a literature review that began at two general points: a Medline search (using the keywords: rural, minority, aging) and our general knowledge of the literature. We searched back for relevant peer-reviewed materials published after 1979 (some papers published before 1980 are included in this review). We expanded our review by an examination of the literature cited in each relevant source. Our search did find many studies that focused on metropolitan minority elders in the Southeast and elsewhere. We also found literature on rural elders of different ethnic backgrounds for other regions (e.g., rural Mexican-American elders in the Southwest or Native-American elders on the Great Plains). However, these are outside of the purview of this review.

The limited research on rural minority elders in the southeast United States is revealed in the way that several authors have tried to develop generalizations about the rural Black elderly population. In the absence of a substantial literature, some authors have developed conclusions by combining the results of studies with samples that are composed of urban Black elders, with the results of studies with samples of rural White elders. For example, the reasoning is that if urban Black elders have extensive kin networks and strong family support, and if rural White elders have stronger family support than urban White elders, then rural Black elders must have very strong family support. Ralston uses this approach when she tries to make some generalizations about health promotion programs for rural Black elders [6]. Wood and Wan [7] use this reasoning when they try to generalize about family care giving to rural Black elders, and Kivett [8] uses this approach in her review of the literature on informal supports among rural minority elders. However important these attempts are in using available data to make generalizations on which future research or current programs for rural minority elders can be based, they do not provide the strength that studies focused directly on the rural minority elderly would have.

We divide the rural minority aging research literature for the southeast United States into four groups. First, there are large multivariate analyses that include measures of rural and urban, and of minority status. The primary focus of these studies is to examine variation among elders in demographic characteristics such as marital status, household composition [e.g., 9], or medical conditions such as diabetes, hypertension, mental health, or heart disease [e.g., 10-12]. However, in these studies, residence and ethnicity are usually only two of many variables that are included in the analysis, rather than the focus of the study (an exception is [9]). These studies tell us very little about what it means to be a rural minority elder in the Southeast, about the health of these rural minority elders, or about the support and needs of rural minority elders.

Most of the published work in the first group uses data from the Duke Established Populations for Epidemiologic Studies of the Elderly (EPESE) [10, 11, 13-19], also referred to as the Piedmont Health Study. This is one of five sites in the United States (New Haven, Connecticut; East Baltimore, Maryland; St. Louis, Missouri; Piedmont, North Carolina; and east Los Angeles-Venice, California) selected to prospectively study the health of elders in rural and urban communities. The Piedmont EPESE site draws participants from one urban county and four rural counties, providing an opportunity to examine Black-White, and urban-rural differences in the health of elders in North Carolina.

Hays et al. is the best of the published Piedmont EPESE studies to present results that address the effects of minority status on the health of rural elders [9]. Hays and her colleagues consider Black-White and urban-rural differences in household composition stability. They show that rural Blacks have lower household incomes and formal education, are more likely to have a chronic medical condition, are less likely to live alone or only with a spouse, and are less likely to have stable household composition.

Examples of other EPESE studies that examine rural-urban and Black-White differences find that urban residence is a risk factor in depressive disorders and cognitive deficit [11]. Rural Blacks have a higher prevalence of alcohol abuse and dependence [14]. Whites are more likely to use anti-anxiety medication, although urban-rural residence is not predictive of medication use [19]. Galanos et al. observe higher Chance and Powerful Others Locus of Control scores among Blacks and rural residents in the Piedmont sixty-five and older Dental Project [20]. However, in multivariate analysis, urban-rural residence is not predictive of Chance and Powerful Others scores. Fillenbaum et al. found that Black elders used fewer prescription and non-prescription drugs than did White elders [16]. Musick did not find important differences between Black and White rural and urban elders in the influence of religion on subjective health [21]. Finally, in a comparison of EPESE data from New Haven, Connecticut, and North Carolina, Moritz et al. find that diabetes is more common among Blacks in North Carolina than in New Haven, and associations between myocardial infarction, stroke, and physical disability among diabetics differ by race in both sites [18].

The second group of studies compares rural minority elders to urban minority elders in the Southeast. There are three studies in this group. Keil and Saunders compare urban and rural differences in rates of mortality and cardiovascular disease from three studies: the Evans County Heart Study (rural southern Georgia); the Charleston Heart Study (urban South Carolina); and the Pee Dee Heart Study (rural and urban areas around Columbia, South Carolina) [22]. They find higher rates of heart disease among urban Blacks than among rural Blacks. Jackson and Ball compare Black elders in one urban ($n = 62$) and one rural ($n = 70$) county in Georgia on income, health and social service use, family size, and social participation, and they find that rural Black elders use health services less and family support more than do urban elders [23, 24]. Clayton et al. compare rural and urban Black centenarians in Georgia [25]. They find that rural Black centenarians are more depressed, have lower Activities of Daily Living scores, and lower life satisfaction scores than their urban counterparts.

The third group includes those analyses that compare rural minority elders to rural majority elders [26-37]. The studies in this group cover a diverse set of topics.

Arcury et al. find in one rural North Carolina county that Black adults are less likely to use conventional health care and more likely to use alternative health care to treat arthritis than White adults, and that the use of specific alternative treatments differs between these two groups [26]. Bekhuis et al. analyze data from Black and White elder residents in one North Carolina county with arthritis [27]. They find strong ethnic differences in the perceptions of health according to differences in ethnicity, church affiliation, and belief in God's control over all aspects of life.

Kivett considers Black-White differences in life situations [32] and in the grandfather [33] role among elders. She finds that older rural North Carolina Blacks are more likely than older Whites to perceive their income as inadequate, to live with a daughter, and to have a high level of life satisfaction [32]. Kivett also finds that older rural Black men play a stronger central role as grandfather compared to older rural White men in terms of stronger family ties, higher levels of help to grandchildren, and stronger affection [33].

Groger examines the differences in meaning to land ownership [29, 30] and dimensions of exchange [31] between Black and White elders in a rural North Carolina county. She shows that dimensions of exchange differ between Black and White elders. Black elders received more than they gave in their exchange relationships. The exchanges of Black elders were more apt to be of tangible items (e.g., food, money), while those of White elders were more apt to be intangibles.

In other papers, Krishef and Yoelin compare Black and White rural elder Floridians on sources of income and the use of formal and informal support [34]. Learner and Kivett analyze perceived dietary adequacy differences between Black and White elders in a rural North Carolina county [35]. Yearwood and Dressel consider race relations in a rural Georgia Senior Center [36]. Wood and Parham report on differences between Black and White (as well rural and urban) family caregivers of elders with Alzheimer [37].

The final group of studies include those analyses which focus on the lives and health of rural minority elders [38-50]. As with comparisons between White and minority elders, these studies of rural Black elders cover a range of diverse topics.

Several studies use oral history approaches to record the experiences of rural Black elders. Salber presents the life histories of several Black elders without interpretation [47]. Carlton-LaNey uses the oral histories of eight elderly Black women to show these women have a strong sense of attachment to family, farm, and church [41]. As farm women, they have a strong work orientation that has strengthened and sustained them through difficult life situations. Dula presents the story of "Miss Mildred," an elderly Black woman in a rural Southern community, to describe the cultural and health experiences of female rural Black elders [43]. This woman is portrayed as a deeply religious, hard-working, highly-respected woman. Implications are provided for the health care provider in under-standing this woman as a representative of rural Black elders in the South. Nye draws from the life stories of forty-three Black elders from southwest Virginia to show the important role religion plays in providing continuity in the self-identity of these elders [46].

Groger describes the experiences of thirty-five Black landowners in a rural Piedmont, North Carolina community [30]. She shows that land ownership plays a tremendous role in maintaining family ties and establishing social support networks. Scott and Kivett describe the poor economic situation of widowed rural Black elders in a rural North Carolina county [48]. They discuss the social support systems and service needs of these widowed elders.

Blake discusses traditional beliefs and practices of Black elders on the Sea Islands of South Carolina as they relate to health care, and their reluctance toward the use of Western medicine [40]. Watson examines the use of folk medicine among rural Black elders in six southern states (Alabama, Georgia, Louisiana, Mississippi, South Carolina, and Virginia) [49]. The use of herbal medicine is associated with poor self-rated health, a higher degree of religiosity, and a lower level of formal education.

Several studies have examined health beliefs and behaviors of rural minority elders. Wilson-Ford documents the health behaviors of 407 Black elderly women in Elm City, North Carolina [50]. Her findings suggest heterogeneity in health behaviors, resulting from variations in knowledge of health, health beliefs (such as use of prayer or home remedies), and access to traditional health care. Some behaviors, such as relaxing, praying, and living by religious principles, are highly prevalent, while others such as taking vitamins, using dental floss, and keeping first aid equipment in the home, were very infrequently done. Mathews et al. describe the health beliefs of twenty-eight Black women in eastern North Carolina who presented with advanced breast cancer, showing that beliefs about the causes and effects of medical treatment on cancer deterred these women from seeking care [45]. Arcury discusses the perceived occupational health risks and preventive behaviors of Black farmers in four southeastern states (Kentucky, Mississippi, North Carolina, and Tennessee) [38, 39]. He shows that these older farmers are realistic about the perceived causes of farm accidents, with carelessness considered to be the major problem.

Finally, Griffin describes the experience of abused Black elders in eastern North Carolina [44]. She finds eight themes that can be used in delivering social services. Some of these themes are that poverty is pervasive in situations in which rural Black elders are abused, perpetrators of elder abuse are in dependent relationships with elders, and abuse victims are geographically isolated.

Several trends are apparent in this literature. The first trend is that there are few studies examining the health of rural minority elders and their use of health care services (see Ralston's review of health promotion among rural Black elders [6]). This trend is very troubling as more knowledge of the current health and health services use of minority elders is needed for providing adequate services for these elders.

Second, all of these studies examine older rural African Americans. There are no studies on other rural minority group elders in the southeast United States. We have seen that Blacks are the overwhelmingly predominant minority group in this region. Yet, there is a substantial number of Native American elders in North Carolina and Hispanic elders in Florida. While there are no published studies of these minority groups, at least one study is in progress. This study, funded by the National Institute on Aging and under the direction of Sara A. Quandt, is examining nutrition among African American, Native American, and European American elders in two rural North Carolina counties.

Due to the small number of studies and the wide variety of topics addressed, the literature on rural minority elders in the southeast United States is fragmented.

The few studies are on a wide range of issues. A few topics have received significant attention by specific scholars, such as Blazer et al.'s [11, 14, 15] analyses of mental health, and Groger's analyses of land ownership and exchange [28-31]. But most issues have not been addressed by more than a single investigator, and often only in a single paper. Therefore, there has not been the empirical development that leads to a comprehensive understanding for any topic.

There are also no comprehensive community-based analyses of the multiple aspects of minority elders' lives, such as that which Rowles presents for Whites in a West Virginia community [51-57]. Our knowledge of minority elders' lives is splintered, in many cases it is based on how minority elders differ in some aspect (like depression) from majority elders. The closest such work for minority elders is Groger's series of papers for a North Carolina community [28-31].

Studies of rural minority aging in the southeast United States cover a very limited geographic area. The majority of these studies have been conducted in North Carolina. These include the Piedmont EPESE [e.g., 11], the several studies of Kivett [e.g., 32, 33], the research of Groger [e.g., 28, 30], and several others. Parks does use data collected in Arkansas, Mississippi, and Tennessee [58]. However, Parks' sample is small (170 in each state) and the sample selection procedures are not reported. Further, data analysis and interpretation are incomplete, relying largely on the presentation of many bivariate tables with no tests of statistical significance. Our review of the U.S. Census data shows that there are substantial parts of non-metropolitan Georgia, Alabama, Mississippi, and Louisiana in which a very large part of the elderly population is composed of minority group members. However, almost no research has focused on the minority elderly population in these states.

Finally, a positive aspect of this rural minority aging research literature is that a variety of research methods are being used. While several investigators have used fixed response interview and quantitative analysis approaches [e.g., 14, 33], others have used in-depth, qualitative designs [e.g., 36, 41, 45], and some have used integrated qualitative and quantitative designs [e.g., 31].

SPECIAL CONSIDERATIONS FOR RESEARCH
ON RURAL MINORITY ELDERS

Researchers who plan to investigate the lives and health of rural minority elders must consider a number of important factors in the research endeavor. These include issues of general research design, measurement, data collection, and data analysis.

Research Design Issues

The most basic issue in the design of research on rural minority elderly is the conceptual basis of what is a minority, and the way minority is used in the selection of study participants and in data analysis. In current common usage, individuals are part of a minority group if they are a member of a "race" or "ethnic group" which is different from the majority. In the United States the majority race and ethnicity is currently referred to as White, or European American. When research on minority rural aging is conducted, we need to ask if the research is attempting to understand the influence of "race" (a concept that purports to differentiate people in terms of some set of biological characteristics) on aging or on the life and health of elderly persons. Is the research attempting to understand the influence of "ethnicity" (a concept that differentiates people in terms of some set of cultural characteristics) on aging and on elders? Is the research attempting to understand the influence of "racism" (a concept that addresses the way groups and individuals are denied fair access to the reward system in a society) on aging and on elders? Finally, are minority status, race, or ethnicity being used as a surrogate measure of other factors, such as low income and poverty?

There is a growing literature on the definition and use of the concepts race, racism, ethnicity, and minority. We accept the developing consensus that "race" is not a legitimate scientific concept which measures biological differences [3, 59, 60]. Rather "race" is a social variable that denotes a common socio-political and geographic history among a group of individuals [4]. In the language of the cultural anthropologist, race is a "folk-taxonomy" that members of society use to group themselves. As such, it must only be studied in terms of the beliefs of those individuals, rather than as a means of biological grouping. Ethnicity is a cultural variable that most importantly denotes a common set of beliefs and behaviors, as well as a common history and geographic origin. Individuals who share an ethnicity see themselves as belonging to a group; they are Italian Americans, or Mexicans, or Lumbee, or Haitian. However, membership or identification with an ethnic group may change over the lifetime of an individual, or from generation to generation within a family. LaVeist differentiates two types of racism, structural (or institutional) racism, which is a policy that is injurious to a group, and individual racism, which is the application of influences with personal prejudice [4]. Both types of racism effect the life and health of individuals and may be the focus of study.

LaVeist succinctly explains the need to be explicit in the definition of these concepts in studying minority groups.

> It would be helpful if researchers would make explicit whether they regard race as measuring cultural factors, exposure to racism, other social factors, or biology . . . We must advance this research beyond proxy measures. If race is measuring culture, then we need to find better and more direct ways to measure culture. If race is measuring exposure to racism, we must learn to rigorously measure exposure to racism. And, if one contends that race is biology, then it is incumbent upon them to make explicit what the race differences in biology are [4, p. 26].

Following from this argument of LaVeist (as well as the position of Kaufman and Cooper [3]), minority status and ethnicity should not be used as surrogate measures for other variables. Such variables as educational attainment, income and poverty status, racism, and specific beliefs and behaviors should be specifically measured, rather than using ethnicity or minority status as inexact proxies. Standards of empirical research demand such specific measurement. To use ethnicity or minority status as surrogate measures for individual characteristics is to commit the ecological fallacy.

Related to the definition of race and ethnicity, an additional general design issue for research that intends to examine rural minority elders is the need to consider intra-group variation. Not all rural Black elders, or Native American elders, or Hispanic Origin elders are the same. The members of any one of these groups are not all poor, do not all use alternative health care, nor do they all have the same diseases. As Ralston points out, the direction of research on minority aging is not only on how minority and majority elders differ, but on the variation among minority elders [6]. Only by learning about intra-group variation will we be able to design programs that address the needs of all rural minority elders.

Understanding the importance of ethnic differences, and accurately defining what we mean by ethnic or minority group, becomes even more important with recent changes in requirements of the U.S. Public Health Service for all research grants. These guidelines now require that research and programs receiving financial support from any U.S. Public Health Service agency (the National Institutes of Health, the Centers for Disease Control and Prevention, etc.) include minority group members and women. Projects that do not include minority group members and women among their target populations must strongly justify their exclusion [61, 62].

The historical context in which the minority elderly were born and came of age is another important design issue. Many of the oldest minority elders grew up in the era of Jim Crow and segregation. This historical context continues to have a profound influence on all aspects of the lives of these elders. For example, Groger and Kunkel found that Jim Crow laws which led to

> Black elders' unequal access to landownership [that] had consequences in a number of domains. They were less likely than whites to own their homes; they had considerably lower incomes and derived incomes from fewer sources; and they were less likely to have been born in the community [31, pp. 284-285].

While the next generations of rural minority will not be as affected by the structural racism of Jim Crow, their historical context may well still include the effects of individual racism, as well as the changing population structure (e.g., the increasing diversity of the minority population with the greater immigration and settling out of Hispanic Origin individuals) of the rural communities in which they live.

Qualitative research designs, quantitative research designs, and research that incorporates qualitative as well as quantitative methods into their design are all appropriate for projects that examine the life and health of rural minority elders. Excellent examples of both quantitative [e.g., 9] and qualitative [e.g., 31] studies of rural minority elders are included in our literature review. Each approach has its strengths, and each will provide different insights (see Arcury et al., Chapter 6, pp. 109-126 in this volume for a discussion of qualitative methods in rural aging research).

Finally, those who are considering quantitative research on rural minority elders must consider whether data sets exist that contain the necessary information to address their research problem. LaVeist reviews available data sources for aging research on minority groups [63]. The Public Health Service Task Force on Minority Health Data has cataloged Public Health Service (PHS) data sets with minority data [64].

Measurement Issues

There are two major measurement issues that must be addressed in the design of research examining rural minority elders. The first is determining how individuals are to be assigned to membership in one ethnic group or another. We have already seen that there is no strictly biological basis for assigning minority group or ethnic group membership to an individual. Any number of methods can be used to assign group membership. Each individual can be asked to select a group to which they belong. While this sounds simple enough, how does the researcher handle an individual who has one parent from one group, the other parent from another group, and who states unequivocally that he or she is a member of both groups. Another method for assigning group membership, is to let the groups themselves decide who is a member. In addition to the tautological problem of deciding who in the minority groups will decide if an individual is a member of the group, there are the inevitable problems that will result if the individual and the group differ on the assignment of membership. Finally, the investigator can determine group membership based on some set of predetermined criteria (geographic ancestry, skin color, beliefs, religious affiliation). This has the likely chance of placing an individual in one ethnic group when neither the group nor the individual agree. Overall, our experience is that in the vast number of cases, ethnic group membership will be easily arrived at. Our caution to the investigator is to consider and define the criteria to be used, rather than to assume that everybody knows who is an African American, a Native American, or a European American.

The second important measurement issue is the cultural appropriateness of any scale or instrument the investigator decides to use [e.g., 65, 66]. Many of these instruments have been developed with individuals who are European American and have a middle class lifestyle. Many of these measures have been found to lack validity for minority populations. The National Institutes of Health has recognized this problem, and has funded projects to develop culturally appropriate measures.

Data Collection Issues

Several data collection issues must be considered in primary research on rural minority elders. The first of these is language or dialect. Because some minority elders have only recently migrated to the United States, or they have lived isolated from the majority society, they may speak another language. Examples include Haitians and Cajuns, both of whom speak a Creole French, with the former including recent migrants, and the latter including isolated communities. Even if the minority elders speak English, their dialect may include words and grammatical forms with meanings very different from those used by the college educated researchers. Those investigating Hispanic elders must be aware of dialect differences among individuals with different national origins; for example, dialect differences between individuals of Cuban versus Mexican ancestry. The researcher must therefore learn the language or dialect of the study population, or include individuals on the research team with the appropriate language and translation skills.

Other data collection issues for primary research involve the ethnicity of the investigator, the ethnicity of interviewers, and the age of the interviewers. Should interviewers be matched to the ethnicity and age of the respondent? Our opinion is that such matching is not essential. Good interviewers are able to develop rapport with any respondent. The age, ethnicity, and gender of the interviewer is important only when we consider the interview situation or the topic. We would not use male interviewers to interview older women about such topics as urinary incontinence, sexual activity, or how they maintain personal safety and security, no matter what the ethnic group. Nor should female interviewers attempt to interview older men about such topics. No interviewer, no matter the gender, age, or ethnicity should ever be placed in a dangerous situation. What a dangerous situation is may differ by gender.

On the issue of matching respondent and researcher ethnicity, we concur with Wood and Wan who state,

> Minority researchers may have fewer problems than majority researchers in attempting to conduct studies in a minority community. However, maintenance of scientific objectivity in the face of one's own ethnic loyalty and expectations from the community for support and advocacy can place conflicting demands on the minority researcher . . . the important criteria for conducting effective research in minority aging are methodological expertise in gerontology, a solid interdisciplinary foundation in the content area, and

understanding of the subject population. Sensitivity to ethnic and cultural issues, awareness of one's own ethnocentrism, and respect for cultural differences are more important than the racial background of the researcher [7, p. 51].

We also agree with Wood and Wan that in larger projects that involve a number of investigators and interviewers, the involvement of minority investigators and field staff will improve community acceptance of the research project [7].

Investigators focusing on rural minority elders must be aware of and sensitive to the influence of historical factors while attempting to gain the acceptance of rural, ethnic minorities for participation in research projects. These people have been excluded from most past research and they have often been subjected to ridicule from those projects that have considered them. More importantly, the legacy of the Tuskegee Syphilis Study makes many minority people unwilling to be involved in any research project. Dating from 1932, and finally forced to conclude in 1972, the Tuskegee Syphilis Study examined the natural history of syphilis in 400 rural Black men in Alabama. The purpose of this study was withheld from the participants, and they were not told about antibiotic treatment for the disease when it became available in the 1940s [67-69]. This study has tainted the acceptance of research among minority groups.

Analysis Issues

In addition to being clear in the definition of ethnicity, racism, or race in the selection of study participants, it is also important that these concepts be used appropriately in data analysis. Simply including a dichotomous variable with the values "White" and "non-White" in a multivariate model is not analyzing the effects of ethnicity on the phenomenon being investigated. The investigator must be explicit as to why measures of ethnicity are being included in the analysis, and be sure that the measures used are actually measures of ethnicity, racism, or race.

Equally important in analyses of minority elders is the need to include some measure of wealth. As found in the review of census data, almost half of all minority elders in rural southeastern United States counties have incomes below the poverty level. Analyses which do not adequately measure and include measures of wealth or poverty can never be sure if any results are due to ethnicity or wealth. At the same time, as Groger and Kunkel note, it may never be possible to totally disentangle the effects of culture and socioeconomic status. "Insofar as these inequalities may have elicited culture-specific responses and coping strategies—notably patterns of informal support—it may be futile to attempt to disentangle the interactive effects of culture and of economic status on informal support" [31, p. 28].

Finally, the effects of life course must be factored into any analysis. As we noted in our discussion of historical context, those in difference cohorts, even among the elderly, became adults and aged in different historical periods which will influence the life courses they bring into old age. This point is illustrated by the analysis of Rowles in his discussion of the changing health culture of older Appalachians [57]. Rowles argues that in this population, those who are now old, especially the very old, use alternative medicine and restrict use of conventional health care. This is a result of not having had access to conventional health care when they were younger. Those who are now the young old, and those who will be attaining elder status over the next decade will have lived during a time when conventional health care has been more accessible, even to the rural poor. Therefore, we need to be careful in assuming the characteristics of one cohort of elderly will be the same in future cohorts.

IMPORTANT DIRECTIONS FOR FUTURE RESEARCH

Based on current demographic data, existing research results and our discussion of research design issues, we see several important directions for future research on rural minority elders. The first is the need for comprehensive, community-based studies of rural minority elders that develop detailed, holistic explanations of their lives, health, and use of health care. Such comprehensive analyses are needed so that we can see how the different components of life are patterned for minority elders of diverse ethnic backgrounds. These studies are needed so that we can begin to understand exactly how being rural as opposed to being minority affects the lives and health of rural minority elders. They are also needed to inform the interpretations of results from survey investigations focused on single topics (such as studies of informal support, use of formal services or health beliefs across the Southeast). Finally, comprehensive community-based analyses are needed to delineate the implications of any changes in public policy.

The geographic distribution of studies of the lives and health of rural minority elders must be expanded. The majority of this research has been conducted in North Carolina, yet there are several other states in which the minority elders compose a significant part of the rural elderly population. Minority elders in these other states have had to deal with different histories, laws and policies, and services structures. Research must be conducted with rural minority elders in these other states so that, through comparison, we will be able to differentiate what is minority in rural minority aging from the specific history of a particular state.

Research on rural minority elders must consider changes in the numbers and proportions of different ethnic groups in the region. In particular, elders of different Hispanic ethnicities may increase in rural Southeast counties in the coming decades. This increase is not reflected in the 1990 census data. However, our reconnaissance of rural counties in North Carolina shows a recent settling out of Hispanic migrants. As these individuals age, and as their older relatives come to join them, the number of Hispanic elders will increase.

Research indicates that racism accounts for lower quality medical treatment received by African Americans as compared to European Americans [70]. There is every reason to expect that racism has a negative effect on the medical treatment received by rural minority elders today, as it has in the past. Racism affects the access of rural minority elders to other services, as well as other aspects of their lives. Groger and Kunkel note the effects of Jim Crow laws on home ownership of African American elders [31]. Research is needed that directly examines the effects of racism on all aspects of the lives and health of minority elders.

Direct research on the informal support network of rural minority elders is extremely important. Some analyses report that rural Black elders in the Southeast receive very high levels of support from family as well as neighbors and friends [7]. Other analyses show that informal support is variable among rural Black elders [e.g., 30]. Before programs are developed that assume or expect a universal high level of informal support, research is needed to establish the real support levels and how they may be changing in light of economic and demographic changes that are occurring in all rural communities.

Like informal support, religion and churches are reported to play extremely important roles in the lives of rural minority elders, particularly rural elder Blacks [e.g., 7, 71, 72]. Much more research is needed to substantiate the exact role of organized religion in the lives of rural minority elders, the strength and resilience of church-based bonds, and the limits of religion in the lives of these elders. Research must also differentiate the importance of religious feelings and attitudes among rural minority elders from the roles of organized churches.

Finally, research needs to quantify the prevalence of alternative medicine use among rural minority elders, and test whether there are significant differences in this prevalence when minority elders are compared to majority elders. Several authors argue that due to the historically limited access that minority elders have had to conventional medical care in the rural South (as well as in other areas of the country), this population has maintained the use of traditional and folk medicine [49]. There are several excellent discussions of alternative medicine use among rural minority elders [73]. However, studies have not examined the prevalence of these practices among rural minority elders. Arcury et al. find in a study comparing rural North Carolina African and European American elders in the use of alternative and conventional treatments for arthritis that members of both groups use conventional and alternative treatments [26]. African and European Americans differ in the types of alternative treatments used, and more African Americans use some of the alternative treatments.

DISCUSSION AND CONCLUSIONS

Minority elders comprise a significant part of the rural elderly population across a major part of the southeast United States. Most of these minority elders are African Americans, and a high proportion are poor. Several excellent studies have examined aspects of the lives and health of rural African American elders [e.g., 28-30]. However, given the size, complexity and changes among rural minority elders in this region, our pool of knowledge is extremely shallow.

The design of research focused on rural minority elders must consider a number of special issues. These include realistic definitions of minority group and ethnicity, and consideration of the influence of racism in rural minority aging. Researchers of rural minority elders should be aware of the diversity within this population. The historical context of the lives of rural minority elders must also be considered.

With the importance that minority populations have had to rural Southern society, it is particularly shocking how little research-based knowledge we have of rural minority aging in this region. The lack of comprehensive community-based studies of rural minority elders particularly needs to be addressed. With so much of the rural minority aging research limited to North Carolina, it is also imperative that future research projects be conducted in other parts of the region with large minority elderly populations.

The current interest in issues facing minority groups, and the effects of being a minority group member on health status that results from the structural impediments placed on minority individuals by society is indeed a positive movement. Research on minority aging must be an important part of this trend if we are to ensure successful aging for all members of our society.

REFERENCES

1. M. S. Harper (ed.), *Minority Aging: Essential Curricula Content for Selected Health and Allied Health Professions,* Health Resources and Services Administration, Department of Health and Human Services, DHHS Publication No. HRS (P-DV-90-4), U.S. Government Printing Office, Washington, D.C., 1990.
2. M. Hewitt, Defining "Rural" Areas: Impact on Health Policy and Research, in *Health in Rural North America: The Geography of Health Care Services and Delivery,* W. M. Gesler and T. C. Ricketts (eds.), Rutgers University Press, New Brunswick, New Jersey, 1992.
3. J. S. Kaufman and R. S. Cooper, In Search of the Hypothesis, *Public Health Reports, 110,* pp. 662-666, 1995.
4. T. A. LaVeist, Why We Should Continue to Study Race . . . But Do a Better Job: An Essay on Race, Racism and Health, *Ethnicity & Disease, 6,* pp. 21-29, 1996.
5. R. C. Wimberly, L. V. Morris, and D. C. Bachtel, The Southern Rural Black Belt and Political Initiatives, in *Rural Development and A Changing USDA,* Tuskegee University, Tuskegee, Alabama, 1994.
6. P. A. Ralston, Health Promotion for Rural Black Elderly: A Comprehensive Review, *Journal of Gerontological Social Work, 20,* pp. 53-78, 1983.

7. J. B. Wood and T. T. H. Wan, Ethnicity and Minority Issues in Family Caregiving to Rural Black Elders, in *Ethnic Elderly and Long-Term Care,* Charles M. Barresi and D. E. Stull (eds.), Springer, New York, pp. 39-56, 1993.

8. V. R. Kivett, Informal Supports Among Older Rural Minorities, in *Aging in Rural America,* C. N. Bull (ed.), Sage, Newbury Park, California, 1993.

9. J. C. Hays, G. G. Fillenbaum, D. T. Gold, M. C. Shanley, and D. G. Blazer, Black-White and Urban-Rural Differences in Stability of Household Composition Among Elderly Persons, *Journal of Gerontology: Social Sciences, 50B,* pp. S301-S311, 1995.

10. J. D. Beck, G. G. Koch, R. G. Rozier, and G. E. Tudor, Prevalence and Risk Indicators for Periodontal Attachment Loss in a Population of Older Community-Dwelling Blacks and Whites, *Journal of Periodontology, 61,* pp. 521-528, 1990.

11. D. Blazer, L. K. George, R. Landerman, M. Pennybacker, M. L. Melville, M. Woodbury, K. G. Manton, K. Jordan, and B. Locke, Psychiatric Disorders: A Rural/Urban Comparison, *Archives of General Psychiatry, 42,* pp. 651-658, 1985.

12. D. A. Revicki and J. P. Mitchell, Strain, Social Support, and Mental Health in Rural Elderly Individuals, *Journal of Gerontology: Social Sciences, 45*:6, pp. S267-S274, 1990.

13. J. Cornoni-Huntley, D. G. Blazer, M. E. Lafferty, D. F. Everett, D. B. Brock, and M. E. Fanner, *Established Populations for Epidemiologic Studies of the Elderly,* Vol. II, Resource Data Book, NIH Pub. No. 90-495, National Institutes of Health, Washington, D.C., 1990.

14. D. Blazer, B. A. Crowell, Jr., and L. K. George, Alcohol Abuse and Dependence in the Rural South, *Archives of General Psychiatry, 44,* pp. 736-740, 1987.

15. D. Blazer, B. Burchett, C. Service, and L. K. George, The Association of Age and Depression Among the Elderly: An Epidemiologic Exploration, *Journal of Gerontology: Medical Sciences, 46,* pp. M210-215, 1991.

16. G. G. Fillenbaum, D. C. Hughes, A. Heyman, L. K. George, and D. G. Blazer, Relationship of Health and Demographic Characteristics to Mini-Mental State Examination Score Among Community Residents, *Psychological Medicine, 18,* pp. 719-726, 1988.

17. G. G. Fillenbaum, R. D. Horner, J. T. Hanlon, L. R. Landerman, D. V. Dawson, and H. J. Cohen, Factors Predicting Change in Prescription and Nonprescription Drug Use in a Community-Residing Black and White Elderly Population, *Journal of Clinical Epidemiology, 49*:5, pp. 587-593, 1996.

18. M. J. Moritz, A. M. Ostfeld, D. Blazer, D. Curb, J. O. Taylor, and R. B. Wallace, The Health Burden of Diabetes for the Elderly in Four Communities, *Public Health Reports, 109,* pp. 782-790, 1994.

19. M. Swartz, R. Landerman, L. K. George, M. L. Melville, D. Blazer, and K. Smith, Benzodiazepine Anti-Anxiety Agents: Prevalence and Correlates of Use in a Southern Community, *American Journal of Public Health, 81,* pp. 592-596, 1991.

20. A. N. Galanos, R. P. Strauss, and C. F. Pieper, Sociodemographic Correlates of Health Beliefs among Black and White Community Dwelling Elderly Individuals, *International Journal of Aging and Human Development, 38,* pp. 339-350, 1994.

21. M. A. Musick, Religion and Subjective Health Among Black and White Elders, *Journal of Health and Social Behavior, 37,* pp. 221-237, 1996.

22. J. E. Keil and D. E. Saunders, Jr., Urban and Rural Differences in Cardiovascular Disease in Blacks, *Cardiovascular Clinics, 21*:3, pp. 17-28, 1991.
23. J. Jackson and M. Ball, A Comparison of Rural and Urban Georgia Aged Negroes, *Journal of the Association of Social Science Teachers, 12*, pp. 30-37, 1966.
24. J. J. Jackson, Aged Negroes: Their Cultural Departures from Statistical Stereotypes and Rural-Urban Differences, *Gerontologist, 10*, pp. 140-145, 1970.
25. G. M. Clayton, W. N. Dudley, W. D. Patterson, L. A. Lawhorn, L. W. Poon, M. A. Johnson, and P. Martin, The Influence of Rural/Urban Residence on Health in the Oldest-Old, *International Journal of Aging and Human Development, 38*, pp. 65-89, 1994.
26. T. A. Arcury, S. L. Bernard, J. M. Jordan, and H. L. Cook, Gender and Ethnic Differences in Alternative and Conventional Remedies Use Among Community Dwelling Rural Adults with Arthritis, *Arthritis Care and Research, 9*, pp. 384-390, 1996.
27. T. Bekhuis, H. Cook, K. Holt, J. Scott-Lennox, R. Lennox, L. Price, and J. G. Fryer, Ethnicity, Church Affiliation and Beliefs About the Causal Agents of Health: A Comparative Study Employing a Multivariate Analysis of Covariance, *Health Education Research, 10*, pp. 73-82, 1995.
28. B. L. Groger, Growing Old With or Without It: The Meaning of Land in a Southern Rural Community, *Research on Aging, 5*, pp. 511-526, 1993.
29. B. L. Groger, The Meaning of Land in a Southern Rural Community: Differences between Blacks and Whites, in *Farm Work and Field Work: American Agriculture in Anthropological Perspective*, M. Chibnik (ed.), Cornell University Press, Ithaca, New York, 1987.
30. L. Groger, Tied to Each Other Through Ties to the Land: Informal Support of Black Elders in a Southern U.S. Community, *Journal of Cross-Cultural Gerontology, 7*, pp. 205-220, 1992.
31. L. Groger and S. Kunkel, Aging and Exchange: Differences Between Black and White Elders, *Journal of Cross-Cultural Gerontology, 10*, pp. 269-287, 1995.
32. V. R. Kivett, The Importance of Race to the Life Situation of Rural Elderly, *Black Scholar, 13*:1, pp. 13-20, 1982.
33. V. R. Kivett, Centrality of the Grandfather Role Among Older Rural Black and White Men, *Journal of Gerontology: Social Sciences, 46*, pp. S250-258, 1991.
34. C. H. Krishef and M. L. Yoelin, Differential use of Informal and Formal Helping Networks among Rural Elderly Black and White Floridians, *The Journal of Gerontological Social Work, 3*, pp. 45-59, 1981.
35. R. M. Learner and V. R. Kivett, Discriminators of Perceived Dietary Adequacy Among the Rural Elderly, *Journal of the American Dietetic Association, 78*, pp. 330-337, 1981.
36. A. Yearwood and P. Dressel, Interracial Dynamics in a Southern Rural Senior Center, *The Gerontologist, 23*:5, pp. 512-517, 1983.
37. J. B. Wood and I. A. Parham, Coping with Perceived Burden: Ethnic and Cultural Issues in Alzheimer's Family Caregiving, *Journal of Applied Gerontology, 9*, pp. 325-339, 1990.
38. T. A. Arcury, Risk Perception of Occupational Hazards Among Black Farmers in the Southeastern United States, *Journal of Rural Health, 11*:4, pp. 240-250, 1995.

39. T. A. Arcury, Occupational Injury Prevention Knowledge and Behavior of African-American Farmers, *Human Organization, 56,* pp. 167-173, 1997.
40. J. H. Blake, "Doctor Can't Do Me No Good": Social Concomitants of Health Care Attitudes and Practices Among Elderly Blacks in Isolated Rural Populations, in *Black Folk Medicine: The Therapeutic Significance of Faith and Trust,* W. H. Watson (ed.), Transaction Books, New Brunswick, New Jersey, 1984.
41. I. Carlton-LaNey, Elderly Black Farm Women: A Population at Risk, *Social Work, 37:*3, pp. 517-523, 1992.
42. I. Carlton-LaNey, The Last Quilting Bee, *Generations, 17:*2, pp. 55-58, Spring/ Summer 1993.
43. A. Dula, The Life and Death of Miss Mildred: An Elderly Black Woman, *Clinics in Geriatric Medicine, 10:*3, pp. 419-430, 1994.
44. L. W. Griffin, Elder Maltreatment among Rural African-Americans, *Journal of Elder Abuse & Neglect, 6:*1, pp. 1-27, 1994.
45. H. F. Mathews, D. R. Lanin, and J. P. Mitchell, Coming to Terms with Advanced Breast Cancer: Black Women's Narratives from Eastern North Carolina, *Social Science and Medicine, 38,* pp. 789-800, 1994.
46. W. P. Nye, Amazing Grace: Religion and Identity Among Elderly Black Individuals, *International Journal of Aging and Human Development, 36,* pp. 103-114, 1993.
47. E. Salber, *Don't Send Me Flowers When I'm Dead: Voices of Rural Elderly,* Duke University Press, Durham, North Carolina, 1983.
48. J. P. Scott and V. R. Kivett, The Widowed Black, Older Adult in the Rural South: Implications for Policy, *Family Relations, 29,* pp. 83-90, 1980.
49. W. H. Watson, Folk Medicine and Older Blacks in the Southern United States, in *Black Folk Medicine: The Therapeutic Significance of Faith and Trust,* W. H. Watson (ed.), Transaction Books, New Brunswick, New Jersey, 1984.
50. V. Wilson-Ford, Health-Protective Behavior of Rural Black Elderly Women, *Health and Social Work, 17,* pp. 28-36, 1992.
51. G. D. Rowles, Growing Old 'Inside': Aging and Attachment to Place in an Appalachian Community, in *Transitions of Aging,* N. Datan and N. Lohmann (eds.), Academic Press, New York, 1980.
52. G. D. Rowles, The Surveillance Zone as Meaningful Space for the Aged, *The Gerontologist, 21:*3, pp. 304-311, 1981.
53. G. D. Rowles, Observations from Appalachia, *Journal of Environmental Psychology, 3,* pp. 299-313, 1983.
54. G. D. Rowles, Between Worlds: A Relocation Dilemma for the Appalachian Elderly, *International Journal of Aging and Human Development, 17:*4, pp. 301-314, 1983.
55. G. D. Rowles, Geographical Dimensions of Social Support in Rural Appalachia, in *Aging and Milieu: Environmental Perspectives on Growing Old,* G. D. Rowles and R. J. Ohta (eds.), Academic Press, New York, 1983.
56. G. D. Rowles, The Rural Elderly and the Church, *Journal of Religion and Aging, 22,* pp. 79-98, 1986.
57. G. D. Rowles, Changing Health Culture in Rural Appalachia: Implications for Serving the Elderly, *Journal of Aging Studies, 5,* pp. 375-389, 1991.
58. A. G. Parks, *Black Elderly in Rural America: A Comprehensive Study,* Wyndham Hall Press, Bristol, Indiana, 1988.

59. A. H. Goodman, The Problematics of Race in Contemporary Biological Anthropology, in *Biological Anthropology: The State of the Science,* N. T. Boaz and L. D. Wolfe (eds.), International Institute of Human Evolutionary Research, Bend, Oregon, 1995.
60. A. A. Herman, Toward a Conceptualization of Race in Epidemiologic Research, *Ethnicity & Disease, 6,* pp. 7-20, 1996.
61. National Institutes of Health, *Outreach Notebook for the NIH Guidelines on Inclusion of Women and Minorities as Subjects in Clinical Research,* National Institutes of Health, 1994.
62. National Institutes of Health, NIH Guidelines on the Inclusion of Women and Minorities as Subjects in Clinical Research, *NIH Guide for Grants and Contracts, 23*:11, 1994.
63. T. A. LaVeist, Data Sources for Aging Research on Racial and Ethnic Groups, *The Gerontologist, 35,* pp. 328-339, 1995.
64. Public Health Service Task Force on Minority Health Data, *Directory of Minority Health Data Resources of the Public Health Service,* Office of Minority Health, Public Health Service, U.S. Department of Health and Human Services, 1992.
65. M. Dignon, P. Sharp, K. Blinson, R. Michielutte, J. Konen, R. Bell, and C. Lane, Development of a Cervical Cancer Education Program for Native American Women in North Carolina, *Journal of Cancer Education, 9,* pp. 235-242, 1994.
66. R. B. Warnecke, C. Estwing Ferrans, T. P. Johnson, G. Chapa-Resendez, D. P. O'Rourke, N. Chavez, S. Dudas, E. D. Smith, L. Martinex Schallmoser, R. P. Hand, and T. Lad, Measuring Quality of Life in Culturally Diverse Populations, *Journal of the National Cancer Institute Monographs, 20,* pp. 29-38, 1996.
67. W. J. Curran, The Tuskegee Syphilis Study, *The New England Journal of Medicine, 289,* pp. 730-731, 1973.
68. R. H. Kampmeier, Final Report on the "Tuskegee Syphilis Study," *Southern Medical Journal, 67,* pp. 1349-1353, 1974.
69. H. Edgar, Outside the Community, *Hastings Center Report, 22*:6, pp. 32-35, 1992.
70. M. E. Gornick, P. W. Eggers, T. W. Relly, R. M. Mentnech, L. K. Fitterman, L. E. Kucken, and B. C. Vladeck, Effects of Race and Income on Mortality and Use of Services Among Medicare Beneficiaries, *The New England Journal of Medicine, 335,* pp. 791-799, 1996.
71. J. W. Hatch and K. A. Lovelace, Involving the Southern Rural Church and Students of the Health Professions in Health Education, *Public Health Reports, 95,* pp. 23-25, 1980.
72. National Institutes of Health, *Churches as an Avenue to High Blood Pressure Control,* NIH Publication No. 92-2725, U.S. Department of Health and Human Services, Public Health Service, Washington, D.C., 1992.
73. J. Kirkland, H. F. Mathews, C. W. Sullivan III, and K. Baldwin (eds.), *Herbal and Magical Medicine: Traditional Healing Today,* Duke University Press, Durham, North Carolina, 1992.

CHAPTER
9

Trajectories of Health in Aging Populations

Elizabeth C. Clipp, Glen H. Elder, Jr., Linda K. George,
and Carl F. Pieper

This chapter examines several methodological approaches to monitoring temporal patterns of health in later life that may be applied to rural populations. Relatively traditional approaches to longitudinal investigation (e.g., the establishment of age norms) are compared to recent analytical developments (e.g., hierarchial linear modeling) in both concept and empirical patterns. Beyond methodological description and illustration, however, lies an attempt to impart a "way of thinking" about health processes, as dynamic sequences of stability and change, conditioned by elements of person and context. To the extent that patterns of health can be captured both within and between older individuals in rural populations, planners and providers gain precision in targeting health services to those in need.

The notion of health as a dynamic process is central to clinical practice. Clinicians are trained to think longitudinally (e.g., the "history" component of the history and physical examination) and typically follow their patients over time with attention to symptom or functional changes in relation to baseline records. As such, practitioners can easily identify patients with relatively stable health histories. Some of these persons, endowed with good physical or mental constitution, rarely, if ever seek medical care. Another smaller group of persons are ill, or live with impairments associated with chronic disease through much of their lives. Still other lives are characterized more by changes in health states, the severity of which correspond to illness type, severity, extent of recovery, and nature of residual impairment. For some, health transitions of this kind are rare as in the case of a healthy individual who experiences a major coronary event with recovery in midlife. In other instances, more frequent or sporadic declines correspond to multiple acute illnesses or exacerbations of chronic problems. Such life course patterns of health unfold as a unique blending of genetics and life experience.

However it is difficult to relate such clinical observations, rich in heterogeneity, to epidemiologic and population-based health research. There are several reasons for this. First, population-based research reveals little of the whole person, owing to its emphasis on indicators such as general and specific mortality rates, disability levels, life expectancy, and contacts with the health care system. Similarly, the focus in such research tends to be on patterns of group change that may or may not be relevant at the individual level. And finally, population-based research focuses on disease states rather than on natural histories of diseases or illness courses. Moreover, individuals with similar clinical profiles may have entirely different long-term outcomes.

In this chapter we focus on the concept of "health trajectory" as part of a strategy that will allow us to bring population-based health statistics together with the richness and diversity of clinical patterns. We begin by examining relevant literature on health assessment over the lifespan to consider the more traditional ways that patterns of temporal health have been captured. When possible, we focus on studies with application to rural populations. However, longitudinal studies of rural elderly are notably rare. One exception is the Established Populations for Epidemiological Studies of the Elderly (EPESE) which will be discussed later in this chapter.

The literature review is followed by a discussion of the concept of trajectory as it has emerged from life course studies [1-3] and in our own empirical work [4-7]. We then compare and contrast two approaches for delineating trajectories: a typological or "person-centered" approach which requires clinical judgment by trained raters, and hierarchical linear models (HLM), a state-of-the-art approach for modeling the level and rate of within-individual change over time.

Finally, we describe a new project which uses data from the Established Populations for Epidemiologic Studies of the Elderly (EPESE) and combines both approaches, typological and HLM, to examine patterns of health and health service use in a longitudinal sample of rural and urban elderly.

TRADITIONAL APPROACHES TO LONGITUDINAL HEALTH ASSESSMENT

Longitudinal studies offer the greatest promise for obtaining reasonably conclusive answers to questions regarding temporal health processes. Multiple times of measurement are essential for examining the relationship between physiological and behavioral characteristics and the subsequent development of illness and disability or good health and longevity. Most of the larger, well-known longitudinal studies which emphasize health assessment take an "age norm" approach to data organization, an approach that reveals little of the natural history of illness and function *within* individuals or subgroups of individuals over time.

An age norm approach focuses on the establishment of age norms in order to describe normal, healthy aging from a multidisciplinary perspective. Examples of this approach include the Baltimore Longitudinal Study of Aging [8], the Duke Longitudinal Studies [9], the Boston Normative Aging Study [10], and the Institute of Human Development Studies [11]. Although none of these studies has focused on rural populations, these studies offer significant diversity in design, subject selection, and methods of health assessment.

This diversity is a source of both strength and weakness. The strength lies in the broad range of indicators used to measure physical and emotional health, but this range provides an incomplete portrait of health at the group level. Individuals are fragmented into age-related health processes such as lung function, cognitive performance, personality dimensions, reaction time and serial changes in cholesterol levels. From this perspective, health may be conceptualized as a number of interrelated biopsychosocial processes, but analytically the person is broken into disparate variables, each of which typically has a course. Data are organized by successive waves and are usually analyzed by plotting group means and percentages over time or by correlating earlier health states with later ones.

A second approach to longitudinal health assessment, which may be termed a "typological" or "health pattern" approach [4], moves away from reducing health to component processes and toward constructing broad within-individual patterns of health-related processes and behavior. Although examples of pattern approach studies among rural populations are lacking, this perspective may be appreciated in the Bonn Longitudinal Study of Aging [12, 13] whose investigators aimed to establish the relevance of differential gerontology as a science of aging patterns; the Grant Study which focuses on the components of adaptation and emotional health [14]; and the Berlin Aging Study [15] with theoretical orientations that include differential aging, continuity versus discontinuity of aging, and range and limits of plasticity and reserve capacity.

Verbrugge's research, more than most individual programs in the last decade, uniquely captures the reality of health dynamics. Her creative approaches to issues of gender, aging, institutionalization, disability, morbidity, mortality, longevity, and disablement [16-25] exemplify the potential of thinking in terms of health trajectories. Using fine-grained health diary data on 165 older persons, she and Balaban [26] plotted individual patterns of disability and activity up to two years after hospitalization among persons with chronic illness. Verbrugge recently proposed a move toward measurement of "transition rates" from one state of disability to another [25, 27]. Once captured, disability dynamics will tell us much about processes of functional loss and gain.

Verbrugge's perspective offers numerous examples of *transition* analysis with emphasis on the timing and duration of specific health events. By contrast, *trajectory* analysis, described more fully in the next section, focuses on the dynamic sequence of such transitions over the life course. Abbott and Hrycak contend that there is no standard method for analyzing whole sequences of events, such as a trajectory, but methods for examining transitions at one point in time are widespread [28].

In summary, there are basically two approaches to longitudinal health assessment. The first, "age norm approach," focuses on specific aspects of physical or emotional health (illness categories, diagnoses, bodily functions) and seeks to establish norms for various functions across age cohorts. The second approach, "health pattern" or "typological" involves the conceptualization and description of individual patterns such as coping, functional impairment, or disability. Longitudinal studies of aging tend to take an age norm approach (between-individual) or a pattern approach (within-individual) to health assessment. The concept of health trajectory is a lineal descendant of the pattern approach in the sense that typologies are specified. However, trajectories gain precision and are distinguished by a consideration of event *sequences,* providing a relatively new, and perhaps more fruitful way of thinking, about health dynamics.

TRAJECTORIES OF THE LIFE COURSE AND HEALTH

Life course theory maintains that experiences earlier in life shape the long-term as well as the short-term paths our lives will follow. Efforts to capture such dynamics have led to a focus on individual patterning over time through analysis of trajectories and transitions [1-3]. Trajectories represent the long view of human functioning and thus depict pathways defined by aging processes. By contrast, transitions are relatively short-term periods of change. In this sense, health transitions represent specific health events or periods of change such as episodes of acute illness, accidents, or changes in function. Such health transitions are embedded in overall health trajectories and impart to them distinctive form and meaning.

Using a trajectory approach, for example, it is possible to focus on a sample of aging men, in their mid-sixties at Time 1, with an identified chronic disease such as Stage B prostate cancer and, controlling for comorbidities and other influences, follow the natural history of their functioning over a ten-year period. Some men will decline abruptly; others more slowly. Some will die and others will remain stable or improve. What factors account for these various trajectories?

These and similar questions were raised when the first and second authors of this chapter joined others in a recasting of the Lewis Terman archive at Stanford University, the oldest, ongoing longitudinal study in the world, to achieve valid and reliable measures of physical and emotional health. The Terman study began in 1922 with approximately 1,500 school children who were selected for their high IQs—greater than 134. Their birth years ranged from 1903 through 1920. Follow-ups were conducted in 1928, 1936, and every five years up to 1960. After 1960, the next wave of follow-ups began in 1972 and continued in 1977, 1982, and 1986. The data are available through the Inter-University Consortium for Political and Social Research [30-34].

Because work with the Terman data was a first approach to trajectory delineation, efforts focused on the subsample of Terman men ($N = 857$) for whom detailed physical and emotional health codes had been obtained from 1940 to 1986, a time frame that began when the men were approximately thirty-five years old and extended into their seventies and early eighties. Although the Terman data are not amenable to the study of rural health issues, the methodology can readily be used in other longitudinal studies that feature rural/non-rural populations such as the EPESE data. Therefore, some detail follows on the process of recasting the Terman archive for purposes of more generally explicating a trajectory approach.

For many years the Terman archive was reputed to have "inadequate" health data. In reality, however, this assessment applied only to the existing codes which provide self-rated health at one point in time. In many other ways, aspects of the mens' health were well-described across time, from about 1940 into the 1980s, especially when the men were asked to describe ways in which their health had changed from one survey to the next (see [35] for method results). Using these original surveys, new codes were developed (inter-rater reliability typically exceeded .90) for state, transition, and trajectory measures of emotional and physical health including acute and chronic disease categories, postwar illnesses and injuries, number of contacts with the health care system, mortality data, and patterns of ulcer disease, generalized anxiety, depression, suicide, and alcoholism.

Based on the new codes, a model of physical and emotional health trajectories was introduced, spanning forty-five years of adult life on the 857 Terman men [4]. The mode, shown in Figure 1, is based on the assumption that physical and emotional health are separate but interrelated processes characterized by periods of stability and change over the life course. Initially, qualitative data analysis was used to identify and describe health patterns that characterized most individuals; quantitative analysis enabled differentiation of health trajectories by individual and medical characteristics.

As depicted in Figure 1, results of this work included the identification of five physical and six emotional health profiles. Individuals in the *Constant Good Health* category consistently received "good" or "excellent" physical health ratings at each survey and during intervals between surveys. In terms of emotional health, these men typically describe problems as challenges and consistently report being happy and content with life. If sudden death occurred as in a plane crash or fatal heart attack with no prior symptoms, the individual is still coded as constant good health (i.e., morbidity rather than mortality is coded). On

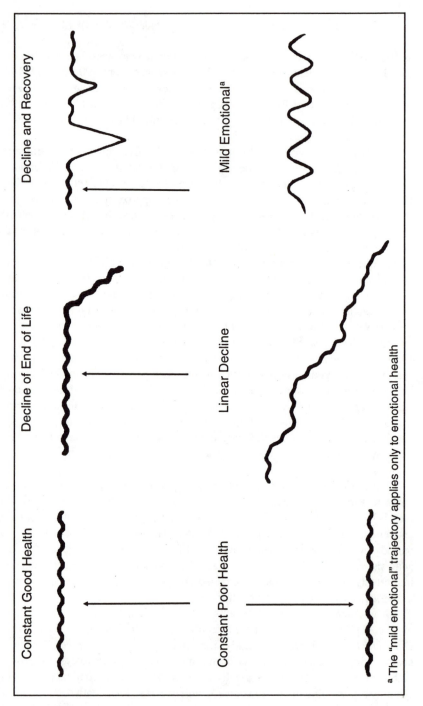

Constant Good Health

Decline of End of Life

Decline and Recovery

Constant Poor Health

Linear Decline

Mild Emotional[a]

[a] The "mild emotional" trajectory applies only to emotional health

Figure 1. Physical and emotional health trajectories.

the other hand, *Constant Poor Health* became a category that described individuals whose health was coded as "fair" or "poor" at each survey and across intervals between surveys. The majority of individuals with this trajectory had histories of chronic, disabling physical or emotional illness. These persons may "perk up" for short periods, but the overall level of health is stable and low.

Three trajectories characterized by decline were identified. Individuals with *Decline at End of Life* experienced relatively uneventful health histories followed by their first major health event, physical or emotional, from which they never fully recovered. This trajectory may have ended with death or the 1986 survey, depending on which occurred first. By contrast, individuals with *Decline and Recovery* experienced one or more significant physical or emotional health problems with evidence of recovery. These declines may or may not have been related but, after each, there was evidence of return to baseline. The last decline group was termed *Linear Decline* because members demonstrated marked or subtle physical or emotional health decline over the majority of their adult life. Slight periods of recovery may have been noted, but the overall trend for these persons was down.

The final category, *Mild Emotional,* applies only to emotional health and describes individuals who, on multiple surveys, report or are described by others as having mild emotional problems without evidence of treatment. Although these individuals continue to function in family and work roles, it is clear from their case files that mild emotional problems are a continual source of distress.

Regarding physical health, most of the Terman men were equally likely to demonstrate any one of the patterns. There was much less variation, however, across patterns of emotional health—most men enjoyed high levels of well-being across their adult lives. This contrast suggests a randomness to physical infirmity, especially among members of this cohort who came of age prior to the advent of health promotion and risk prevention. Their high levels of emotional health were perhaps a benefit of their relatively privileged backgrounds (the Terman sample is biased because of selection on high IQ in childhood) and greater opportunities.

Based on characteristic sequelae of various chronic conditions, the mens' major areas of physical impairment (e.g., cardiovascular disease, cancer, stroke) were examined in relation to the trajectories. This analysis provided support for the conceptual validity for the model. For example, men with cancer tended to have physical trajectories characterized by decline at the end of life. Trajectories of men with histories of stroke were best described as decline and recovery or partial recovery.

An interest among some members of our group regarding the effects of military experience in later life [36-39] led to an analysis of the trajectories by veteran status. Unfortunately, cell sizes across various trajectories were too small for analyses of specific types. However, we were able to get some indication of physical health differences between veterans and nonveterans by collapsing the six physical health trajectories into two [6]. The "positive trajectory" category included men with trajectories of constant good health, decline and recovery, and decline at the end of life associated with age-related changes (e.g., arthritis, sensory decline). The "negative trajectory" category included men whose health trajectories were characterized by sporadic illness, linear decline, constant poor health, and decline at the end of life associated with marked disease (e.g., heart disease, cancer).

By thinking in terms of positive versus negative health profiles, we examined the life stage principle which suggests that the impact of a historical event on the life course of a cohort reflects the stage at which the change or transition was experienced [2]. Specifically, it was hypothesized that the late mobilized men, over the age of thirty-two years at entry, were at greatest risk of a disrupted life course and subsequent health impairment.

This hypothesis was supported and the less favorable health outcome was attributed to the older veterans' experience of social disruption and dislocation during the war years and in the postwar transition. Social disruption most likely placed veterans at risk of physical illness through negative affective and physiological states (e.g., feelings of loss of control) over an unspecified period of time [40]. It is also possible that older entrants may have been more likely to have experienced a variety of later-life disruptions such as retirement, bereavement, and loss of social support, which accounted in part for their relatively worse health. However tentative, the implications of this work suggest the potential of a trajectory approach.

The method by which a trajectory approach could be applied to questions of rural aging would begin by locating appropriate longitudinal data sets and examining basic comparisons of health trajectories among rural and non-rural populations. Although studies of this type are lacking, the potential for trajectory analysis exists with data sets such as the Piedmont Health Survey in which nearly half the community-dwelling sample ($N = 3921$) is rural and over-sampled for elderly respondents. Controlled baseline comparisons between rural and non-rural respondents revealed, for example, that major depressive disorders are twice as frequent among non-rural dwellers [41]. Would trajectories of depression over time with identical controls suggest the same differential? Longitudinal patterns of depression would greatly enhance our understanding of the natural course of this illness among rural and non-rural populations.

In the next section we discuss the trajectory approach currently being used with the EPESE population in terms of both typology identification and hierarchical linear models with emphasis on applications in longitudinal research on aging populations.

MEASUREMENT ISSUES IN TRAJECTORY RESEARCH

One of the most appealing features of trajectories is that they capture an intermediate (between-individual and group) level of complexity—an issue that merits at least brief attention. There are three types of chance—group level, between-individual (based on correlational analysis), and within-individual (hierarchical linear models—HLM). The types of statistical procedures traditionally used to model change over time are designed to characterize group change (e.g., repeated measures MANOVA, standard time series regression). Unfortunately, use of such techniques ignores within-individual change [e.g., 42].

As early as the mid-1940s, investigators recognized that aggregate statistics often told a story that did not fit the experiences of sample members. For example, Kohler studied performance in a simple learning task [43]. Typically, subjects in his study exhibited the following trajectory: an initial period of random performance, followed by insight into the problem, followed by a steady stream of high performance. At the individual level, then, performance curves were jagged at first, increased sharply at the time of insight, and then smoothed off with perfect or near perfect performances. The aggregate curve, however, indicated a smooth progression because subjects differed in the time needed to gain insight into the learning task. Similar problems were reported by Baloff and Becker, leading to their article on the futility of aggregating individual learning curves [44]. As Flaum et al. recently noted in a study of the course of schizophrenia, traditional statistical techniques "treat individual differences in growth curves as noise rather than as features of interest" [45, p. 486].

As described below, there are statistical techniques designed to capture individual patterns of change and stability. The problem with total reliance on such techniques is that it is nearly impossible to summarize results in a parsimonious manner. For example, if we had no choice but to plot a separate growth curve for each of the Terman men, for example, we would have more than 850 curves to analyze. What is needed is a way to parsimoniously report results at an intermediate level of complexity, a higher level of aggregation than the individual case, *without* losing the rich heterogeneity of individual patterns.

Trajectories offer a potential mechanism for meeting this goal. Two attractive, yet conceptually and analytically distinct approaches to ascertaining health trajectories in aging populations, include the *typology approach,* which was discussed earlier with reference to the Terman sample, and *Hierarchical Linear Models Approach* (HLM) (see Figure 2). The goal of the typology approach is to use reliable clinical judgments to identify a set of trajectories within an identified health domain such as cognitive functioning or depression—a discrete number of categories that adequately characterizes patterns of change and stability over time. As noted below, appropriate statistical techniques (e.g., cluster analysis, multiple discriminant analysis, logistic regression) can then be used to assess the degree to which identified trajectories are related to, predicted by, or predict other fixed or time-varying factors of interest.

The second approach, HLM, generates a trajectory for each individual and, instead of identifying groups, focuses in usual statistical fashion on issues of central tendency and dispersion. Relative to traditional, group-based statistical

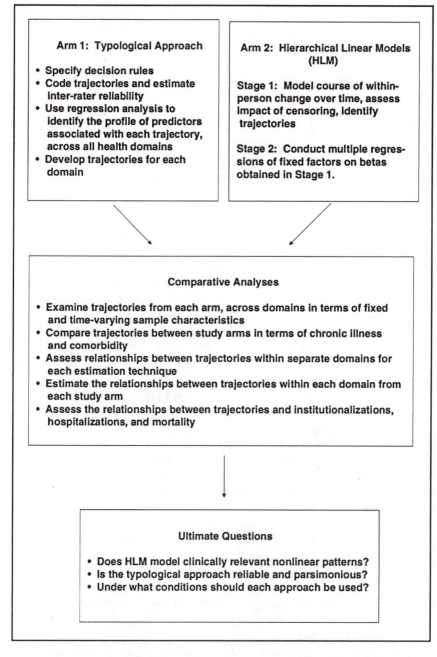

Figure 2. Health Trajectory Project: Study Arms and Process.
Domains: Perceived Health, Functional Health, Cognitive Status, Depression.

procedures, Hierarchical Linear Models have advantages beyond the ability to model individual change. First, using HLMs, estimation in the presence of missing data is possible and measurement at varying time intervals is not problematic. Second, unlike repeated measures models where compound symmetry is assumed, these models allow the incorporation of different and possibly more appropriate error structures. Essentially, HLM models estimate the typical level and the typical rate of within-individual change in behavior or health in a population [see 46 for example]. In addition to the term "HLM," such models have been described as multilevel models or mixed effects models [47].

A recent study by Crystal and Sambamoothi illustrates the advantage HLM (multilevel models) demonstrates over traditional analytic approaches (e.g., single-level models) in describing the natural history of functional status among persons with symptomatic HIV disease [48]. Results from HLM indicated a significant month-to-month worsening of functional status which was masked by between-person variation in single-level models. HLM indicated that although impairment increased over the disease course, it followed a variable and episodic course rather than a consistent decline.

In the next section we describe our current work that systematically compares the methods (trajectory typologies vs. HLM) using a large regional sample of aging men in rural and urban North Carolina. We do so on substantive grounds and in terms of the costs and benefits of each method to health and health services research.

HEALTH TRAJECTORIES AMONG OLDER MEN: A STUDY IN PROGRESS

Based on earlier experience in recasting the Terman archive to obtain health trajectories, we approached the current project with several specific questions. What are the major trajectories of health that characterize the lives of most aging men? What personal and social factors, chronic diseases and serious life events, such as military experience, distinguish these patterns? To what extent do health trajectories differ for African Americans and Whites, for rural and urban populations, for veterans and nonveterans? To answer these questions, we targeted as our sample the Established Populations for Epidemiologic Studies of the Elderly (EPESE) data, a longitudinal, multisite (Harvard, Yale, University of Iowa, and Duke) research program funded by the National Institute on Aging (NIA). We chose to focus on elderly from the Duke site as the study population because of its oversampling of African Americans and rural residents.

The sampling frame for the Duke EPESE project is a five-county area in north central North Carolina. By Census Bureau definitions, one county (Durham) is urban; the other four counties (Franklin, Vance, Granville, and Warren) are rural. The population of the urban county is approximately equal to that of the four rural counties combined. A four-stage probability sampling design was used to obtain a community-based sample of 4,162 persons age sixty-five and older at the baseline interview. To facilitate racial comparisons, stratification procedures were used to insure that 55 percent of the sample consisted of African Americans (who represent 36% of the population in the 5 counties). The response rate at the baseline survey was 80 percent. Sample weights can be used to generate a demographic profile identical to that for the five-county area, based on Census Bureau data. The weights include adjustments for the oversample of African Americans, for households of varying sizes (1 person per household was recruited, regardless of size), and for differential nonparticipation. Sampling procedures are outlined by Blazer et al. [49].

The EPESE research design is longitudinal, with seven annual interviews. Detailed, face-to-face interviews were conducted at the baseline, year-four, and year-seven interviews. Most data for the trajectory analyses derive from these in-person interviews. Telephone surveys (in-person visits for those without phones) were conducted in years two, three, five, and six. As of this writing, all seven interviews are complete—data collection for the third in-person interview ended in June 1993. Adjusted response rates (i.e., excluding mortality) exceeded 98 percent for the four telephone interviews and 90 percent for the in-person follow-up interviews. Actual sample sizes at the Duke site for the seven waves of data are: 4,162, 4,098, 3,698, 3,561, 3,226, 2,715, and 2,445. Although the baseline sample was restricted to community-dwelling older adults, subsequent interviews have included follow-up to nursing homes and other long-term institutions.

In addition to the seven annual interviews, surveillance of the EPESE cohort will continue for five additional years. The primary focus of the surveillance efforts will be health-related transitions: hospitalizations, institutionalization, and mortality. Health Care Financing Administration (HCFA) records (for Medicare-eligible health care) and state Medicaid records will be the primary sources of information about use of hospitals and long-term care facilities. State vital statistic records, supplemented by the National Death Index (for participants who die outside of North Carolina), will be used to obtain mortality data. All deaths recorded thus far have been verified with death certificates; this procedure will also be followed during the surveillance interval.

Given the detailed accounts of health and functioning in the EPESE data, we have the opportunity to chart health trajectories over nearly a decade within four major domains: *Perceived Health* (standard self-reports), *Functional Health* (activities of daily living, bed days, days of limited activity, clinical ratings), *Cognitive Status* (SPMSQ), and *Depression* (CES-D). Currently, these trajectories are being determined simultaneously in two study arms. One mode of inquiry relies on the typology approach [4], with the second line of study using identical indicators of the four health domains in Hierarchical Linear Models (HLM). After the trajectories have been determined using both approaches, we will proceed with a series of comparative analyses in which trajectories from various health domains are examined in relation to fixed and time-varying sample characteristics. There are several steps in this process.

The primary focus of our preliminary efforts with the EPESE data is a labor-intensive trajectory coding. This preparation involves variable construction for each major health domain. Specifically, the EPESE database includes multiple indicators for two of the four health domains: functional health and self-perceived health. The dimensionality of the indicators within each domain is assessed, algorithms are developed for the scales, and the relative constancy of the scales is assessed across multiple waves.

The results of this analysis may indicate that at baseline, the indicators within a domain form one factor. If multiple factors are obtained, both the typology and the HLM approaches will utilize a multivariate design to assess separate trends for the multiple components of the domain. For example, we expect "bed days," days of limited activity, ADLs and IADLs to comprise a single latent construct. Should this not be the case, functional health will be considered multidimensional and trajectories for each functional health dimension will be examined.

A second step involves the development of summary sheets. After indicators for each health domain are decided upon, a statistical program will be written to generate summary sheets for each individual, depicting a time × health domain matrix. Each row of the summary sheet records the indicators across the four health domains at each survey wave; each column records any one domain over the decade.

As a third step, the major trajectories that characterize most individuals within each of the four domains are identified collaboratively among members of the research group. Following summary sheet construction and trajectory specification within each domain, a detailed codebook is developed that provides trajectory definitions, substantive examples of each code and decision rules for coding each trajectory, handling missing data, and dealing with ambiguous cases systematically. Examples of this approach exist for identifying trajectories of health [4] and retirement [5]. Greater detail on each step of this approach appears in Chapter 3, *Working With Archival Data* [35].

The final stage involves actual trajectory coding. The best-fitting health trajectory within each domain (perceived health, functional health, cognitive status, and depression) will be identified for each male in the EPESE sample. At this point the study splits into two paths, characterized by the two methodological approaches. From the typology side, two doctoral-prepared raters (ECC and LKG) will conduct a precoding phase (100 cases) intended to identify problems with trajectory definitions and decision rules. In the actual coding phase, each rater independently codes at least 5,892 trajectories (at least 4 per subject) which are automatically entered into a computer file. Trajectories are coded for all time points until death, after which respondents will be considered censored.

Inter-rater reliability estimates are made using kappa because the trajectories are categorical [50, 51]. Kappa is preferable to chi-square and percentage agreement because it strictly measures agreement, whereas the other statistics include all types of association. Kappa also is preferable because it corrects for chance agreement, especially important when the marginal distributions in a table are highly skewed. Following each reliability check, discrepant codes are resolved in consensus conferences.

Using the Hierarchical Linear Model (HLM) approach (also referred to as Growth Curve, Empirical Bayes, and Random Regression models), the three parameters of trajectory analysis (level, slope, and variance) are examined to identify the course of change [47, 52-54]. As explicated by Bock [52] and others, the first stage in hierarchical regression models is to model the course of change (within-person analysis) for each individual over the near decade period. The impact of censoring on trajectories is assessed, particularly when the censoring is not random (e.g., people are censored because they die, become proxies, or drop out).

Working separately within each arm of the study (typology and HLM), the trajectories provided by each approach are examined in relation to fixed sample characteristics. From the typology side, the extent to which factors such as race, age, marital status, veteran status, and rural vs. non-rural residence relate to different profiles of health are determined. Because of our interest in veterans, we also will compare the health trajectories of veterans and non-veterans. Additional comparisons will be made within the sample of veterans to determine the degree to which trajectories differ for veterans with and without service-connected disabilities, and those who do and do not use the VA Medical System as their usual source of care.

Based on earlier research [6], we hypothesize that veterans will be disproportionately represented among trajectories characterized by poor (level) or declining (slope) health relative to nonveterans. Moreover, for those analyses that examine variability within the veteran subsample, we expect to find that those veterans who had service-connected disabilities and those who use the VA as their usual source of care will be most likely to exhibit trajectories marked by poor health (level) and declining health (slope).

If it is found that veterans and nonveterans are differentially distributed across health trajectories, subsequent analyses that add time-varying social factors and chronic diseases to the models will be especially important. Results of these analyses will indicate whether veteran status is related to the health trajectories when other factors are statistically controlled. It is expected that such controls will reduce, but not eliminate, the hypothesized relationship between veteran status and negative health trajectories.

By contrast, on the HLM side, "HLM stage two" involves multiple regressions of the same fixed factors (race, age, marital status, veteran status, and rural vs. non-rural residence) on the betas obtained in HLM stage one to answer questions such as, "is the slope of the cognitive trajectory at all conditional on race, rural/non-rural residence, veteran status, or age?" In essence, these second-stage analyses in HLM employ between-person and/or time-invariant variables to determine the degree to which the patterns of individual change are so related.

Working within each arm of the analyses (typology approach and HLM), trajectories provided by each method are next examined in relation to time-varying predictors. From the typology side, this allows a determination of the extent to which acute and chronic health events, social support, and serious life events such as bereavement influence the course of health. From the HLM side, the question is, "what time-varying factors such as acute and chronic illness or social support account for the betas obtained in HLM stage one (the individual trajectories)?" Using HLM, different parameterizations will be tested systematically to determine the data fit. The simplest model is that of linear decline.

However, clinical experience suggests that higher-older polynomials and nonlinear functions may be needed to adequately characterize most of the identified trajectories. For example, if a nonlinear pattern such as "decline and recovery" is identified, this pattern will be modeled as a quadratic equation. The timing in such changes in the curve are hypothesized links to health events such as stroke, hip fracture, or myocardial infarction. Previous research in this area [4] suggests that health changes are not always linear. Overall, the assumption is made that trajectories will be driven, in part, by the context of people's lives (rural/non-rural residence) and events that people experience over the course of living (e.g., medical insults, serious life events, social change including war). In both arms of the study, fixed variables that are significantly related to the trajectories are included as controls.

It is important to note that in both approaches, typological and HLM, data about chronic physical illnesses are excluded from the initial depiction of the trajectories—only domain indicators are used (self-rated health, cognitive status, functional status, and depression). After the trajectories are characterized, comparisons can then be made among trajectories in terms of patterns of chronic illness and comorbidity. This approach was successful in earlier work [4]. Clinically, this step also permits the formulation of tentative conclusions regarding the extent to which trajectories are "disease driven," as compared to representing more gradual processes of cumulative frailty. Our expectation is that the onset and/or worsening of chronic diseases (e.g., heart disease, cancer) will be related to some trajectories, especially those of more rapid decline, but that other trajectories, characterized by cumulative age-related frailty, will not be closely related to specific chronic diseases.

In addition to rich longitudinal data on health, the EPESE data also offer extensive information on health service use, an important time-varying factor for these analyses. The analyses targeted here will focus on relating health trajectories across the four domains to health service use. The types of health services to be examined are: outpatient care for physical health problems, outpatient care from mental health professionals, emergency room visits, hospitalizations, and institutional care. Each type of health service can be examined in terms of any care vs. no care and/or in terms of volume of use (e.g., number of outpatient visits, number of hospitalizations, and hospital days). In addition, separate analyses will examine differences in health service use between rural versus urban elderly.

Finally, all of these preliminary analyses, from both study arms, will come together through: 1) Assessment of the relationships between the trajectories for the separate domains for each estimation technique; 2) assessment of the correlation between trajectories estimated by different methods within a domain; and 3) assessment of the relationship of the trajectories to mortality. To accomplish the first task for the trajectory method, the individuals for k categories for domain i (i = 1,4) are classified with the k' categories for domain j for each of the four domains. Log-linear models are then employed to assess association between the four sets of multinomial responses [55, 56]. Here the obvious measure of interest is the change in odds for a particular category and domain given a similar category in other domains.

For the trajectories defined by HLM, the trajectories can be correlated by multivariate correlational techniques—including principal components and cluster analysis. At a second stage, the trajectories as defined by typology analysis are compared with trajectories defined by HLM. Here again, any of the several multivariate discriminant techniques (e.g., Discriminant Analysis and Logistic Regression) are appropriate. Finally, the sets of trajectories defined by the two techniques are used to assess future outcomes including institutionalization, hospitalization, and mortality. Survival analysis as implemented under the Cox proportional Hazards model is an appropriate strategy for these analyses [57].

It may be worth noting that the results of the correlational analysis above between trajectories created by the typological approach and those identified using HLM may be of greater substantive interest than the correlation of two sets of related variables. HLM, as a quasi-Bayesian technique, adjusts the predicted trajectory for an individual to incorporate information about the group depending on the amount of "information" contained about the individual by group membership. By contrast, the typology approach utilizes only information about the individual.

If the group contains information useful in the prediction of a trajectory, the HLM approach may be a more powerful technique in the validity check of the method—prediction of subsequent morbidity and mortality. HLM allows all degrees of slope while the trajectory approach does not—a degree of refinement that may increase power. On the other hand, the typology method, because it easily blends clinical insight into the analytic structure, can more easily arrive at appropriate non-linear functions than the more statistically-based HLM. Thus, unless care is taken to appropriately express the model under HLM to incorporate these non-linear clinical insights, the phenomenon of potentially crucial interest may be modeled as "error." This will lead to more power for the trajectory approach in the morbidity and mortality analyses.

In summary, results from the typology approach may suggest that HLM does not model clinically relevant nonlinear patterns. The HLM analyses may suggest that the typology approach is unreliable or less parsimonious. Results from the typology side may argue strongly that individuals can be grouped into meaningful patterns; the HLM side may argue that knowledge of central tendency in a sample is what matters and that differences between individuals are just a matter of degree. Which approach is better? We are currently preparing to put this question to empirical test.

DISCUSSION

The substantive and statistical issues inherent in the examination of health trajectories in aging populations using two very different, state-of-the-art methodologies are indeed challenging. Conceptually, a focus on health trajectories provides an opportunity to move beyond traditional longitudinal models that elucidate age norms or group patterns, but ignore individual variability and important sources of heterogeneity. Unlike traditional approaches, use of health trajectories focuses attention on the dynamics of within-individual change rather than changes occurring between individuals. By disaggregating within-individual variation from between-individual variation, trajectory modeling provides a more accurate view of illness-related change over the life course.

Methodologically, the use of hierarchical linear models permits identification of patterned heterogeneity, while simultaneously doing justice to the richness of individual change. Although the concept of trajectory is attractive, relatively complex statistical models are required to translate the concept of trajectory into empirical operation. A comparison between the typology approach and hierarchical linear models will provide research illustrations of interest to a wide audience of scientists, including those working with longitudinal data focused on issues other than health.

Clinically, a trajectory approach will provide several types of "fine-grained" data about the courses and outcomes of various health domains during late life: 1) patterns of within-individual rather than between-individual change, 2) health indicators in four domains (perceived health, functional health, cognitive status, and depression), 3) relationships between health trajectories and personal, social and clinical factors including chronic disease and residential location, and 4) associations between health trajectories and sources and volume of health service use.

A trajectory approach also holds significant potential for answering certain time-dependent research questions pertaining to rural aging. It is estimated that over eight million elderly live in nonmetropolitan areas of the United States [58] and, more importantly for longitudinal data collection purposes, they continue to live in such communities over the course of their later years. Very little information based on research findings currently exists on how functioning changes as individuals age in rural communities, and how social and physical contexts support or undermine these processes.

Potential applications of a trajectory approach to rural aging populations include the identification of service-use patterns in relation to physical health trajectories, rural/non-rural differences in how informal assistance to frail elders changes over time in relation to patient needs, the incidence of new medical conditions and functional losses among elderly in rural and non-rural communities, migration patterns of aging populations over time toward medical and social interventions, and length of time that rural and non-rural elders are within a specific ADL-deficit state before becoming more dependent.

Consider, as a more specific example, the concept of "aging in place," and the current movement toward "assisted living" for frail elderly persons [59]. These terms have captured this country's attention in a search for more humane and less costly alternatives to nursing home or other institutional care. The primary goal of assisted independent living is to maintain older persons in independent living environments and to enable frail elderly to function independently. In terms of cost effectiveness, this is a challenging model to implement in rural areas because home health agencies are less available and the services such agencies provide are crucial components of the assisted living model.

However, before dealing with issues of service need and accessibility, research is needed to determine whether or not enhanced environments such as assisted living have beneficial effects on functioning. To date, there has been no research on longitudinal patterns of competence and functional status of elderly living in enhanced environments, in either urban or rural settings. Under what conditions are such environments cost effective and, for how long do they allow elders to maintain independent living in their communities? Answers to these questions are best approached using longitudinal data on health and health service use among rural and non-rural elderly, and by thinking beyond central tendencies of the group to individual trajectories and the factors that shape them.

ACKNOWLEDGMENTS

The authors gratefully acknowledge support for this work from a VA Merit Review Award (Elizabeth Clipp); a grant from the National Institute of Mental Health (MH41327, Glen Elder); a Contract with the U.S. Army Research Institute (Glen Elder); a Research Scientist Award (MH00567, Glen Elder); a Contract (N01-AG-1-2102, Linda George and Carl Pieper with the National Institute on Aging); Grant (R01 AG12765, Linda George and Carl Pieper); and a Center (P60 AG11268, Linda George and Carl Pieper).

REFERENCES

1. G. H. Elder, *Children of the Great Depression,* University of Chicago Press, Chicago, 1974.
2. G. H. Elder, Perspectives on the Life Course, in *Life Course Dynamics,* G. H. Elder (ed.), Cornell University Press, Ithaca, pp. 23-49, 1985.
3. G. H. Elder, The Life Course, in *The Encyclopedia of Sociology,* E. F. Borgatta and M. L. Borgatta (eds.), Macmillan, New York, 1991.
4. E. Clipp, E. Pavalko, and G. Elder, Trajectories of Health: In Concept and Empirical Pattern, *Behavior, Health and Aging,* 2:3, pp. 159-179, 1992.
5. G. Elder and E. Pavalko, Work Careers in Men's Later Years: Transitions, Trajectories, and Historical Change, *The Journal of Gerontology: Social Sciences, 48,* pp. S180-S191, 1993.
6. G. Elder, M. Shanahan, and E. Clipp, When War Comes to Men's Lives: Effects on Family, Work and Health, *Psychology and Aging, 9*:1, pp. 5-16, 1994.
7. G. Elder, L. K. George, and M. J. Shanahan, Psychosocial Stress over the Life Course, in *Psychosocial Stress: Perspectives on Structure, Theory, Life Course, and Methods,* H. B. Kaplan (ed.), Academic Press, Orlando, Florida, pp. 247-292, 1996.
8. N. W. Shock, R. C. Greulich, R. Andres, D. Arenberg, P. Costa, E. G. Lakatta, and J. D. Tobin, *Normal Human Aging: The Baltimore Longitudinal Study of Aging,* NIH Publication No. 84-2450, U.S. Government Printing Office, 1984.
9. E. W. Busse and G. M. Maddox, *The Duke Longitudinal Studies of Normal Aging 1955-1980,* Springer, New York, 1985.
10. D. J. Ekerdt, Normative Aging Study, in *The Encyclopedia of Aging,* G. L. Maddox, R. C. Atchley, L. W. Poon, G. S. Roth, I. C. Siegler, and R. M. Steinberg (eds.), Springer, New York, pp. 485-487, 1987.
11. L. M. Bayer, D. Whissell-Buechy, and M. Honzik, Health, in *Present and Past in Middle Life,* D. H. Eichorn, J. A. Clausen, N. Haan, M. P. Honzik, and P. H. Mussen (eds.), Academic Press, New York, 1981.
12. H. Thomae, Patterns of 'Successful' Aging, in *Patterns of Aging. Findings from the Bonn Longitudinal Study of Aging,* H. Thomae (ed.), S. Karger, New York, pp. 147-161, 1976.
13. U. M. Lehr, Longitudinal Studies: Europe, in *The Encyclopedia of Aging,* G. L. Maddox, R. C. Atchley, L. W. Poon, G. S. Roth, I. C. Siegler, and R. M. Steinberg (eds.), Springer, New York, pp. 415-416, 1987.
14. G. E. Vaillant, *Adaptation to Life,* Little, Brown and Co., Boston, Massachusetts, 1977.
15. P. B. Baltes, K. U. Mayer, H. Helmchen, and E. Steinhagen-Thiessen, The Berlin Aging Study (BASE): Overview and Design, *Ageing and Society, 13,* pp. 483-515, 1993.
16. L. M. Verbrugge, Recent Trends in Sex Mortality Differentials in the United States, *Women and Health, 5,* pp. 17-37, 1980.
17. L. M. Verbrugge, Women and Men: Mortality and Health of Older People, in *Aging and Society: Selected Reviews of Recent Research,* M. W. Riley, B. B. Hess, and K. Bond (eds.), Lawrence Erlbaum Assoc., Publishers, Hillsdale, New Jersey, pp. 139-174, 1983.

18. L. M. Verbrugge, A Health Profile of Older Women with Comparisons to Older Men, *Research on Aging, 6,* pp. 291-322, 1984.
19. L. M. Verbrugge, Longer Life but Worsening Health? Trends in Health and Mortality of Middle-Aged and Older Persons, *Milbank Memorial Fund Quarterly, 62,* pp. 475-519, 1984.
20. L. M. Verbrugge and J. H. Madans, Social Roles and Health Trends of American Women, *Milbank Memorial Fund Quarterly, 63,* pp. 691-735, 1985.
21. L. M. Verbrugge, Gender and Health: An Update on Hypotheses and Evidence, *Journal of Health and Social Behavior, 26,* pp. 156-182, 1985.
22. L. M. Verbrugge, From Sneezes to Adieux: Stages of Health for American Men and Women, in *Health in Aging: Sociological Issues and Policy Directions,* R. A. Ward and S. S. Tobin (eds.), Springer, New York, pp. 17-57, 1987.
23. L. M. Verbrugge, Exploring the Iceberg: Common Symptoms and How People Care for Them, *Medical Care, 25,* pp. 539-569, 1987.
24. L. M. Verbrugge and D. L. Wingard, Sex Differentials in Health and Mortality, *Women and Health, 12,* pp. 103-145, 1987.
25. L. M. Verbrugge and A. M. Jette, The Disablement Process, *Social Science and Medicine, 38,* pp. 1-14, 1994.
26. L. M. Verbrugge and D. J. Balaban, Patterns of Change in Disability and Well-Being, *Medical Care, 27,* pp. 128-147, 1989.
27. L. M. Verbrugge, Recent, Present, and Future Health of American Adults, *Annual Review of Public Health, 10,* pp. 333-361, 1989.
28. A. Abbott and A. Hrycak, Measuring Resemblance in Sequence Data: An Optimal Matching Analysis of Musicians' Careers, *American Journal of Sociology, 96,* pp. 144-185, 1990.
29. G. Elder, The Life Course and Human Development, in *Handbook of Child Psychology 1,* R. M. Lerner (ed.), W. Damon (general ed.), Wiley and Sons, New York, 1996.
30. H. L. Minton, Charting Life History: Lewis M. Terman's Study of the Gifted, in *The Rise of Experimentation in American Psychology,* J. G. Morawski (ed.), Yale University Press, New Haven, pp. 138-162, 1988.
31. M. H. Oden, The Fulfillment of Promise: 40-Year Follow-Up of the Terman Gifted Group, *Genetic Psychology Monographs, 77,* pp. 3-93, 1968.
32. L. M. Terman, *Genetic Studies of Genius: I. Mental and Physical Traits of a Thousand Gifted Children,* Stanford University Press, Stanford, California, 1925.
33. L. M. Terman and M. H. Oden, *Genetic Studies of Genius: IV, The Gifted Child Grows Up,* Stanford University Press, Stanford, California, 1947.
34. L. M. Terman and M. H. Oden, *The Gifted Child at Mid-Life,* Stanford University Press, Stanford, California, 1959.
35. G. Elder, E. Pavalko, and E. Clipp, *Working With Archival Data: The Study of Lives,* Sage Publications, Newbury Park, California, 1993.
36. E. Clipp and G. Elder, The Aging Veteran of World War II: Psychiatric and Life Course Insights, in *Aging and Posttraumatic Stress Disorder,* P. E. Ruskin and J. H. Talbott (eds.), American Psychiatric Press, Washington, D.C., 1994.
37. G. Elder and E. Clipp, Combat Experience and Emotional Health: Impairment and Resilience in Later Life, *Journal of Personality, 57:*2, pp. 311-341, 1989.

38. G. Elder and E. Clipp, Combat Experience, Comradeship, and Psychological Health, in *Human Adaptation to Extreme Stress: From the Holocaust to Vietnam,* J. P. Wilson, Z. Harel, and B. Kahana (eds.), Plenum, New York, pp. 131-156, 1988.
39. G. Elder and E. Clipp, Wartime Losses and Social Bonding: Influence Across 40 Years in Men's Lives, *Psychiatry, 51*:2, pp. 177-198, 1988.
40. C. L. Coe and S. Levine, Psychoimmunology: An Old Idea Whose Time Has Come, in *Sociophysiology of Social Relationships,* P. Barchas (ed.), Oxford University Press, New York, 1993.
41. G. Blazer, L. K. George, R. Landerman, M. Pennybacker, M. L. Melville, M. Woodbury, K. G. Manton, K. Jordan, and B. Locke, Psychiatric Disorders: A Rural/Urban Comparison, *Archives of General Psychiatry, 42,* pp. 651-656, 1985.
42. J. R. Nesselroade, Interindividual Differences in Intraindividual Change, in *Best Methods for the Analysis of Change,* L. M. Collins and J. L. Horn (eds.), American Psychological Association, Washington, D.C., 1992.
43. E. Kohler, *Gestalt Psychology,* New American Library, New York, 1947.
44. N. Baloff and S. W. Becker, On The Futility of Aggregating Individual Learning Curves, *Psychological Reports, 20,* pp. 183-191, 1967.
45. M. A. Flaum, N. C. Anderson, and S. Arndt, The Iowa Prospective Longitudinal Study of Recent-Onset Psychoses, *Schizophrenia Bulletin, 18,* pp. 481-490, 1992.
46. G. L. Maddox and D. O. Clark, Trajectories of Functional Impairment in Later Life, *Journal of Health and Social Behavior, 33,* pp. 114-125, 1992.
47. A. Bryk and S. Raudenbush, Application of Hierarchical Linear Models to Assessing Change, *Psychological Bulletin, 10*:1, pp. 147-158, 1987.
48. S. Crystal and U. Sambamoothi, Functional Impairment Trajectories Among Persons with Symptomatic HIV Disease: A Hierarchical Linear Models Approach, *Health Services Research, 31,* pp. 467-486, 1996.
49. D. G. Blazer, B. Burchett, C. Service, and L. K. George, The Association of Age and Depression among the Elderly: An Epidemiological Exploration, *Journal of Gerontology: Medical Sciences, 46,* pp. M210-M215, 1991.
50. J. Cohen, *Statistical Power Analysis for the Behavioral and Social Sciences,* Lawrence Erlbaum and Associates, Englewood Cliffs, New Jersey, 1989.
51. J. L. Fleiss, *Statistical Methods for Rates and Proportions,* John Wiley and Sons, New York, 1973.
52. D. Bock, Measurement of Human Variation: A Two-Stage Model, in *Multiple Analysis of Educational Data,* R. D. Bock (ed.), Academic Press, New York, 1989.
53. J. Strenio, H. Weisberg, and A. Bryk, Empirical Bayes Estimation of Individual Growth Curve Parameters and Their Relationship to Covariates, *Biometrics, 39*:1, pp. 71-86, 1983.
54. J. Ware, Linear Models for the Analysis of Longitudinal Studies, *The American Statistician, 39*:1, pp. 95-101, 1985.
55. Y. Bishop, S. Fienberg, and P. Holland, *Discrete Data Analysis,* MIT Press, Cambridge, Massachusetts, 1975.
56. L. Goodman, The Analysis of Cross-Classified Data having Ordered and/or Unordered Categories: Association Models, Correlation Models, and Asymmetry Models or Contingency Tables With or Without Missing Entries, *Annals of Statistics, 13*:1, pp. 10-69, 1985.

57. D. R. Cox, Regression Models and Life Tables (with discussion), *Journal Royal Statistical Society, B, 34,* pp. 187-202, 1972.
58. R. Coward, N. C. Bull, G. Kukulka, and J. M. Galliher (eds.), *Health Services for Rural Elders,* Springer, New York, 1994.
59. D. Tilson (ed.), *Aging in Place: Supporting the Frail Elderly in Residential Environments,* Scott, Foresman and Company, Glenview, Illinois, 1990.

CHAPTER
10

Methodologic Rigor and Therapeutic Obligation: The Dialectic in Community Research

Carol C. Hogue

Is there an insoluble contradiction between rigor in controlled clinical trials and health professionals' desire to serve individuals and groups in the community where the research is conducted? Are the tensions greater in rural settings, where services for older adults are often thin and public and professional experiences with research are limited?

INTRODUCTION

In this chapter we will describe the development of a controlled clinical trial conducted with a rural older adult population, illustrating the dialectic between methodologic rigor and therapeutic obligation, and giving examples of successful resolution of tensions.

Kessler and Levin, in the classic work on community as epidemiologic laboratory, suggest criteria for selecting a community for research: unusual prevalence of disease or of suspected risk factor, administrative convenience, favorable community relations, availability of demographic data on the community, and needs of public health service programs [1]. Because of increasing skepticism about research on the part of lay and professional citizens, an increasing amount of research conducted, greater understanding of the ethical conduct of research, and a more sensitive attitude toward populations studied, which are Kessler and Levin's criteria, are now the tip of the iceberg. Successful community-based research today, particularly with a vulnerable population, such as elders in a rural county distant from the university, requires much more to honor both the demands of methodologic rigor and the requirements of service.

DEVELOPMENT OF THE STUDY

The interactive effects of biological aging, chronic disease, and inactivity, mediated through losses in neurologic control, motor performance, and energy metabolism, place elderly persons at risk for functional decline incompatible with psychological well-being, performance of social roles, and maintenance of self-care at home. This functional decline has recently been labeled frailty [2] or preclinical disability [3, 4]. Older persons with arthritis, the most prevalent chronic condition in later life, are at high risk for functional decline because they tend to limit their activity [5-7]. This limitation of activity leads to mobility problems in older adults, and mobility difficulty predicts falls [8, 9], hip fracture [10], and other adverse outcomes. Residents of rural communities have high rates of arthritis [11, 12], more poverty [13], and fewer available services than urban dwellers [14]; thus they are at particularly high risk for disability.

The purpose of our research was to determine whether a sixteen-week training program designed to increase muscle strength, flexibility, aerobic capacity, and speed of task completion, as well as knowledge about, acceptability of, and support for exercise would lead to continued physical activity for rural sedentary older adults with symptomatic arthritis of the weight-bearing joints.

We spent several years doing groundwork in preparation for our research in Johnston County—a large rural county in eastern North Carolina. We needed to become acquainted with the community before we could develop collaborative relationships. We needed to develop our measurement instruments and procedures in ways that would be acceptable in the county and to us, and we needed to pilot our procedures.

Johnston County, with an area of 800 square miles, had about 70,000 residents when we began our work. The majority of residents (66%) lived in completely rural areas, with the remainder in small towns. The population of the largest town was approximately 8,000. Thirty percent of the residents were ethnic minority persons, 17 percent were sixty or older, 40 percent had less than $10,000 annual income, and 53 percent of persons over the age of twenty-five had less than a high school education.

Students and faculty from the University of North Carolina in Chapel Hill began working in Johnston County in the 1970s under the leadership of a medical anthropologist, Tony Whitehead, and later, his colleague in the School of Public Health, Harold Cook. After several years they formalized their research, training, and service activities as a Rural Health Research Center. The Center, which had initial funding from the UNC Center for Health Promotion and Disease Prevention, and from the UNC Multipurpose Arthritis Center, became the focal point for several new projects in the county. The mission of the Center was to conduct studies to improve health and prevent disease in Johnston County. Two local advisory committees with different perspectives and authority were formed: a community advisory group of "everyday people," and a professional advisory group of businessmen, physicians, and other professionals. Members were selected not only because of their individual competence and interest, but also because they each represented a constituency. This "representative" membership gave us an opportunity to express our valuing their existing leadership structure. The committees gave advice on how to conduct various projects such as focus groups around the county, and a survey. Advisory committee members acted as the link between other members of the community and the projects of the Center, including developing research projects. Feelings and concerns about projects were brought to meetings, and encouragement to participate in projects was taken from the Center to other members of the community. Roper talks of local policymakers and university-based researchers becoming "bound together on an issue" [15, p. 427] such that both the populations being studied and the researcher benefit by a collaborative research relationship. Acknowledging the claims, concerns, and issues of community members makes the product more useful to those it is meant to serve" [16, p. 276]. We were deliberate in seeking and using advice. That persistence and respectful attitude helped community residents feel a sense of ownership for our research. Kaiser and Camp described four conditions for successfully implementing rural aging activities: the presence of key leaders, the involvement of key organizations, the availability of resources, and the development of community-based ownership [17]. We were fortunate to participate in activities largely started by others, especially Harold Cook, and our research benefited from these conditions.

In meeting with community leaders, professionals, and lay people we had to show that we knew something about the community; that we had respect for the values of groups in the community; that our research had the potential to benefit participants, their families, and others in the community; and that we would involve members of the community in all phases of the research from the planning to the reporting of results. We spent time with many people, giving them reasons to trust us before we began our research.

Our research team, an interdisciplinary group of university faculty from nursing, geriatric medicine, rheumatology, exercise physiology, physical therapy, occupational therapy, biostatistics, and health psychology, had to learn to work together to design and conduct a sound study worthy of funding from the National Institute of Health (NIH). Some members of our team had never visited Johnston County before the study began, but all visited during the conduct of the study, some very frequently. We needed a strong design incorporating population-based sampling, random assignment to treatment groups, a sample large enough to have sufficient power to test hypotheses, reliable and valid measurement strategies that would also be acceptable to participants, and appropriate analytic strategies for an intervention study with multiple outcomes. We needed to show that we could make the needed measurements and that our intervention would have the expected intermediate outcomes of increased physical performance.

We met with both community advisory groups and we convened a separate focus group twice to get advice about our intended procedures and our data collection instruments. We learned that we could expect African-American and White elderly rural residents to be willing to exercise together, but that we might encounter resistance if we tried to form groups with highly variable socio-economic status. We learned that if we wanted older rural residents to attend our research intervention sessions three times each week, we had to provide trans-portation. We learned that in that county at that time, Senior Centers were not frequented by more advantaged people. We were advised that some participants would not have comfortable clothing and shoes for exercise and would not be able to afford to purchase them. We learned that language such as "strenuous activity" should be changed to "things that make you sweat a lot." Other lan-guage was simplified to make it accessible to more people, and examples of experiences included in widely-used research interview schedules were reviewed for their appropriateness in that setting. The length of data collection instruments was reviewed with attention to both respondent burden and need for reliable information. We were advised not to expect participants to record information in health diaries.

The National Institute on Aging, through the Sheps Health Research Center and its North Carolina Rural Aging Project, provided initial funding of our pilot study, with supplemental funding from the National Institute of Arthritis and Musculoskeletal Diseases through the Thurston Arthritis Center. That fund-ing from two UNC Centers, a great deal of contributed faculty time over two years, and generous contributions from individuals and organizations in Johnston County allowed us to conduct an effective pilot. Examples of contributions from the community for the pilot work included space for testing and the intervention in the Senior Center in the largest town, a van and driver to pick up and deliver our subjects, and advice from an Emergency Medical Technician who helped us arrange for emergency procedures with the local fire department (procedures that were never needed during seven years of research with a vulnerable population). We purchased a large wooden shed for storing our equipment during the pilot, and we gave the shed to the Senior Center when we completed our work there.

CONDUCT OF THE PILOT STUDY

The purpose of the pilot study was to collect both process and outcome data to strengthen sampling, interventions, and data collection for larger con-trolled studies to follow. A group of deconditioned elderly persons with chronic disease were studied by direct observation of physical performance and by inter-view self-reports immediately before and after a twelve-week behavioral training program and again three-and-a-half months later. Behavioral training included exercise to improve functional aerobic capacity, muscle strength, and flexibility. In addition, the behavioral training included psychoeducational strategies to increase knowledge about exercise and activity. Subjects learned problem-solving skills for dealing with barriers to adherence with the exercise regimen, developed a sense of competence, established habits, and experienced reinforcement from a buddy, the exercise group, and the leader. The fourteen subjects were at least sixty-two years old, were sedentary, but were able to walk at least fifteen feet and climb three or more stairs, had physician approval to participate, had a family member or friend for support, and were not severely cognitively impaired.

The intervention, conducted in a group of twelve, was tailored to individuals at a Senior Center. The remaining two subjects exercised in the home of one subject so we could examine the feasibility of home exercise. Progressive, light resistance exercises for all major muscle groups, with aerobic training building to 40 to 70 percent functional aerobic capacity, and the psychoeducational strategies to build commitment to exercise during and after the organized intervention were administered by a nurse clinician. The nurse clinician was assisted by a lay person, a vigorous eighty-three-year-old woman from the county, a peer exercise facilitator, and an older adult role model. The intervention was conducted three times each week in two-hour sessions.

Prior to, and twice following the intervention, physiologic, psychologic, and functional evaluations were performed. Physiologic measures included blood pressure, heart rate, and aerobic capacity (submaximal tests on a Monark 818E bike ergometer, with the Amundson step procedure, and with the Smith and Gilligan Chair Step Test). Psychologic measures included measures of predicted adherence, social support, mood, and self-esteem. Functional measures included tests of static and dynamic muscle strength, gait, balance, and flexibility.

The peer exercise facilitator made two home visits to each participant's buddy or support person. The first visit included a description of the content, benefits, and demands of the exercise program, a request for support and encouragement of the exerciser, a short discussion about ways of helping, and a brief message about coaching without nagging. The second home visit, at the end of the intervention, focused on the participant's progress in the exercise program and the importance of continued exercise and activity, and on obtaining another commitment to encourage continued exercise.

At all three measurement times (before, at the end, and three-and-a-half months after the intervention) variables were measured by direct observation and self-report. At the final three-and-a-half month follow-up data collection, a relatively unstructured interview was also conducted to ascertain facilitators and barriers to exercise after the supervised training period. Process data were collected by asking subjects their perceptions of the program, taking attendance, and having the trainer and the peer exercise facilitator keep logs describing what was done in each session and how it was received.

An example of the log kept by the senior exercise facilitator is the following entry for the second day of the intervention.

> All participants came back with a "Let's go" attitude. Some complained of sore leg muscles, but others remarked "I slept better," "I didn't feel any soreness." Some had to sit after the first few minutes. EB sat, SD was slow and sat, LP came in with a headache and complained of fatigue, but she exercised for a while.

Following a suggestion of Bandura, a videotape of sessions early, mid-way, and late in the training program was made [18]. The videotape was used in the subsequent controlled trial, the larger study, both for recruiting and as a means of increasing participants' exercise self-efficacy by viewing coping models [18]. According to Bandura's theory, a coping model presented on videotape will encourage new participants in the program to identify with people like themselves who are obviously struggling and uncoordinated in beginning exercise. Later in the program, the videotaped participants display increased competence which should offer hope of mastery to those viewing the tape and increase their exercise self-efficacy.

FINDINGS FROM THE PILOT STUDY

Fifteen men and women (86% female, 57% black, mean age 73 years) began the study. Half had less than nine years of education (range 5 to 12 years). Most had arthritis (79%) and/or hypertension (71%), two had diabetes, two had strokes, several had myocardial infarctions, one had early Parkinson's disease, several had joint replacements, and several had lower-extremity fractures. Functionally, the subjects had considerable muscle weakness, especially in the quadriceps, and they had poor flexibility in shoulders and hips. Only two subjects exercised as often as once a week.

One sixty-nine-year-old woman dropped out after the second week because even the simplest group activities were too strenuous for her. As fourteen of the fifteen subjects completed the program, overall completion rate was 93.3 percent. Among the fourteen subjects who completed the training, attendance was 90.6 percent. Late in the follow-up period one subject was hospitalized for ten days for studies that confirmed a diagnosis of lung cancer.

The pilot showed modest gains in the expected direction, with slight declines at follow up (T3), but better results at follow up on many parameters than at baseline (T1) [19]. The gain in aerobic capacity is both statistically significant ($t = 3.68$, $df = 7$, $p < .01$) and clinically significant. A gain in METS from 4.4 to 5.4 means that the average person at T1, functioning at maximal aerobic capacity, could make a bed, and that the average person at T3 could also be an active gardener. The total psychosocial and physical scores on the Sickness Impact

Profile (SIP) improved significantly from T1 to T3 ($t = 4.39$, $df = 13$, $p < .001$; $t = 3.66$, $p < .001$; $t = 2.47$, $p < .05$). Subjects reported far less impact of illness on their activities and feelings after the intervention and three-and-a-half months later. Self-esteem scores improved ($t = 3.10$, $df = 13$, $p = .01$) and then declined to pre-intervention levels.

This was a small sample of volunteers with no controls, but the results were useful. The pilot experience also suggested that training of frail older adults could be done in a small group setting. Bike ergometry was found to be feasible and preferable to step test or chair step. Several clinical functional tests were found to be conceptually strong, but in need of strengthening by measuring time and by quantifying levels of performance. We learned that rural elderly participants with little education could learn new concepts such as problem solving and goal setting. The social experience of the group is important, and the support person adds reinforcement. The transition to home/independent exercise should begin earlier, last longer, and increase in intensity. The investigative team was well-received in the community. Feature stories with photographs appeared in local and statewide newspapers. The newspaper articles included anecdotal reports of participants' progress.

DISCUSSION

The pilot work described above led to design and funding by the National Institute for Nursing Research at the National Institutes of Health, a controlled clinical trial of the piloted intervention. The resultant study, "Reducing Frailty in Older Adults with Arthritis," would not have been possible without the learning experiences of the pilot work and the community experiences that preceded the pilot. The controlled trial, which was completed by ninety-eight Johnston County residents (mean age 72 years, 52% white, 85% female, with an average of 10 years of education), is nearing completion. Our potential participants for the controlled trial came from prevalent cases of hip or knee arthritis in an ongoing population-based study of the incidence of osteoarthritis in Johnston County [12]. Interventions and data collection are completed. Data analysis is in process and shows a significant impact of the intervention on the physical health status of participants. In addition to completing the data analysis and planning our return to Johnston County to report our findings to the many individuals and groups who helped us, we reviewed our experience in conducting a demanding, complex, population-based clinical trial in a rural community.

As we made our way in the community over the years, we developed a sense of closeness to people that led us to spend time visiting in their homes, visiting them or their family members in hospitals in the county, and in medical centers sixty miles away. We attended community fairs, sent our participants birthday cards, and holiday greetings. Carter et al. noted that because of random assignment to treatment groups, subject recruitment and retention are most difficult in clinical trials [20]. We struggled with our subjects when, even after we thought we had explained randomization to them and their family members, they were very disappointed to be randomized to the control group. While we wanted to please people, we had to follow our randomization procedure without any departure. We did make a decision that married couples or sisters could be randomized as a unit, a consideration that seemed very important to participants and was beneficial to us too. If we had randomized couples as individuals, the potential for "contamination" was very great, so we also benefited.

Krout mentioned the importance of "interdisciplinary and research/practice cross-fertilization of ideas and expertise" in the preface of his 1994 book [14, p. x]. Our research was more demanding because we listened to local physicians even when a few of them were skeptical about the safety of our program for their patients, and because we took the time to take blood pressures, do glucose testing, treat minor joint and muscle flare-ups, and communicate with physicians at the conclusion of the intervention for their patients. These activities undoubtedly contributed to our very low drop-out rate in the controlled trial (7%), and our very high attendance rate (79%).

The myths of rural aging described by Krout remind people at a distance what we see every day in our interactions with people in our rural setting: life is hard [14]. While the strengths of individuals often overcome very difficult situations, life in the country, for both farmers and non-farmers, is far from idyllic or bucolic. When people don't use services, it is generally because the services don't exist, or because there's no transportation, or because the cost is too high—not because large rural extended families make such services unnecessary. The willingness and perseverance of our participants to faithfully attend our intervention sessions and to work hard when many of them had very difficult life situations, reflects the commitment of the community and the skill, wisdom, and caring attitudes of our study personnel. While intervention research is more demanding than cross-sectional survey research, when interventions have the clear potential to improve quality of life of participants, it is easier to "give something" to the community than if the research merely asks for information.

Kihl wrote of the centrality of automobile transportation for all elderly, and she described some alternatives for rural elderly who are less likely to be able to drive their own cars [21]. In our study, we knew early in the preliminary planning that we would have to provide transportation to all testing and training activities; this was a major budget item in our clinical trial. Spending a lot of money on transportation of subjects (and of investigators from the university to the county) meant we didn't have money to hire a couple of staff people we needed, so the investigators had to pick up the slack. A side benefit we never dreamed of is that we were blessed with a wonderful person to drive the fifteen-passenger van we rented. Our driver is a therapeutic person. She was an integral part of our program—someone who actually extended our program by her caring and friendly interaction with all.

While Thorson and Powell write that "research is needed that helps explain the paradox of less adequate health care services but high levels of satisfaction among the rural aged" [22, p. 135], our experience suggests that rural residents are not different from other adults: they respond to surveys in ways that suggest they are satisfied with their health care, but when you speak with the same people, they are far from satisfied. Our participants, who were fortunate enough to have primary care physicians, were often very pleased with their care; a number of our subjects were unable to find a physician who would take new patients. We maintain our connections in the county, and are committed to helping increase the number of primary health care providers there.

Our research took more time, cost more money, and was more complex because of our commitment to collaborate with individuals and groups in Johnston County, but the collaboration was essential; the study could not have been done without it. Beyond that stark fact, we have warm feelings about people, institutions, and a culture that invited us to join them in an endeavor that had meaning for them and for us. We designed and carried out a study with internal validity that has important applications in Johnston County and other rural settings.

REFERENCES

1. I. I. Kessler and M. L. Levin, The Community as an Epidemiologic Laboratory, in *The Community as an Epidemiologic Laboratory,* I. I. Kessler and M. L. Levin (eds.), The Johns Hopkins Press, Baltimore, Maryland, pp. 1-22, 1970.
2. L. Weinbruch, M. Ory, and E. Hadley, *Reducing Frailty and Fall-Related Injuries in Older Persons,* Springer, New York, 1991.
3. L. P. Fried, S. J. Herdman, K. E. Kuhn, G. Rubin, and K. Turanon, Preclinical Disability: Hypotheses about the Bottom of the Iceberg, *Journal of Aging and Health, 3,* pp. 285-300, 1991.
4. L. P. Fried and J. M. Guralnik, Disability in Older Adults: Evidence Regarding Significance, Etiology, and Risk, *Journal of the American Geriatrics Society, 45,* pp. 92-100, 1997.
5. N. M. Fisher, D. R. Pendergast, G. E. Gresham, and E. Calkins, Muscle Rehabilitation: Its Effect on Muscular and Functional Performance of Patients with Knee Osteoarthritis, *Archives of Physical Medicine and Rehabilitation, 72,* pp. 367-374, 1991.
6. M. A. Minor, J. E. Hewitt, R. R. Webel, S. K. Anderson, and D. R. Kay, Efficacy of Physical Conditioning Exercise in Patients with Rheumatoid Arthritis and Osteoarthritis, *Arthritis and Rheumatism, 32,* pp. 1396-1405, 1989.
7. C. C. Hogue, S. Cullinan, and E. McConnell, Exercise Interventions for the Chronically Ill: Review and Prospects, in *Key Aspects of Caring for the Chronically Ill,* E. Tornquist, S. Funk, M. Champagne, and R. Wiese (eds.), Springer, New York, 1993.
8. M. C. Nevitt, S. R. Cummings, S. Kidd, and D. Black, Risk Factors for Recurrent Non-Syncopal Falls: A Prospective Study, *Journal of the American Medical Association, 261,* pp. 2633-2668, 1989.

9. M. E. Tinetti, M. Speechley, and S. F. Ginter, Risk Factors for Falls Among Elderly Persons Living in the Community, *New England Journal of Medicine, 322,* pp. 286-290, 1990.

10. A. Z. LaCroix, J. Wienpahl, L. White et al., Thiazide Diuretic Agents and the Incidence of Hip Fracture, *New England Journal of Medicine, 322,* pp. 286-290, 1990.

11. National Center for Health Statistics, *Current Estimates from the National Health Interview Survey: United States,* DHHS Publication No. PHS 86-1584, Hyattsville, Maryland, 1986.

12. J. Jordan, G. F. Linder, J. B. Renner, and J. G. Fryer, The Impact of Arthritis in Rural Populations, *Arthritis Care and Research, 8,* pp. 242-250, 1995.

13. L. Jensen and M. Tienda, Non-Metropolitan Families in the United States: Trends in Racial and Ethnic Economic Stratification, 1959-1986, *Rural Sociology, 54,* pp. 509-532, 1990.

14. J. A. Krout, An Overview of Older Rural Populations and Community-Based Services, in *Providing Community-Based Services to the Rural Elderly,* J. A. Krout (ed.), Sage Publications, Newbury Park, California, pp. 1-22, 1994.

15. R. Roper, Collaborative Research and Social Change: Applied Anthropology in Action [Review of Westview Special Studies in Applied Anthropology], *Applied Anthropology, 90,* p. 427, 1988.

16. D. Malone-Rising, Rural Research: The Lamille County Experience, in *Rural Health Nursing: Stories of Creativity, Commitment, and Connectedness,* P. Winstead-Fry, J. C. Tiffany, and R. V. Shippee-Rice (eds.), National League for Nursing Press, New York, pp. 273-297, 1991.

17. M. A. Kaiser and H. J. Camp, Rural Elderly: Their Demographic Characteristics, in *Aging in Rural America,* C. N. Bull (ed.), Sage Publications, Newbury Park, California, pp. 45-58, 1990.

18. A. Bandura, Self-Efficacy Mechanism in Physiological Activation and Health-Promoting Behavior, in *Adaptation, Learning and Affect,* J. Madden IV, S. Matthysse, and J. Barchas (eds.), Raven Press, New York, 1986.

19. C. Hogue and S. Cullinan, *Exercise Training for Frail and Rural Elderly: A Pilot Study, Key Aspects of Caring for the Chronically Ill,* Springer, New York, 1993.

20. W. B. Carter, K. Elward, J. Malmgren, M. L. Martin, and E. Larson, Participation of Older Adults in Health Programs and Research: A Critical Review of the Literature, *The Gerontologist, 31,* pp. 584-592, 1991.

21. M. R. Kihl, Rural Elderly: Their Demographic Characteristics, in *Aging in Rural America,* C. B. Bull (ed.), Sage Publications, Newbury Park, California, pp. 84-89, 1990.

22. J. A. Thorson and F. C. Powell, Rural Elderly: Their Demographic Characteristics, in *Aging in Rural America,* C. N. Bull (ed.), Sage Publications, Newbury Park, California, pp. 134-145, 1993.

CHAPTER
11

Informal Caregiving Networks and Community Resource Infrastructure Serving Rural Elderly Populations: Making the Macro-Micro Link

Jean Kincade, Donna J. Rabiner, Gary M. Nelson,
and Mary Anne P. Salmon

Over the past decade, there has been increasing attention paid to the segment of the elderly population that lives in rural areas. To some extent, this is because large numbers of older adults continue to live in these areas [1]. There are also indications that rural older adults experience poorer health, and that rural non-farm older adults report having a higher number of medical conditions, more functional limitations, and greater difficulty performing activities of daily living (ADL) and instrumental activities of daily living (IADL) than do older adults of any other residential group [2]. In addition, it has been found "that there is something distinctly different about aging and family life experiences in rural areas" and both individual and community characteristics contribute to these differences [3, p. 332].

The needs of the rural older adults, as with their urban counterparts, are addressed by overlapping systems of informal and formal care. However, studies have shown that older adults living in rural areas are more likely than their more urban counterparts to have networks consisting exclusively or primarily of informal caregivers [4]. Often these differences are attributed to rural values and greater availability of family and friends. An alternative explanation, however, might be that there is a limited availability of formal services to supplement the efforts of informal networks [5]. Both of these possibilities have practical and policy implications [4].

If the rural value system supports the use of informal caregivers to the exclusion of formal services, more supports need to be given to family caregivers to cope with their responsibilities. Similarly, if informal caregivers are more available, and if their help is preferred to formal services, then efforts need to be intensified to identify those older persons with limited or no informal networks, and to make formal services more affordable, acceptable, and accessible to them. Finally, if rural-dwelling older adults are no more likely to use informal networks than their urban counterparts, yet formal services are less available in rural areas, this may imply that efforts need to be made to improve access to formal services in rural community settings.

Addressing these complex issues remains difficult, in part, because of limitations in the methodological approaches used to explore them. While those who study informal caregiver networks and formal service availability have in common a concern for the well-being of the same set of people (impaired community-dwelling older adults and their families), they tend to approach this outcome quite differently; they ask different questions and, in general, they work at different levels of analysis. Those involved in caregiving research tend to focus on the micro-level, collecting data from the older adults themselves or from their caregivers [4, 6, 7]. They may or may not include questions about whether the family is receiving formal services, but they seldom include measurement of macro-level variables such as the supply and availability of services in the community [8]. When they do attempt to incorporate "system" or macro-level variables into the analysis, however, the result usually has serious statistical limitations.

By contrast, those who study formal service availability and capacity generally conduct their analyses at the macro-level [9-14]. The study questions posed at the macro-level are generally designed to explore the relationship between system-level attributes (e.g., funding sources within the community or agency-type) and access to, and use of formal home- and community-based services [15-19]. The variables included in a macro-level model are generally measured at the aggregated (rather than individual) unit of analysis.

The purpose of this chapter is to review current approaches to the study of informal caregiver networks and formal service availability to older persons in rural communities, highlight problems caused by the theoretical need to include both micro- and macro-level variables, and identify a statistical approach that gives better options for combining observations at multiple levels of analysis. First, several theoretical frameworks will be reviewed to present ways in which researchers conceptualize the integration of micro- and macro-level variables. Second, examples of studies will be reviewed to illustrate attempts to operationalize the theoretical models. Some studies include only micro-level variables with data collected from the older adults themselves or from their caregivers; other studies include only macro-level variables using system-level attributes; in very rare cases, studies include both micro-level variables (individual data) and macro-level variables (system attributes) in the same study without taking into account multi-level relationships. Finally, a new strategy will be discussed to incorporate both individual and system level variables into the analysis of formal and informal care networks.

THEORETICAL FRAMEWORKS ADDRESSING LINKAGES BETWEEN INFORMAL AND FORMAL CARE

Although several theoretical approaches exist for studying the coexistence of formal and informal networks, only a few are comprehensive in their approach. One comprehensive approach has been used by Bass and his colleagues at the Benjamin Rose Institute. They have used a modified conceptual framework originally developed by Andersen and his colleagues [20, 21] to study service utilization in older populations [e.g., 22, 23]. In this modified framework, the Andersen model is expanded to include predisposing, enabling, and need factors of both the impaired older person and the primary caregiver [22]. Thus decisions about use of formal services are based on characteristics of the older person (e.g., physical, cognitive, and functional status), characteristics of the informal support system (e.g., availability and willingness of unpaid helpers), and characteristics of the formal system (e.g., availability and eligibility requirements).

Another comprehensive conceptualization of rural service use was presented by Joseph and Cloutier [24]; this model was an extension of the earlier work of Joseph and Poyner [25]. Joseph and Cloutier focused on the relationship between an older person's needs for care and the potential of the community service sector to satisfy these needs [24]. One part of the model was specific to the individual and the decision to use or not use a service. A second part of the model represented the conventional aggregate approach to the description of usage patterns. A third key part of the model was the linking of individual and aggregate approaches to understand utilization patterns. This linkage was made through a consideration of the behavioral mechanisms that associate the characteristics of services and client service utilization decisions. These behavioral mechanisms included: "action space" or the degree to which the older individuals were mobile, "information" or the quality and quantity of their information about service opportunities, and "informal support networks" or the degree to which the informal network facilitated or impeded the use of community services.

In Cantor's theoretical work on the social system available to older Americans, she envisioned the elderly person at the center of a series of concentric circles containing a range of informal and formal sources of care [26]. Informal care was located close to the center of the circle while formal care was located at the periphery. Her macro-level model emphasized the relatedness of the informal and formal components, the fluidity and overlap of the components of social care that could be affected by a number of trends (e.g., proportion of the population over age 65, health, economic, and social trends, etc.), and placed the older person at the core of the model. In a striking acknowledgment of economic and social reality, informal care was the first concentric circle; Cantor felt that the role of informal care was a critical component in the social service system. Furthermore, although Cantor located the concentric circles in various strategic positions in her model, she stressed the value and contribution of each component of social care in her paradigm. She wrote: "To encompass the broader vision of social care required for the future, a systemwide model is needed. Contrary to the current tendency to consider informal and formal care as separate and often polarized systems, this model stresses the holistic nature of social care and the interrelatedness of the several parts" [26, p. 345].

MICRO RESEARCH USING MICRO-LEVEL VARIABLES ONLY TO ADDRESS LINKAGES BETWEEN INFORMAL AND FORMAL CARE

One approach used to determine the utilization of informal care and formal services in both rural and urban settings is to ask either the elderly care recipient and/or the primary informal caregiver about the receipt of informal care and use of formal services. Three studies provide examples of this approach [4, 6, 7].

Tennstedt, Crawford, and McKinlay used data from the Massachusetts Elderly Health Project to investigate the needs of older people for assistance with daily activities, and the sources and patterns of both informal and formal health care utilization [7]. Towns and cities in eastern Massachusetts were stratified according to size and then sampled with probability proportional to the size of the sixty-five and older population. Information about assistance was collected through interviews with primary caregivers of older adults. Six types of care were investigated: personal care, housekeeping, meal preparation, transportation, managing finances, and arranging for services. No variable was included to indicate the size of town/city in which the respondent lived. Questions were also asked to determine who provided the care (i.e., informal or formal source). They found some evidence of substitution of formal services for informal care but that it was temporary and related to availability of the primary caregiver. Although there were no macro-level measures included in the analysis, the authors acknowledged that, ". . . this study was conducted in a state with a well-established, publicly funded home care program which would have made substitution of formal services for informal care easier" [7, p. 621].

Stoller gathered data through personal interviews with a panel of older people and their informal helpers living in an eight-county nonmetropolitan area in northeastern New York [6]. Only elderly persons who were alive and living in the community at baseline (1979) and at follow-up (1986) were included in the analysis. She wanted to determine whether informal caregivers withdrew support when formal substitutes were available. Variables included in the analysis were: the number of hours of assistance provided by informal caregivers; the scope of assistance provided; the number of hours of personal care provided; formal service use (count of the number of formal services used); the older person's functional status; network characteristics; and other roles played by the informal caregivers. She found no support for the service substitution model (i.e., use of formal services was not associated with either fewer hours or more limited scope of informal assistance). There were no macro-level variables included in the analysis.

Coward, Cutler, and Mullens also used micro-level data to examine the informal and formal networks of care [4]. They relied on the 1984 Supplement on Aging to examine residential differences in the helping networks of older adults. Older adults who, when interviewed, indicated that they had difficulty performing an activity and had received help from another person, were asked to identify their relationship with their care provider. Sources of assistance were then classified into two mutually exclusive groups: "formal care" or "informal care." They found residential differences in the sources of help at different levels of disability and by place of residence (SMSA-central city, SMSA-not central city, and non-SMSA). Severely-impaired older adults residing in nonmetropolitan areas were less likely than their metropolitan counterparts to be receiving help from a formal caregiver and were more likely to be receiving help from informal caregivers exclusively. The authors cautioned, however, that their study provided no indication of why these differences occurred. Two alternative explanations were suggested either: ". . . that severely impaired elders residing in small towns and rural communities simply have fewer formal services available to them. Or, the differences may be a reflection of that often talked about, but seldom empirically documented, reluctance of rural elders to use formal services" [4, p. 48].

These micro-level studies are limited because they only elicit information about informal care and formal service use from the older person and/or his caregiver without including important macro-level variables in the analysis. As a result, we are not able to assess the range of services available to older adults and the selection criteria used to determine eligibility into these types of programs.

RESEARCH USING MACRO-LEVEL VARIABLES ONLY TO ADDRESS LINKAGES BETWEEN INFORMAL AND FORMAL IN-HOME CARE

Four macro-level studies of in-home health service utilization provide examples of ways in which system-level variables have been used to examine the relationship between formal and informal care. Two of these studies assessed use of Medicare-funded services with the state used as the unit of analysis [15, 19]. The third study also looked at Medicare service utilization, but Kenny and Dubay examined service availability by Metropolitan Statistical Area (MSA) and by residential status in each state (aggregated from all non-MSA counties in that state) [16]. The fourth study examined the use of all home health agency services in the state of Wisconsin, this time using the county as a unit of analysis [17].

Each of these studies relied on macro-level measures for state or county characteristics (e.g., region, per capita income, and rurality), and capacity measures (e.g., the number of home health agencies, FTEs of nursing staff, proportion of agencies that are proprietary); some studies also included program-level attributes for formal care agencies (e.g., required spend-down) in the analysis. All four studies controlled for system-level population attributes, such as the proportion of the population in the oldest old categories [15, 17, 19]. Two studies also used additional system-level variables as proxies for client need [15, 17].

In these macro-level studies, informal care was viewed as a potential substitute for formal services, although the caregiver research cited above gives only mild support for that assumption. The percent of women in the labor force was used in each study as a macro-level indicator of caregiving capacity. In half of these studies, a second proxy for caregiving capacity was included in order to assess the impact of living arrangements on service utilization. (Benjamin [15] used the percent of people 65 and older who were married while Kenny and Dubay [16] used the converse idea, percent of people 75 and older who lived alone.)

Benjamin found that both of his proxy measures for the availability of informal care were significant negative predictors of the proportion of Medicare enrollees in a state who received some home health services [15]. That is, states with high proportions of married older adults had smaller proportions using home health services, and states with high female labor force participation had higher proportions receiving home health services. When Swan and Benjamin looked at the number of home health visits per 100,000 older adults in the state in the period 1978 to 1984, they also found that female labor force participation—suggesting a dearth of available informal care—was a significant positive predictor of service utilization [19].

By contrast, Nyman et al. found that the proportion of women in the labor force did not predict the proportion of older adults in Wisconsin counties who received home health services from any funding source [17]. Kenny and Dubay used a different approach from the previously noted Medicare studies; they looked at the relationship between hospital discharge rates and average length of stay, and the characteristics of the home health system and institutional service network [16]. They found that neither the percent of women in the labor force, nor the percent of people seventy-five or older living alone significantly predicted: 1) the proportion of Medicare enrollees receiving any home health services or 2) the average number of visits per recipient. Even so, they specifically noted, "the role that caregivers play in substituting for or complementing Medicare home health service use is likely to be complex and may be better addressed at the household level" [16, p. 34].

RESEARCH USING MICRO- AND MACRO-LEVEL VARIABLES TO ADDRESS LINKAGES BETWEEN INFORMAL AND FORMAL CARE

Another approach used to determine the utilization of informal care and formal services is to include both micro-level interview questions about informal care and formal service use, and macro-level indicators of presence or absence of a service in the analysis. Kemper combined micro- and macro-level indicators into his analysis of factors associated with the amount of formal and informal home care received by elderly disabled persons [8]. He used interview data from the National Long-Term Care Demonstration ("Channeling") data set to determine the number of hours of formal and informal care the older person received, whether the older person had received home medical treatment, and whether the older person had been hospitalized. A macro-level variable—whether the study site had a state program that pays for home care—was used as an indicator of the availability of formal care. When a state home care program existed, Kemper found that: 1) the probability of receiving formal care and the number of hours of formal care were greater, while 2) the probability of receiving resident informal care, and the number of hours were smaller. However, the author cautioned that "these results must be interpreted cautiously: the four sites that had state home care programs may have differed from the six that did not in other respects that account for the differences in the use of formal and informal care" [8, p. 443]. Unfortunately, while Kemper tried to incorporate both micro-level and macro-level variables into his analyses, only one macro-level variable was included in his models, and the multi-level relationship between variables across levels was not examined.

Although the studies described above were designed to address specific issues of relevance to a given unit of analysis, both theoretical and methodological difficulties hamper their usefulness to the gerontological and health services research community at-large. The section that follows describes several strategies that have been used to incorporate both individual and system level variables into the analysis of formal and informal care networks.

ALTERNATIVE STRATEGIES TO COMBINE MICRO- AND MACRO-LEVEL DATA

Multi-level data may be analyzed several different ways. Some researchers have attempted to assess multi-level effects in analysis at the individual-level by including both macro-level unit means and micro-level variables as predictors of individual-level outcomes [27]. Unfortunately, this approach is inadequate since it does not take into account the correlation between the macro-level and micro-level values [28, 29].

As an alternative, some researchers have suggested that the micro-level outcomes be aggregated for individuals within each macro-level unit of analysis (e.g., by community setting), and then, that the data be analyzed at the aggregated (macro) level [30]. While this approach does overcome the problem of correlation between the two units of analysis, inferences may only be made at the macro-level. Therefore, if one is interested in making inferences to micro-level outcomes, problems of cross-level or ecological fallacy will be more likely to occur [29, 31-33]. (See Chapter 2 by Salmon and Ricketts, pp. 17-42, for further discussion of the problems of generalizing to inappropriate units of analysis.) An additional problem is that it will not be possible to explore the extent of individual differences or contextual effects. Because individual-level factors cannot be incorporated into the aggregated model, "one loses the power increase and theoretical insight that one can realize with individual-level variables that explain portions of outcome variability" [28, p. 82].

A different multi-level method treats differences among units at each level as random effects, and differences due to a specific health or program intervention as fixed effects [34, 35]. Under this "mixed-effects" approach, the unexplained (error) variance in the model is subdivided into components due to each separate unit of analysis [36]. While standard statistical methods may be used for some analyses (e.g., those with equal numbers of observations at the macro-level of analysis) [35], with other study designs it is more difficult to divide the error terms into their component parts [37]. One advantage of this "mixed model" estimation technique over more traditional macro-level data methodologies is the micro-level variables may be incorporated into the analysis. This modeling approach also has been used in the context of regression analysis [38] and applied to binary outcomes as well [34].

THE STATISTICAL CONSEQUENCES OF ALTERNATIVE APPROACHES

Those interested in exploring the relationship between formal and informal caregiving networks in rural and urban America often want to incorporate variables from several units of analysis into their conceptual models since such model specifications are more likely to reflect the complex set of relationships found between health system factors (macro-level variables) and the personal characteristics of an older adult and his/her informal care network (micro-level variables). However, if these multi-level relationships are ignored, and these relations between individual- and system-level factors are studied as if only individual-level data were available, incorrect inferences regarding the impact of individual and group-level variables on study outcomes will be more likely to occur [29, 39].

Problems of inference from the macro-level to the micro-level, which are known as the "ecological fallacy," may arise when only macro-level factors are included in analysis even though implications are drawn to individuals at a different (micro) unit of analysis [29]. Similarly, while much less is known about the "individualistic fallacy," when inferences are drawn from micro-level distributions to macro-level phenomena, incorrect implications may result at the aggregated level (e.g., by state, region, or country) of analysis.

From an analytical standpoint, when data with different levels of observation are used to assess the relationship between a set of predictor and outcome variables, it should not be assumed that the observations from one level of analysis are unassociated with observations from a different unit of analysis [28, 40]. Instead, it should be acknowledged that individuals coming from the same macro-level setting will be likely to share common attributes, and that as a result, there will likely be a correlation among individuals living in a given macro-level setting. If investigators choose to include only micro- (or macro-) level variables in their analyses even though they suspect that there will be a correlation between the variables included and those omitted from the analytical model at a higher (lower) unit of analysis, they may violate an important assumption of multivariate model analyses, namely, that the model has been fully specified [41]. Similarly, if investigators are interested in assessing the impact of individual and macro-level variables on a given set of outcomes, but fail to take into account the implications of gathering data from several levels in their analysis, they may have difficulty justifying the validity of study findings since the multivariate model assumption of independence between error terms at different levels of analysis will be seriously called into question.

The violation of the assumption that the error terms between the levels are uncorrelated is particularly problematic since both coefficient estimates and the standard errors of the estimates may be affected [28]. Because it is likely that older adults living within a given local community setting will share some important attributes (e.g., they will have similar access to health care, to local economic opportunities, and be affected by similar changes in the local environment), it is reasonable to expect a significant within group, or "intraclass" correlation among individuals residing in a given community setting.

If investigators erroneously assume that there is no significant intraclass correlation among individuals within a given geographic setting, the standard errors of their estimates may be underestimated (particularly for individual-level variables) and the point estimates, while generally unbiased, may be inefficient [29]. In some cases, even the signs of the coefficient estimates may be misleading [42].

Because of the methodological and theoretical problems associated with either 1) limiting a research analysis to a micro- or macro-level unit of analysis, or 2) inappropriately combining units of analysis in a given statistical model, alternative methodologies have recently been devised to enable individual- and system-level variables to be examined simultaneously in a given model. Multi-level models have been proposed to allow investigators to assess the relationships between a set of characteristics at different levels in order to examine the nature of these effects. In such an analysis, the effects of a given set of predictors at each level are simultaneously considered. These effects may include both predictor variables (main effects) and interactions between the predictor variables at different units of analysis.

As an example, if investigators were interested in studying the impact of a residential stroke rehabilitation program for rural-dwelling older adults on subsequent health and utilization behavior, they might consider the following factors in their conceptual and empirical models: macro-level characteristics of the stroke rehabilitation centers (e.g., per capita funding, staff ratios, the experience of the therapists and the leadership at the rehabilitation centers), other community-level characteristics (e.g., population density, percentage of the population living in nonmetropolitan areas, and proportion of the population over age 65), and micro-level characteristics of the older participants and their informal care networks (e.g., age, gender, race, functional status of the care recipient and care provider, knowledge of services and attitudes about family responsibility). If these researchers were to utilize a multi-level framework to analyze these relationships using this type of data (rather than focusing solely on macro- or micro-level variables in the predictive model), they would be more likely to make correct inferences about the impact of individual- and system-level factors on the outcomes of interest [39].

OPERATIONALIZATION OF A MULTI-LEVEL MODEL

Suppose that researchers having data at two levels of observation anticipated that characteristics of a given program for older adults in some way depended on the community in which it was located, and that this effect varied by community type. In order to estimate a model using multi-level analytic techniques, the researchers would need to follow several preliminary steps. (For a more statistical presentation of this procedure, see Mason et al. [36] and Ringdal [39].) First they would need to define a micro-level equation for each community setting. Continuing with the previous example, if the investigator were assessing health care utilization among rural older adults following the implementation of a stroke rehabilitation intervention, they might operationalize the empirical model with the following micro-level variables for the caregiver and care recipient: age, race, gender, income, functional status, and the treatment group status of the care recipient. In addition, they would assume that these variables were imperfectly measured, so that an error term would also be included as an additional term in each micro-level equation. The micro-level error terms would be assumed to be normally distributed in this type of model.

As a second step, they would describe the macro part of the model. The macro-level model might include variables such as the proportion of the population over age sixty-five, the population density of a geographic setting, the average income of the population served, and proximity to a metropolitan area. One macro-level equation would be specific for each beta coefficient (i.e., unstandardized regression coefficient) in the micro-level model. The left-hand side of each macro-level equation (i.e., the dependent variables in the macro-level model) are the same beta coefficients found on the right-hand side of the micro-level model. Stated differently, if there were ten micro-level variables measuring attributes of caregivers and care recipients, plus an intercept term in the micro-level model (as described above), there would be eleven distinct equations specified as part of the micro-level model. The independent variables (on the right-hand side) of the macro-model would be the aggregated variables hypothesized to directly affect each dependent variable in the macro-level model. The same independent macro-level variables (e.g., population density, proportion of the population over age 65, etc.), and any interaction terms would be used as explanatory variables in each macro-level equation. Furthermore, since the macro-level model also assumes that the group-level variables are measured with error, an error component would be incorporated into each macro-level equation in this part of the multi-level model. The macro errors would be assumed to be multivariate normally distributed and allowed to be correlated, but the micro- and macro-level errors would be assumed to be uncorrelated [36, 39].

Finally, the investigators would substitute each equation from the macro model into the overall macro-level model. In this step, each coefficient in the micro-level would be replaced with the more complex macro-level equation (from step 2). Continuing with the previous example, the macro-level equations (which specify the relationship between the macro-level independent variables and the eleven dependent variables in the macro-level model) would be incorporated into the right-hand side of the micro-level part of the multi-level model. The result of the substitution of each macro-level equation for every coefficient on the right-hand side of the micro-level model is a single equation multi-level model. Special-purpose computer programs, such as ML3 from the Institute of Education at the University of London [43], HLM from the University of Chicago [44], and VARCL [45] are among the programs currently available to estimate such multi-level models.

Multi-level modeling is appropriate for a wide range of applications since it allows for macro- and micro-level errors in analysis. It is also a quite general model, with many applications becoming more widely known as special cases. Although the approach does have some limitations (e.g., special estimation procedures are still needed to handle some discrete micro-level variables, and multi-equation systems and latent variables have yet to be adequately handled in some computer packages), multi-level analysis can be useful in preventing fallacious inferences from one level of analysis to another, and offers a useful tool to researchers interested in handling individual and group data in a theoretically and statistically satisfactory manner.

CONCLUSION

In this chapter we have presented examples of two methodological approaches to the study of informal caregiver networks and formal service availability. The micro-level approach involves collecting information about informal care and formal service utilization directly from the older adult and/or his or her caregiver and only rarely includes macro-level or system variables. The macro-level approach examines relationships between system-level characteristics and use of services using a geographic area (such as county or state) as the unit of analysis. Because of limitations in each of these approaches, results are sometimes contradictory and questions are left unanswered.

A comprehensive understanding of the complex interrelationships between informal caregiving networks and formal service infrastructure is of particular importance in rural areas. There seems to be general consensus that rural older adults experience poorer health [2] and are more likely to depend primarily or exclusively on informal networks than their urban counterparts [4]. What remains unanswered is whether they do this by choice (i.e., they prefer to be cared for by a more readily available informal network) or by necessity (i.e., the formal services are unavailable, inaccessible, and/or unacceptable). How this question is answered could lead to very different policy decisions concerning allocation of resources. We have suggested in this chapter that a multi-level approach could provide answers to this and other important questions. This approach enables researchers to incorporate both macro- and micro-level variables into the analysis to provide a more complete picture of the determinants of formal and informal care for older adults.

REFERENCES

1. W. B. Clifford, T. B. Heaton, P. R. Voss, and G. V. Fuguitt, The Rural Elderly in Demographic Perspective, in *The Elderly in Rural Society: Every Fourth Elder,* R. T. Coward and G. R. Lee (eds.), Springer Publishing Company, New York, pp. 25-55, 1985.
2. R. T. Coward, D. K. McLaughlin, R. P. Duncan, and C. N. Bull, An Overview of Health and Aging in Rural America, in *Health Services for Rural Elders,* R. T. Coward, C. N. Bull, G. Kukulka, and J. M. Galliher (eds.), Springer Publishing Company, New York, 1994.
3. B. J. McCulloch, Aging and Kinship in Rural Context, in *Handbook of Aging and the Family,* R. Blieszner and V. H. Bedford (eds.), Greenwood Press, Westport, Connecticut, 1995.

4. R. T. Coward, S. J. Cutler, and R. A. Mullens, Residential Differences in the Composition of the Helping Networks of Impaired Elders, *Family Relations, 39,* pp. 44-50, 1990.
5. E. P. Stoller and G. R. Lee, Informal Care of Rural Elders, in *Health Services for Rural Elderly,* R. T. Coward, C. N. Bull, G. Kukulka, and J. M. Galliher (eds.), Springer Publishing Company, New York, pp. 33-64, 1994.
6. E. P. Stoller, Formal Services and Informal Helping: The Myth of Service Substitution, *The Journal of Applied Gerontology, 8:*1, pp. 37-52, 1989.
7. S. L. Tennstedt, S. L. Crawford, and J. B. McKinlay, Is Family Care on the Decline? A Longitudinal Investigation of the Substitution of Formal Long-Term Care Services for Informal Care, *The Milbank Quarterly, 71:*4, pp. 601-624, 1993.
8. P. Kemper, The Use of Formal and Informal Home Care by the Disabled Elderly, *Health Services Research, 27:*4, pp. 421-451, 1992.
9. I. E. Gibbons, H. F. Camp, and M. A. Kaiser, Patterns of Long-Term Care Services for Rural Elderly: A Community Approach, *Human Services in the Rural Environment, 14:*3, pp. 6-11, 1991.
10. M. Kaiser, H. Camp, and J. Gibbons, Services for the Rural Elderly: A Developmental Model, *Journal of Gerontological Social Work, 11:*1/2, pp. 25-45, 1987.
11. J. A. Krout, *Area Agencies on Aging: Service Planning and Provision for the Rural Elderly,* Final Report to the Retirement Research Foundation, State University of New York, Fredonia, 1989.
12. J. W. Meyer, R. A. Lusky, and A. Wright, Title III Services: Variation in Use Within a State, *The Journal of Applied Gerontology, 10:*2, pp. 140-156, 1991.
13. G. M. Nelson, Social Services to the Urban and Rural Aged: The Experience of Area Agencies on Aging, *The Gerontologist, 20:*2, pp. 200-207, 1980.
14. P. Taietz and S. Milton, Rural-Urban Differences in the Structure of Services for the Elderly in Upstate New York Counties, *Journal of Gerontology, 34:*3, pp. 429-437, 1979.
15. A. E. Benjamin, Determinants of State Variations in Home Health Utilization and Expenditures under Medicare, *Medical Care, 24:*6, pp. 535-547, 1986.
16. G. M. Kenny and L. C. Dubay, *The Determinants of Market Variation in Home Health Utilization,* Working Papers 3740-02, Urban Institute, Washington, D.C., 1990.
17. J. A. Nyman, A. Sen, B. Y. Chan, and P. P. Commins, Urban/Rural Differences in Home Health Patients and Services, *The Gerontologist, 31:*4, pp. 457-466, 1991.
18. M. A. P. Salmon, G. M. Nelson, and S. Rous, The Continuum of Care Revisited: A Rural Perspective, *The Gerontologist, 33:*5, pp. 658-666, 1993.
19. J. H. Swan and A. E. Benjamin, Medicare Home Health Utilization as a Function of Nursing Home Market Factors, *Health Services Research, 23,* pp. 479-500, 1990.
20. R. M. Andersen and J. F. Newman, Societal and Individual Determinants of Medical Care Utilization in the United States, *The Milbank Quarterly, 51,* pp. 95-124, 1973.
21. R. M. Andersen and L. A. Aday, Access to Medical Care in the US: Realized and Potential, *Medical Care, 16,* pp. 533-546, 1978.
22. D. M. Bass and L. S. Noelker, The Influence of Family Caregivers on Elder's Use of In-Home Services: An Expanded Conceptual Framework, *Journal of Health and Social Behavior, 28,* pp. 184-196, 1987.

23. D. M. Bass, W. J. Looman, and P. Ehrlich, Predicting the Volume of Health and Social Services: Integrating Cognitive Impairment into the Modified Andersen Framework, *The Gerontologist, 32*:1, pp. 33-43, 1992.

24. A. E. Joseph and D. S. Cloutier, A Framework for Modeling the Consumption of Health Services by the Rural Elderly, *Social Science and Medicine, 30*:1, pp. 45-52, 1990.

25. A. E. Joseph and A. Poyner, *The Utilization of Three Public Services in a Rural Ontario Township: An Empirical Evaluation of a Conceptual Framework,* Publication No. 127, University of Guelph, Guelph, Ontario, 1981.

26. M. H. Cantor, Family and Community: Changing Roles in an Aging Society, *The Gerontologist, 31*:3, pp. 337-346, 1991.

27. L. H. Boyd, Jr. and G. R. Iversen, *Contextual Analysis: Concepts and Statistical Techniques,* Wadsworth, Belmont, California, 1979.

28. D. Koepke and B. R. Flay, Levels of Analysis, in *Evaluating Health Promotion Programs: New Directions for Program Evaluation,* M. T. Braverman (ed.), Jossey-Bass, San Francisco, California, 1989.

29. J. W. Falter, Some Theoretical and Methodological Problems of Multilevel Analysis Reconsidered, *Social Science Information, 17*:6, pp. 841-869, 1978.

30. R. S. Barcikowski, Statistical Power with Group Means as the Unit of Analysis, *Journal of Educational Statistics, 6*:3, pp. 69-80, 1981.

31. W. Glick, Problems in Cross-Level Inferences, in *Issues in Aggregation. New Directions for Methodology of Social and Behavior Science,* K. H. Roberts and L. Burstein (eds.), Jossey-Bass, San Francisco, California, 1980.

32. H. Morgenstern, Uses of Ecological Analysis in Epidemiologic Research, *American Journal of Public Health, 72*:12, pp. 1336-1344, 1982.

33. C. Poole, Ecological Analysis as Outlook and Method, *American Journal of Public Health, 84*:5, pp. 715-717, 1994.

34. H. Goldstein, *Multilevel Models in Educational and Social Research,* Oxford University Press, New York, 1987.

35. K. D. Hopkins, The Unit of Analysis: Group Means Versus Individual Observations, *American Educational Research Journal, 19*:1, pp. 5-18, 1982.

36. W. M. Mason, G. Y. Wong, and B. Entwisle, Contextual Analysis Through the Multi-level Linear Model, in *Sociological Methodology, 1983-1984,* S. Leinhardt (ed.), Jossey-Bass, San Francisco, California, pp. 72-103, 1983.

37. G. A. Millikin and D. E. Johnson, Analysis of Messy Data, Vol. 1, *Designed Experiments,* Wadsworth, Belmont, California, 1984.

38. L. W. Sayrs, *Pooled Time Series Analysis,* Sage Publications, Newbury Park, California, 1989.

39. K. Ringdal, Recent Developments in Methods for Multilevel Analysis, *Acta Sociologica, 35,* pp. 235-243, 1992.

40. R. L. Tate, Cross-Level Interaction in Multilevel Models, *Journal of Applied Behavioral Science, 21*:2, pp. 221-234, 1985.

41. D. N. Gujarati, *Basic Encounters* (2nd Edition), McGraw-Hill, New York, 1988.

42. I. G. G. Kreft and E. D. De Leeuw, The Seesaw Effect: A Multilevel Problem, *Quality and Quantity, 22,* pp. 127-137, 1988.

43. R. Prosser, J. Rasbash, and H. Goldstein, *ML3. Software for Three Level Analysis,* User's Guide, University of London, London, 1990.
44. A. S. Bryk, S. W. Raudenbush, R. Cogdon, and M. Seltzer, *An Introduction to HLM: Computer and User's Guide,* University of Chicago, Department of Education, Chicago, 1988.
45. M. Aitkin and N. Longford, Statistical Modeling Issues in School Effectiveness Studies, *Journal of the Royal Statistical Society, 149A,* pp. 1-43, 1986.

CHAPTER
12

Improving Health Care Research for Rural Elderly People Using Advanced Communications Technologies

Mark E. Williams, Thomas C. Ricketts, III
and Bob G. Thompson

Generalist physicians (general internists and family practitioners) caring for elderly people face formidable challenges. Physicians experience great satisfaction in playing a pivotal role in providing preventive care and in intervening during acute illness, but this satisfaction is being eroded by bureaucratic complexity, a rapidly expanding information base and an increasing sense of isolation and being out of touch. This chapter describes how modern telecommunications technology can be applied to this situation to address the specific problems of isolation, the need to process growing amounts of data, and the need to relate to increasingly complex payment and review systems.

BACKGROUND

Caring for frail elderly people is especially challenging in rural areas. The hours are long, peer support is limited, and care is often compromised by the familiar problems of distance, economics, and understaffed service settings. The generalist physician can only spend limited time with elderly patients and is poorly reimbursed for the time spent; this is frustrating in that problems are often complex with interacting medical and social issues. Documentation and other paperwork requirements are staggering. Moreover, most generalist physicians have received little training in geriatrics or in effective collaboration with other professions providing various community services. These issues unfavorably affect both physician recruitment and retention in rural America.

Added to these challenges is the explosion of health care costs and appropriate concerns regarding the containment of health expenditures. Generalist physicians are an easy target for calls to further cut reimbursement for medical services. Because of these pressures many generalist physicians are leaving medical practice, and the generalist training programs in internal medicine and family medicine have seen an alarming drop in applicants to their programs. In addition, health care services tend to be consolidated and not always accessible; a more equitable distribution of services is necessary. Moreover, the demographic changes in American society, documented with each successive census, are creating concern. For the first time in human history, infants in fortunate nations like ours can expect to live well into their seventies and eighties. This demographic revolution increases pressures on resources as it also creates further social change and new opportunities.

The current crisis creates an historic opportunity for testing a new approach to health care. A new model must enrich physician decision making by focusing on cooperation as well as teamwork. It must facilitate *management* of identified medical and social problems by increasing access to relevant information and expertise.

One promising way to address this opportunity is through the application of state-of-the-art communications technology to reshape the health care system. Through high-speed electronic linkage, professionals who might otherwise interact only rarely, can function as a virtual health care team through the rapid exchange of vital information, interactive deliberation, and decision making. A patient's single contact with any team member can be a point of universal access to other team members and to a vast array of services and information. Time and travel are minimized for both patient and provider while more timely and coordinated care is given, and health care costs are dramatically reduced through increased efficiency and expansion of productive activity. It is conceivable and technologically feasible to place this capability in the home to allow house calls, home visits, access to diet and other health care information and even components of the history, physical examination, and diagnostic procedures to be performed.

In response to the need to structure the tertiary medical center in a way that will redirect resources to the treatment of the rapidly increasing portion of the population that is elderly, the University of North Carolina School of Medicine created a Program on Aging in 1979 (see Chapter 1, pp. 3-15). That program has supported a model interdisciplinary team program to assist elderly people facing crises and to use the program and its affiliated off-campus sites as the mechanism to train clinicians to work in a team-oriented environment. One component of the program is the telemedicine project. The telemedicine project makes heavy use of the North Carolina Area Health Education Centers (AHEC) program for transportation and communications support. The AHEC system is also the mechanism that allows the telemedicine project to maximize teaching opportunities since the primary role of AHEC is to support continuing clinical education in rural communities. Before describing the details of the program in eastern North Carolina, it may help the reader to describe what telemedicine is and how it works.

TELEMEDICINE—
AN INTRODUCTION TO THE TECHNOLOGY

The term "telemedicine" has been used to describe a wide range of telecommunications systems, and alternative terms such as "telematics" and "distance care" have been proposed as ways to more specifically describe the various use of telecommunications technology in the health care field. The focus here is on the use of technology for improved health care delivery and the term telemedicine is used throughout. The basic components of a telemedicine system are a signal generator, a carrier of the signal, and a receiving site. The various telecommunications technologies used in telemedicine systems have included simple telephone connections, two-way radio, visual slow-scan, and live two-way video/two-way audio transmission (interactive television). Interactive television provides a television camera and a monitor at each end of a system linked by cable or microwave or a combination of transmission technologies that could include satellite or broadcast systems with restricted access to signals.

Various means of electronic transmission can be used in telemedicine systems. The four most widely considered options for transmission of signals in a telemedicine network are satellite, telephone lines, microwave, and fiber-optic cables. While these modes of transmission have very different infrastructure requirements, the major operational distinction between these modes is bandwidth. Narrowband channels can only transmit audio or still pictures, while broadband channels can transmit moving images. Telephone lines are an example of a narrowband channel, and television a broadband channel. The bandwidth required for one television channel can be as much as 1,000 times greater than that for a telephone channel, and television signals are routinely transmitted using satellite and, more and more commonly fiber-optic cable.

Each of these modes has advantages and disadvantages, but the option of fiber-optic cable is gaining in popularity. Fiber-optic systems provide a high-quality method of transmission that is becoming less expensive and higher in quality as the cost of "codec" equipment falls (codec is shorthand for "coding and decoding" and is the hardware that translates video, sound, or data into the electronic signals that travel over the fiber system and decodes the digital signal for use at the remote or receiver site) and the installation of fiber-optic cable is extended across the country. The codec required for operation of fiber-optic transmission has become dramatically smaller in size, decreasing ". . . from equipment that would require two flatbed trucks and five persons to transport to equipment that can be lifted by one person. The codec's reliability and quality, which have been criticized in telemedical applications in the past, also have improved" [1].

Another development which makes the option of fiber-optic cable more acceptable is the fact that fiber-optic cable networks have recently been expanding. To some extent, this may be a result of the lower costs of codec equipment. In many rural areas telephone lines follow railroad right-of-way and regional telephone companies have expedited installation of fiber-optic cable using existing rights-of-way. As a result, fiber-optic networks should facilitate the delivery of medical care and education to rural communities located along railroad lines. There is also an underused infrastructure of existing wide-band fiber-optic systems installed for specific purposes (defense, secure communications) that can be used with telemedicine systems but are not because they are not well known by potential users [2].

The capacity of the system varies according to the type of technology used. Diagnostic aids that are available through telemedicine systems include a remote tilt-zoom camera for patient observation, a patient viewing microscope, an x-ray machine, a stethoscope, electroencephalogram (EEG) equipment, electrocardiogram (ECG) equipment, and fiber-optic endoscopes. Blood slides can be transmitted, and vital signs and metabolic functions can be observed. Visual observations can be made over the system, and medical record and laboratory data can be exchanged. Auxiliary items like facsimiles, laser printers, and videocassette recorders can also be included in telemedicine systems. More specialized equipment is available for certain medical applications, such as radiology.

Commercially available systems for teleradiology include high-speed digitalization of radiographs, data compression, local storage, automatic transmission, selective retrieval, image enhancement, and interfacing with conventional computer systems [3]. The result is that assuming appropriate attention is paid to technical details, teleradiology can be quite easily and accurately performed over most systems. X-rays can be observed in a standard viewing box and, with a remote control zoom lens, the physician can see a close-up of any portion of the film.

Several medical specialties have used telemedicine systems successfully. These include radiology, psychiatry, gastroenterology, dermatology, and neurology. Psychotherapy, speech therapy, allergy, and nutrition counseling have also been performed over telemedicine networks. Telemedicine technology has many applications in addition to remote diagnosis. Telemedicine can be used for supervision of patient care, patient education, and to provide patients with a way of communicating with distant family members while in the hospital. Medical professionals can use it for teleconferencing, education, and consultation. Teleconferencing allows group discussion of research objectives, protocol development, and data analysis at reasonable cost [3, 4]. Telemedicine systems also have uses in administration, data management, and communication between administrators. Many diverse locations can be connected by telemedicine links. Examples include nursing homes, prison health clinics, neighborhood health centers, mobile clinics, airport emergency rooms, hospital surgical suites, classrooms, physician offices, and administrative conference rooms [3].

These applications of telemedicine highlight an aspect of telemedicine systems that is often ignored: the organizational structure created to accommodate the technological system. In contrast to the variety of experiments done in the area of telecommunications technology, relatively little consideration has been given to the development of an organizational structure that is capable of efficiently utilizing telemedicine technology. While there is increasing agreement that improvement of medical care will not be made merely be adding professionals, and that it will require a restructuring of the patterns of health care, no consensus has been reached regarding the new system configurations [3].

TELEMEDICINE AND RURAL AREAS

Telemedicine has been described as a promising way to redress the imbalance in the availability of health care resources for rural residents and the federal government and many states have begun to devote considerable resources to its development [2, 5]. The federal government is supporting telemedicine projects through its Office of Rural Health Policy (ORHP), the National Library of Medicine, the U.S. Department of Agriculture, and the Health Care Financing Administration [3]. States are setting up fiber-optic communications networks with the explicit purpose of creating rural-oriented telemedicine systems; the states of Iowa and Texas are two signal examples [2]. Other states are using telemedicine systems in a consortium structure with multiple systems that are loosely coordinated to improve health care delivery to rural communities [6].

In North Carolina, the state has developed the largest digital network in the world and the legislature has appropriated developmental money to help with early adoption of the technology. A public-private alliance has emerged to assist in the use of that system for health care needs. The North Carolina Health Information and Communications Alliance (NCHICA) involves a voluntary group of hospitals, professional associations, clinics, telecommunications firms, and data processors who are interested in maximizing the use of telecommunications using the Internet and fiber systems. The N.C. Information Highway system and the NCHICA alliance have helped the University of North Carolina and the East Carolina University Schools of Medicine to receive five-year ORHP grants to develop systems. The project described here has been supported, in part, by this grant mechanism.

The adoption of telecommunications technologies in health care have been irregular and are largely dependent upon the need for the technology and the ease

Table 1. Likely Benefits of an Integrated Telecommunication System of Health Care for Older Population in Rural Communities

User	Likely Benefits
Patients	Improved access, better delivery of services, more responsive; informal care
Local Practitioners	Reduced isolation, more time spent providing care, improved supervision of other health-care workers, reduced paperwork
Local Settings	Efficient billing, reduced redundancy, expanded service delivery; ability to serve more people
Regional Centers	Improved service delivery, access to new guidelines, expanded catchment area, reduced redundancy
Tertiary Referral Centers	Disseminated expertise, reorientation to community concerns, significant research potential, critical appraisal of guidelines and care options
State and Federal Agencies	Dissemination of guidelines, effective monitoring of care, evaluation of policies, outcomes research

with which the users, both clinicians and patients, can relate to the new way of doing things. Any system that will meet with wide acceptance will have to provide the physician and other health care workers with a system which, with a simple command on a computer-like terminal, can provide access to vital information and "face-to-face" communication with other professional resources. On a good telemedicine system, the practitioner can view on the monitor any portion of the complete medical record of a patient (including medical, nursing, social information and radiographs, laboratory studies, the electrocardiogram, etc.). Using another command which, given current technology, can be a voice command, the appropriate documentation of a patient visit is generated and sent to the payer. At a prearranged time, the physician participates in a video conference with other team members (e.g., nurse, social worker, pharmacist) to review various patient issues and to develop a more comprehensive plan of care. There is more time to devote to individual patients and for team conferences because time-consuming documentation is handled by the system. In selected circumstances, international experts might be asked to join the team meeting to provide special expertise. Individual medical questions are addressed by accessing large medical databases (such as the National Library of Medicine), or discussing the case with a colleague via video conference. Continuing education is provided by watching Continuing Medical Education (CME) courses and interactive self-study modules. Similarly, other team members benefit from increased interaction with one another for planning and problem-solving. Service delivery gaps resulting from referral delays are minimized. Care is better monitored. And beyond these and other obvious benefits to professionals, the most significant benefits accrue to the patients themselves.

The concept of applying advanced telecommunications services in health care may significantly improve efficiency, quality, and access to services while simultaneously lowering health care costs. Systems employing telecommunications technology can more equitably distribute health care resources. However, these advantages need to be demonstrated and the best possible situation in which to demonstrate them may be in providing complex geriatric care to frail elderly people living in an isolated rural setting. This is a complex clinical area and one that can test the capacity of telecommunications thoroughly and, at the same time, provide the demand for the high-density data and audio-visual contacts that existing systems are able to provide. A responsive, effective telecommunications system employed in this setting will be easily transferable to other settings.

A fully implemented telecommunications system will have links between patients, local health care workers (physicians, nurses, social workers, etc.), regional hospitals, tertiary referral centers and medical schools, and state and federal agencies. While it is beyond the scope of this chapter to fully explore the nature and extent of these interactions, several immediate benefits seem likely (see Table 1).

The system offers much more than telephones and FAX machines—the most common technologies currently used to overcome distance in medical care. Fundamentally, a clinical interview can verify an observable physical finding (e.g., Does the thyroid gland appear enlarged?) or obtain an interpretation of a clinical observation (e.g., What is this pigmented skin lesion? Is this tremor characteristic of Parkinson's disease?). This is similar to the process whereby clinicians in medical centers and larger group practices request informal "verifying consultations" from their on-site colleagues. Even more powerful, having one or more expert diagnosticians in virtual proximity to participate in a clinical interview can assist the busy practitioner in identifying pivotal features in an elderly person's complex presentation of illness. For example, the clinical interview and examination are still the gold standard for diagnosing dementing illness such as Alzheimer's disease.

Medical observation is an active, creative process which assesses the connections between a person's appearance, dress, language, and behaviors to reach an impression (diagnosis) which is explanatory and verifiable. This impression reflects the person's unified presentation of self, combined with specific observable clues of past events: diseases, occupations, experience, losses, and pleasures; the effects of the passage of time revealed through lines and scars. Until now, it has not been possible to share interactively complex clinical observations and insights of this degree of subtlety across distances. In addition, simply reducing the massive burden of paperwork through an integrated health care database would be a major attraction for even the most self-sufficient practitioners.

The potential problems and limitations of advanced technologies also need to be examined. Strategies to maintain data security and access to sensitive personal information must be rigorously evaluated to insure confidentiality, and to safeguard invasion of privacy. In addition, telemedicine systems are initially expensive. Equipment costs can exceed $100,000 and service charges are around $50,000 a year for each fully interactive site on a network. These costs place real financial barriers to the development of advanced telecommunications systems in most rural communities. Moreover, the billing criteria for clinical services are not uniformly established or available by some payers. There are proposals before Congress to require payment for telemedicine service provided under Medicare [7] and the state of California has enacted the Telemedicine Development Act of 1996 that solves some of the problems of regulation and licensing that are necessary elements of a reimbursement system for telemedicine [8].

Psychological barriers could also limit the full use of advanced technology. Some people feel threatened and intimidated by sophisticated technology. The lack of direct physical contact could cause others to mistakenly think the technology creates an impersonal relationship between patient and physician. Physicians and hospitals may fear a loss of control and income as networks extend far beyond local geographies. Telemedicine advocates must be sensitive to these and other concerns. Considerable research opportunities exist in exploring the psychology and economics of telemedical applications.

THE UNC APPROACH TO TELEMEDICINE

The University of North Carolina at Chapel Hill has moved forward with an application of telemedicine technology in a rural area of eastern North Carolina. That demonstration is a collaborative effort involving The Program on Aging in the UNC School of Medicine, and clinicians and administrators in two rural North Carolina counties, Northampton and Halifax. This is a rich collaboration of groups with technological, clinical, service delivery, and rural expertise.

Northampton and Halifax counties, located approximately 100 miles from UNC, Chapel Hill, are the ideal places to test the feasibility of a telemedicine project. Two of the poorest rural counties in North Carolina, they have a combined population of almost 80,000. The elderly population (over 65) is over 15 percent of the population. A profile in 1980 indicated that 40 percent of the population is underemployed, 30 percent live below the poverty level, 34 percent have less than an eighth-grade education (including considerable illiteracy), and 34 percent live in substandard housing. Over half of the residents of the two counties are African American. About 17 percent of residents over sixty-five are believed to be functionally impaired. Health Professional supply statistics indicate that Northampton County has seven physicians and a primary care physicians to population ratio of 1:4,133, well above the standard for designation as a shortage area [9]. Halifax county is better served with health care resources, having a primary care physician-to-population ratio of 1:2,129 in 1995.

Working in this area is a dedicated consortium of health professionals, the Rural Health Group, Inc., which centers its activities in Jackson, North Carolina. Their mission is to provide access to quality health care without regard to ability to pay and to identify community health problems and develop solutions. The consortium's headquarters are at the Roanoke-Amaranth Clinic in Jackson. The Program on Aging at the University of North Carolina at Chapel Hill, which is the focal point for the telemedicine project, has enjoyed a rich working relationship with the Rural Health Group during the recent past. Since 1991, geriatric team consultations have been regularly provided in the community and several collaborative research projects have been located in the area making use of the Roanoke-Amaranth clinicians and patients. This model of a tertiary care university medical center reaching out to a rural, minority community-oriented practice to provide support and services, provided a test bed for the application of telemedicine principles, and in 1993, planning began for a fiber-optic link between Chapel Hill and Jackson.

The original plan called for the use of an interactive video link with the Jackson center and its new long-term care facility to replace the in-person geriatric assessments which involved the transportation of teams of clinicians from Chapel Hill to Jackson on a monthly basis. The plan was expanded as the capabilities of the telemedicine link were better understood and the system started undergoing testing.

THE BENEFITS OF TELEMEDICINE AND THE RURAL ELDERLY POPULATION

This unique rural generalist physician setting was ideal for the application of a system that is meant to optimally benefit rural communities and was seen primarily as a demonstration of telemedicine feasibility before offering it to other primary care practices. The guiding principles for its development were to construct a system that could be easily used from the time of its installation, and that complements the real practice of medicine in rural areas where there is a need for consultation and decision making for isolated practitioners.

The installation of the system began in 1994 and by the fall of 1994 the North Carolina Rural Telemedicine System (NC-RTS) was established to implement the program. It made use of the North Carolina Information Highway, a state-supported, public-private partnership that fostered the development of fiber-optic lines and involved the linking of schools, hospitals, clinics, government agencies, libraries, and data handlers. The NC-RTS initially involved a node at the Hampton Woods long-term care facility which is part of the Roanoke-Amaranth Community Health Center organization. That link was supplemented with other nodes at the Community Health Center clinic itself, the Halifax Memorial Hospital in Roanoke Rapids in Halifax County, a 190-bed community hospital, and Our Community Hospital in Scotland Neck, a 60-bed hospital with less than 20 beds operating as acute-care beds, also in Halifax County.

The program has operated consults, conferences, and training since the winter of 1994-1995 and is now expanding its schedule of on-line work from an average of less than four hours per week to a twenty-hour per week load. The system is not meant to be a hub-and-spoke system centered on Chapel Hill; rather, the structure allows for communications between any and all elements for consultation and education. The distributed nature of the system is meant to be its strength, with the object of giving the rural component equal membership and a sense of ownership and control within the larger system [10, 11]. The system is now in the process of evaluating its effectiveness and to make such an evaluation meaningful. The program has tried to understand telemedicine as an innovation that does not necessarily replace, one-for-one, the in-person clinical encounter, but as a new technology that has its own strengths in terms of clinical data and information capture and as a medium of communication between people.

Testing the effectiveness of such a system requires an evaluation that looks at five representative areas of health care interactions: direct care delivery, obtaining consultations, supervising physician's assistants, patient education, and medical student teaching.

Direct Care Delivery

Practicing physicians have received little training in the effective use of community-based non-medical services. In addition, most health care financing (especially Medicare) contains disincentives for both patients and physicians to use the most effective and least costly type of care for frail elderly people. This is coupled with inadequate reimbursement to the generalist physician for complex ongoing patient management tasks beyond the immediate cause for the office visit. Moreover, a caring physician may invest considerable time and energy only to discover that the patient is not eligible to receive needed services. A key argument for the expanded use of telecommunications is that the generalist can provide more direct care; the technology can reverse the trend toward increasing time and effort spent managing paper rather than people. Properly applied, the system will focus on the patient provider relationship and will produce maximum benefit of this relationship by increasing the amount of time spent with patients.

The UNC system has been used for direct patient interactions and the delivery of care to acute and chronic patients. The advantages of the system are just now being described, but it is clear that the system is essentially a different approach to patient care and not a substitute for direct, personal care.

Consultations

It would be very helpful to patients if expert consultations could be obtained without expensive, time-consuming transportation. Many times patients need to see another physician or allied health professional, but do not require a detailed hands-on evaluation. Individuals with complex needs for care could be co-managed much better if they could be seen by their private physician and consultant at the same time. Obvious examples include the care of patients with Alzheimer's disease, psychiatric illness, or skin conditions. The system would also be helpful for technical assistance such as reviewing radiographs with an expert radiologist or pathologic specimens with a pathologist. This aspect of the UNC system is also in a developmental stage. The system has allowed specialists to view patients and to work with referring clinicians at a distance. The challenge is to optimize the scheduling of patients to be able to take advantage of the availability of remote specialists during a well-managed encounter.

Physician-Assistant Supervision

A major issue for rural practitioners is supervising physician assistants and nurse practitioners. Licensing boards are caught between the impulse toward tighter supervision of these health professionals at a time when fewer physicians are going into rural communities. The ability to effectively supervise care from an off-site location would be very helpful in the oversight conundrum. In addition, more detailed histories could be obtained and physical findings confirmed prior to developing a plan of care. Research shows that some physician extenders appreciate the increased access to physician specialists that telemedicine systems provide. Nurses who were surveyed about their attitudes toward the telemedicine system they were involved with in northern Ontario felt that telemedicine provided them with needed backup in time of emergencies or difficult diagnoses. Whereas rural health care delivery programs in the past often required that physicians travel to the distant areas where health care was needed, telemedicine systems reduce this need for travel.

Patient Education

Like Americans everywhere, people in rural communities have significant needs for health education. However, small clinics often do not have the capability or capacity to hire educators for all locations. A shared educator, especially with expertise in nutrition or drug review, would be supportable using a telemedicine system and the demand would be high for elderly patients. This aspect is one that holds much promise as use of the system shows that retention of the education message may be greater using telemedicine, and the possibility for repeat use of videotaped sessions can intensify the message and significantly improve compliance. The use of telemedicine as a patient education tool has not been completely evaluated for its effectiveness, nor have the advantages it provides been fully exploited. The UNC project will focus more on this in the future.

Medical Student Teaching

There is more and more emphasis on the development of community-based primary care teaching for medical students and students in other health professions. However, contact with tertiary systems for teaching and student evaluation needs to be developed in such a way that the student is not traveling long distances. Video conferences on selected topics or preceptor observation of student-patient interaction could be scheduled. This system would be particularly useful at the resident level.

Already, the UNC project has shown great promise for this as many students from a wide range of disciplines have been able to watch live interactions and participate in them, as well as view recordings of interactions, and benefit from the lessons learned earlier. Telemedicine as a clinical teaching tool also appears to be underused. There needs to be much more work in the adaptation of its systems, its resources to the classroom, and to the practical preparation of the broadest range of clinical professionals.

As exciting and powerful as these new interactions and applications might be, advanced communications technology offers even more. The old paradigm of distance communication is a passive, linear, and time-shifted encounter. Rather, with high-speed fiber-optic telecommunications technology we have a new approach in which distance is no longer a barrier to interpersonal interaction. With high resolution monitors and real time video, we can appreciate more intimate aspects of a person's self-expression. Teaching allows us to join the advances in database technology with the element of the human presence and emotion to enhance the interaction.

The nature of the telemedicine consult, as many have been quick to realize, is not the same as in-person encounters. The difference between watching an event live, and then watching it on a television using video recording, is apparent to even naive observers. However, video can actually recreate the clinician-patient encounter as it fixes the clinician on the screen, necessarily held there by the requirements of the unsophisticated viewer. Television tends to focus attention "artificially" and the viewer has many distractions. This may be the first time the patient has seen clinicians so focused on their problem. At the same time, the clinician can see the patient in a referent setting, that is a place where they are more "normal" in their behavior and the filters of the stress of travel, and the adjustment of behavior when "at the doctor's office," are taken away. The patient has the opportunity to replay an encounter and to clear up misunderstandings that may have arisen in the brief office encounter. The clinician can replay the event to compare future progress or teach others or themselves.

Telemedicine is not a replacement activity for clinical medicine, but an application of technology that, in itself, offers superior opportunities for caregivers. This is often forgotten when evaluations attempt to balance the costs and benefits of what are assumed to be equivalent systems of care when, in fact, they are fundamentally different.

REFERENCES

1. D. McCarthy, The Virtual Health Economy: Telemedicine and the Supply of Primary Care Physicians in Rural America, *American Journal of Law & Medicine, XXI*:1, pp. 111-130, 1995.
2. T. Randall, *Reaching Rural: Rural Health Travels the Telecommunications Highway,* Federal Office of Rural Health Policy, Rockville, Maryland, 1994.
3. M. J. Field (ed.), *Telemedicine: A Guide to Assessing Telecommunications in Health Care,* National Academy Press, Division of Health Services, Institute of Medicine, Washington, D.C., 1996.
4. Advisory Committee on Telecommunications and Health Care, *Findings and Recommendations,* Federal Communications Commission, Washington, D.C., October 15, 1996 (mimeo).
5. R. W. Stahlhut, The Appropriate Use of Computers and Telecommunications in Medicine, *Adolescent Medicine: State of the Art Reviews, 5*:3, pp. 427-439, 1994.
6. E. B. Perrin, L. G. Hart, S. M. Skillman, B. Paul, M. A. Hanken, and J. Hummel, *Health Information Systems and Their Role in Rural Health Services; Issues and Policy Recommendations,* Rural Health Working Paper Series, #41, WAMI Rural Health Research Center, Seattle, Washington, 1996.
7. U.S. Senate, *The Comprehensive Telehealth Act of 1996, 104th Congress, 2nd Session, S. 2171,* Congressional Record, September 30, 1996, S 11984.
8. California, *The Telemedicine Development Act of 1996,* Chapter 864 Statutes of 1996.
9. *North Carolina Health Professions Data Book, 1995,* Cecil G. Sheps Center for Health Services Research, University of North Carolina at Chapel Hill, Chapel Hill, North Carolina, 1996.
10. M. E. Williams, Geriatric Medicine on the Information Superhighway: Opportunity or Road Kill? *Journal of the American Geriatrics Society, 43*:3, pp. 184-186, 1995.
11. M. E. Williams, The North Carolina Rural Telemedicine System, *Carolina Health Services Review, 3,* pp. 165-169, 1995.

CHAPTER
13

Conclusion

Wilbert M. Gesler, Donna J. Rabiner,
and Gordon H. DeFriese

The overall goal of this book has been to make a variety of research methodologies more understandable and accessible to health care practitioners and academics involved in researching the health care problems of older adults who live in rural areas. In this concluding chapter, we will look back at what the authors of the individual chapters have done to facilitate this goal by examining several themes that cross-cut the chapters. The themes are: 1) research pluralism, 2) theory and practice, 3) community-academic collaboration, 4) interdisciplinary study, and 5) generalizability. The intent is to summarize much of the material, provide new ways to look at the overall project, and, most importantly, to demonstrate the applicability of the substance of the discussion to research projects beyond those discussed in the preceding text. Our efforts will be judged successful if other investigators extend our work and our ideas in as wide a variety of contexts as possible.

RESEARCH PLURALISM

Recognizing the complex nature of our topic, we sought contributions which dealt with a wide array of research approaches. In other words, we wanted to satisfy as many practical research needs as possible while contributing to the professional literature on rural aging issues. The result was a multifaceted approach with research pluralism along several dimensions. Perhaps the most obvious dimension formed the basic tripartite structure of the volume: definition and presentation of health problems, measurement of levels of illness and health, and evaluation of health care practices. In Part I we demonstrated how researchers might survey "the lay of the land" by using various existing data sources to identify what the problems of a group of rural older adults might be. Comparable databases are available in many areas of the country, researchers should identify what may be at-hand and utilize the information as fully as possible. Part II discussed ways in which problems or issues could be measured; again comparability is fairly common. Part III addressed how health care programs put into place to help older rural adults could be evaluated for their effectiveness.

The second dimension sought to juxtapose qualitative and quantitative research. This is a tenable project in its own right and the contrast helped to highlight a number of critical issues likely to be encountered in all manner of rural research. As a reflection of the health-related studies carried out over the last several decades, most of the methods discussed were quantitative in nature. The research strategies detailed in Chapter 9 on health trajectories and Chapter 11 on using multi-level models are especially noteworthy as examples of recent trends in quantitative methodologies. At the same time, as Chapter 6 pointed out, qualitative research methods definitely have an important and unique contribution to make and we expect them to be used increasingly in health care studies. It goes without saying that the nature of the question being asked should determine the selection of appropriate methodologies. And, of course, both strategies may be used in the same research project to address comparable or distinct questions by means of a process qualitative researchers refer to as triangulation.

The third dimension has to do with the scale of analysis. Chapter 3 discussed the effect on study results of geographic scale or type of geographic unit (e.g., county, state) being analyzed. In Chapter 4 on migration, national and local level data sources were contrasted. Micro-scale informal caregiving networks and macro-scale formal resource structures were compared and blended in Chapter 11. The fourth and final dimension we will mention here is based on the distinction between primary and secondary data. Chapter 2 outlined comprehensively where to find and how to use secondary data. Chapters which described specific research projects used secondary data, but more often depended on such primary data as structured and unstructured interviews.

THEORY AND PRACTICE

Research should be guided by both a sound theoretical underpinning and be of practical utility. We tried to combine theory and practice in every phase of our work and our analyses. That is, we delved into the literature for background ideas and have gone into the field to see how these ideals play out in the everyday lives of rural older adults. Whenever possible, we asked contributors to discuss the main concepts which have been developed over the years and that underpin their particular topic. As examples, in Chapter 3 the concept of distance decay was briefly touched upon, in Chapter 4 the authors discussed some of the factors which induce people to migrate, Chapter 8 examined racism as a cause for inequities in health service provision for minority older adults, the authors of Chapter 9 provided a theoretical basis for their methods of tracing trajectories of health, and in Chapter 11 there was a discussion of the relative merits of macro- and micro-level studies.

Each chapter was also written with the goal of providing material that would be of practical utility to readers. Thus, for example, Chapter 2 catalogued a wide range of useful databases such as atlases and census volumes, Chapter 5 explained how effective community-university research collaborations could be established and maintained, the authors of Chapter 6 detailed the ways in which focus groups and in-depth interviews could be conducted and analyzed, Chapter 7 demonstrated how a Geriatric Team Consultation worked while the basic issue of defining ethnicity was discussed in Chapter 8. In Chapter 10, the author explained how research could both be rigorous and help to provide good health care in a community, and Chapter 12 outlined the potential benefits of tele-medicine for patients and practitioners in the rural communities of the future.

COMMUNITY-ACADEMIC COLLABORATION

Perhaps the most significant contribution that this volume makes to the study of the health of older adults in rural areas is an approach, taken by several contributors, that was based on collaboration between members of the communities being researched and researchers from various universities. One of the basic premises upon which the North Carolina Rural Aging Program (NC•RAP) was established was the need for both investigator and the investigated to bring their expertise to research projects and come away with their varying needs met and their respective views heard. Community residents and scholars acted together in framing research questions, collecting data, interpreting results, implementing findings, and broadening one another's horizons.

We stressed the fact that mutual understanding had to be developed over an extended period for collaboration to be fruitful in terms of serving the needs of older adults and providing quality research data. We detailed the establishment of two community "laboratories," one in Johnston County, the other in Halifax and Northampton Counties, in Chapter 5 and provided details of projects carried out in these places in Chapters 7, 10, and 12. These cooperative ventures were not without their hurdles; however, shared goals and patience generally paid dividends. Our strong feeling is that research conducted using a collaborative model will be both valid and relevant. Certainly it provides more meaningful and equitable participation for those elderly respondents who provided much needed information for our research agenda.

INTERDISCIPLINARY STUDY

The NC•RAP group consciously strove to be a multidisciplinary enterprise. The feeling was that such a complex issue as health care for rural older adults is best approached from as many angles as possible and with a participatory framework kept at the forefront. We believe that we successfully blended people with expertise from four different areas. First were residents of the three counties where research projects were carried out. Only a few of these people became authors of chapters; hundreds of others, however, served as consultants, interviewers, and interviewees. Most were given the opportunity to make their views and reactions known. Second, there was close collaboration with the Program on Aging in the University of North Carolina School of Medicine. Medical personnel involved in research and writing chapters included doctors, nurses, geriatricians, and other health care providers. The third group involved were academics in Schools of Public Health; these included members of departments of Epidemiology and Health Policy and Administration. Finally, the social sciences of health were well represented by anthropologists, geographers, social workers, and sociologists.

The commonly held view that people from different disciplines will have great difficulty in cooperating on research projects was belied by the research carried out and, indeed, the writing of this book. At least three reasons may be put forward for this success. First, the University of North Carolina and its sister institutions, Duke and Wake Forest, have a history of interdisciplinary ventures. Second, NC•RAP, sponsored by the Cecil G. Sheps Center for Health Services Research, made a concerted effort to encompass scholars and community residents who had the requisite knowledge and interest to participate in conducting particular studies or contributing book chapters. And, third, the book was conceived and developed at several meetings of NC•RAP, attended by most of the first authors, other authors, and researchers on various component projects.

GENERALIZABILITY

Many, if not most, readers of this book will be concerned about how well the methods discussed will apply to other situations besides those described here. We are convinced that, although the specific examples used to illustrate points are unique, the ways of going about doing research on rural older adults can be applied elsewhere in the United States and perhaps outside this country. The ways in which research questions are posed, data are collected, results are analyzed and interpreted, and research findings are implemented in communities have universal application. The blending of methodologies is equally applicable in other contexts and we found that our efforts to do so brought palpable dividends.

We feel we have provided enough distinct research dimensions so that some combination of these dimensions will be applicable to a wide range of research needs (e.g., an evaluation project using qualitative primary data at the micro-scale). We have placed our research methodologies on a sound theoretical footing so that readers can be confident that the research they do is based on recognized scholarly practice. At the same time, we feel that our field work can be repro-duced to obtain practical outcomes in many different settings. The types of collaboration discussed here between North Carolina universities and rural com-munities may not always be feasible, but the relevance and validity which cooperation between researched and researcher provides has the potential to be manifest under a variety of circumstances. The amount of interdisciplinary inter-action achieved by NC•RAP may not be possible elsewhere, but again, it is a worthwhile goal. In sum, we look forward to others using the strategies on which the preceding chapters were built and which have served us so well in their own research endeavors.

Contributors

Thomas A. Arcury, Ph.D., Senior Research Associate, Center for Urban and Regional Studies, and Research Fellow, Cecil G. Sheps Center for Health Services Research, University of North Carolina at Chapel Hill.

Ronny A. Bell, Ph.D., Assistant Research Professor, Department of Public Health Sciences, Section on Epidemiology, Bowman Gray School of Medicine, Wake Forest University.

Iris B. Carlton-LaNey, Ph.D., Associate Professor, School of Social Work, University of North Carolina at Chapel Hill.

Elizabeth C. Clipp, Ph.D., Associate Research Professor, Department of Medicine, Division of Geriatrics, Duke University Medical Center, and nurse scientist, Geriatric Research, Education and Clinical Center (GRECC), Durham VA Medical Center.

Harold L. Cook, Ph.D., Research Fellow, Cecil G. Sheps Center for Health Services Research, University of North Carolina at Chapel Hill.

Gordon H. DeFriese, Ph.D., Professor of Social Medicine, Epidemiology and Health Policy and Administration, and Director, Cecil G. Sheps Center for Health Services Research, University of North Carolina at Chapel Hill.

Glen H. Elder, Jr., Ph.D., Howard Odum Professor of Sociology and Fellow, Carolina Population Center, and Research Professor of Psychology, University of North Carolina at Chapel Hill.

Susan A. Gaylord, Ph.D., Research Associate, Program on Aging, School of Medicine, University of North Carolina at Chapel Hill.

Linda K. George, Ph.D., Professor of Sociology, and Associate Director, Center for the Study of Aging and Human Development, Duke University Medical Center.

Wilbert M. Gesler, Ph.D., Professor of Geography, Senior Research Fellow, Cecil G. Sheps Center for Health Services Research, University of North Carolina at Chapel Hill.

Carol C. Hogue, Ph.D., Associate Professor and Associate Dean for Graduate Studies, School of Nursing, University of North Carolina at Chapel Hill.

Rebecca H. Hunter, M.Ed., Research Associate, Program on Aging, School of Medicine, University of North Carolina at Chapel Hill.

Jean E. Kincade, Ph.D., Assistant Professor of Public Health Nursing, School of Public Health, and Research Fellow, Cecil G. Sheps Center for Health Services Research, University of North Carolina at Chapel Hill.

Charles F. Longino, Jr., Ph.D., Wake Forest Professor of Sociology and Public Health Sciences, Wake Forest University and the Bowman Gray School of Medicine, and Director, Reynolda Center on Aging.

Jane H. McCaleb, M.D., Family Physician, Roanoke-Amaranth Community Health Group, Medical Director, Rural Health Group, Inc., Associate Professor of Family Practice, School of Medicine, University of North Carolina at Chapel Hill, and Director of Student Teaching, Area L AHEC.

Gary M. Nelson, D.S.W., Associate Professor and Director, Family Forum and the Center for Aging Research and Educational Services (CARES), School of Social Work, University of North Carolina at Chapel Hill.

Carl F. Pieper, D.P.H., Assistant Professor of Biometry, Department of Community and Family Medicine, and Director of Computing and Statistical Laboratory, Center for the Study of Aging and Human Development, Duke University Medical Center.

Donna J. Rabiner, Ph.D., Research Health Scientist, National Center for Health Promotion, Veterans Administration Medical Center, Durham, North Carolina, Assistant Research Professor, Center for the Study of Aging and Human Development, Duke University Medical Center, and Program Coordinator, North Carolina Rural Aging Program, Cecil G. Sheps Center for Health Services Research, University of North Carolina at Chapel Hill.

William D. Remmes, B.A., Administrator, Rural Health Group, Inc., Jackson, North Carolina.

Thomas C. Ricketts, III, Ph.D., Associate Professor of Health Policy and Administration and Social Medicine, Schools of Public Health and Medicine, and Deputy Director for Health Policy Analysis, Director, North Carolina Rural Health Research Program, Cecil G. Sheps Center for Health Services Research, University of North Carolina at Chapel Hill.

Mary Anne P. Salmon, Ph.D., Aging Research Specialist and Clinical Instructor, Family Forum, School of Social Work, University of North Carolina at Chapel Hill.

Lucy A. Savitz, Ph.D., M.B.A., Adjunct Assistant Professor of Health Policy and Administration, School of Public Health, and Research Fellow, Cecil G. Sheps Center for Health Services Research, University of North Carolina at Chapel Hill.

Mark H. Smith, Ph.D. Assistant Research Professor, Department of Public Health Sciences, Section on Social Sciences and Policy, Bowman Gray School of Medicine, Wake Forest University.

Bob G. Thompson, Communications Engineer, Program on Aging and Department of Biomedical Engineering, School of Medicine, University of North Carolina at Chapel Hill.

Mark E. Williams, M.D., Professor of Medicine and Director, Program on Aging, School of Medicine, University of North Carolina at Chapel Hill.

Peggy S. Wittie, M.S., Doctoral candidate, Department of Geography, University of North Carolina at Chapel Hill.

Index

Abbott, A., 180
Abuse or neglect, 22, 163
Academic institutions and
    community-based research
    laboratories, 97-99 (*See also*
    Community-based research
    laboratories)
Accessibility of health care services, 45,
    57-61 (*See also* Geographic aspects
    of health care)
Activities of daily living (ADLs), 4, 19,
    189, 209
African Americans (*See* Minority aging in
    the Southeast U.S.)
Age norm approach to longitudinal health
    assessment, 180
Aggregate analysis and meaning, 82-83,
    185
Aging and census data, 25-26 (*See also*
    Older adults in rural areas: *various*
    subject headings)
Agriculture, U.S. Department of, 229
Alcohol abuse, 161
Althouse, R., 113
Alzheimer's disease, 162
Amenity migration, 71, 74-75
American Association of Retired Persons
    (AARP), 10
American Journal of Epidemiology, 37
American Journal of Public Health, 37
Analysis issues for minority aging in the
    Southeast U.S., 169-170
Andersen, R. M., 211
Anderson, N. C., 185

Approximating research questions with
    data at hand, 28
Arcury, T. A., 99, 161, 163, 171
Area agency on aging (AAA), 18
Area Health Education Centers (AHECs),
    144
Arndt, S., 185
Arthritis, 100
Assigning group membership, 167
Association of Schools of Public Health,
    101
Atlases, compiling, 18-19
Automobile transportation, 206
Availability of health care resources,
    56-57, 58*f*-59*f*

Ball, M., 161
Baloff, N., 185
Bandura, A., 204
Bandwidth and telemedicine, 227
Bar charts, 32*f*
Bass, D. M., 211
Becker, S. W., 185
Behavioral mechanisms and utilization
    patterns, 211
Behavioral training, 202-203
Bekhuis, T., 161
Beliefs, health
    chronic disease, 115-119
    Interdisciplinary Geriatric Evaluation
        Clinic, 138
    longevity in a multicultural population,
        119-122

Other Titles in the
SOCIETY AND AGING SERIES
Jon Hendricks, Series Editor

Health & Economic Status of Older Women:
Research Issues and Data Sources
A. Regula Herzog, Karen C. Holden and Mildred M. Seltzer

Special Research Methods for Gerontology
M. Powell Lawton and A. Regula Herzog

Aging Public Policy: Bonding the Generations
Theodore H. Koff and Richard W. Park

The Old Age Challenge to the Biomedical Model:
Paradigm Strain and Health Policy
Charles F. Longino, Jr. and John W. Murphy

Surviving Dependence: Voices of African American Elders
Mary M. Ball and Frank J. Whittington

Staying Put: Adapting the Places Instead of the People
Susan Lanspery and Joan Hyde

Of Related Interest

Defining Acts: Aging as Drama, *Robert Kastenbaum*

Dorian Graying: Is Youth the Only Thing Worth Having?
Robert Kastenbaum

12/21/99